RAILWAYS

THEIR LIFE AND TIMES

———◆◇◆———

Facts, Figures and Curiosities about
Trains from Steam to High Speed

ROBIN BROMBY

Highgate Publishing
Sydney

RAILWAYS: THEIR LIFE AND TIMES.
FACTS, FIGURES AND CURIOSITIES ABOUT TRAINS FROM STEAM TO HIGH SPEED

First published 2017 by Highgate Publishing
P O Box 481, Edgecliff NSW 2027, Australia

www.highgatepublishing.com.au

National Library of Australia Cataloguing-in-Publication entry:

Creator: Bromby, Robin, 1942– author.

Title: Railways : their life and times : facts, figures and curiosities about trains from steam to high speed / Robin Bromby.

ISBN: 9780992595661 (paperback)
ISBN: 9780992595654 (ebook : Kindle)

Notes: Includes bibliographical references.

Subjects: Railroad trains--Australia--Miscellanea.
Steam-engines--Australia--History.
Railroads--Australia--History.

Cover design by Debbie O'Byrne, JetLaunch
Cover image: New South Wales Government Railways locomotive M 78 saved from the scrapheap. It is seen here at the Thirlmere museum south of Sydney in 1983 but was later restored and moved indoors as a static exhibit. *Robin Bromby*

Typeset in Bembo 11.5/14pt by Cannon Typesetting

Contents

Introduction

O N THE AFTERNOON OF 19 July 1929 Berkshire type 2-8-4 locomotive No. 4113 of the St. Louis & San Francisco ("Frisco") Railroad was fired, coupled to a freight train consisting of fifty-five wagons and driven out of the Kansas City yards. Over the next twenty-five days, it would succeed in an attempt to establish a new rail record for continuous operation of a locomotive without once having dropped its fire.

Two years earlier the Great Northern Railroad of St Paul, Minnesota, had set a record of driving a locomotive over more than 3,500 miles (5,630 km) without the fire being relit. Now, in 1929, 4113 made five round trips between Kansas City, Missouri, and Birmingham, Alabama, on the same fire and more than doubled the old record, travelling 7,350 miles (11,826 km).

The locomotive consumed 975 tons of coal, 1.5 million gallons of water, made 13,780,000 freight miles, was manned successively by sixty different crews and arrived at the finishing post, Kansas City, three and a half hours ahead of schedule. The fire was never drawn, the boilers were not washed, and no repairs were done during that 7,350-mile effort. The locomotive could have continued its run for a longer time but federal rules required that, every thirty days, steam locomotives had to drop their fires and have the boilers checked.

Newspapers across America picked up the story—about 1,800 of them—and even *Time* magazine wrote up the exploit. Said the *Philadelphia Public Ledger*: "Unsung and almost unnoticed, No. 4113 gives an endurance performance that will delight every superintendent of motive power who dreads "engine failure"—and all of them do'. And the *St Louis Star*, which described 4113 as 'this 560,000-pound portable power plant' was reassured by the run in that 'electric motors and gas engines have not yet displaced steam. As long as cheap coal is available for the railroads, the modern efficient steam locomotive seems likely to hold its place for heavy haul'.

David L. Forsythe, Frisco's equipment foreman, rode every mile, getting some sleep back in the caboose between stints on the footplate. Forsythe at the end pointed out that the run had to be stopped for regulatory reasons. He was, not surprisingly, getting tired of riding what he called 'that old hog'; rather, he was looking at getting a full night's sleep.

As the twentieth century's third decade approached, newspaper headlines were being captured by amazing achievements in the air, or by a passenger liners setting a new records for the trans-Atlantic crossing. In 1929 aerial refueling had been developed to a stage where aircraft could remain aloft for days (the St Louis Robin flew a continuous 420 hours and seventeen minutes) and, at sea, the passenger liner *Bremen* took the Blue Riband, setting a new record of four days, seventeen hours and forty-two minutes for crossing the Atlantic to New York.

Railway achievements, by contrast and by this time in the twentieth century, no longer attracted the excitement that they once had (and, really, it was not until high-speed rail became possible that the public's imagination and patronage was rekindled).

Built by Baldwin Locomotive Company in 1923, No. 4113 with its two pilot wheels, eight driving wheels and four trailer wheels, was equipped with a Baker valve gear, a Chicago K45 lubricator, and a radial stay-type firebox.

But this was not a just a vainglorious exercise. No. 4113 remained a working locomotive all during this exercise, hauling paying freight for the entire run.

4113, champion locomotive. *Photo courtesy Charles Dix.*

The railroad company's staff magazine provides one of the most comprehensive accounts of the endurance run. At the beginning of this record attempt, fire was built in the firebox at 3.00 p.m. on 19 July and, at 7.00 p.m., 4113 pulled out Kansas City hauling Train No. 131, 'fast meat and merchandise freight train to Birmingham'. The first return leg to Kansas City saw No. 4113 almost eclipse the 1927 record: hauling Train No. 136, its freight including Florida perishables, the locomotive brought the distance travelled to 2,940 miles. That previous record of 3,500 miles was passed on the next run to Birmingham, by which time the locomotive had notched up 3,690 miles.

By the time it departed on its fourth leg, the train was being greeted at stations at which it stopped by crowds and newspaper reporters. Then, on the last scheduled leg, the staff magazine recalled that 'an eager crowd of railway men waited in the Frisco yards at Kansas City in the early morning hours of 13 August … The roadhouse force came out *en masse* to greet her. At 1.47 a.m. her headlight shone around the powerhouse at the end of the yards, and promptly at 1.50 a.m. she halted just west of the roundhouse … Flashlight pictures were taken and many rousing cheers sent into the night. Then the 4113 pulled gently into the roundhouse. At 3.00 a.m. that morning her fires were extinguished for the first time since 19 July.'

An inspection showed no mechanical problems after the endurance run.

* * *

This book sets out to be an evocation of the world of railways over more than a century—the achievements and the failures, the impressive and the quirky, the big picture and the minutiae.

Such as? Such as stations that never saw a train; the national rail company whose main aim is happy passengers (who would have thought?); the long drawn out battle between steam and diesel (and between coal and oil for steam, not to mention exploding locomotives); Christmas rail horrors; model railways being made a scapegoat for national policies; the tangling and the untangling of Russia's rail system; China's initial reluctance to embrace rail (compared to the present)—not to mention the interminable gauge issue.

Throw in 'fact panels' that reveal which European country has the greatest station concentration, who travelled on concession fares on Italian railways in the 1960s, the sorry figures showing Albania's rail decline, rail's death toll over the decades, how much rolling stock was manufactured in the United States in 1923, Hitler's rail fantasies in 1941, the growth of high speed rail and subway systems in the twenty-first century, profiles of selective national railway networks (including Canada and Madagascar)—snapshots, if you will, of the colour and movement of railways, past and present.

* * *

FAST FACT: THE DEMISE OF STEAM IN AMERICA

Locomotive types on Class I railroads in the U.S.

	Steam	Electric	Diesel
1939	41,117	843	510
1959	754	465	28,295

Rail's Greatest Champion?

IT IS DIFFICULT TO think of any greater champion of the railways than John Betjeman. He used his position as a poet and writer to extol the charms of railways, from the architecture of the magnificent stations that were constructed in the first railway age (he led the campaign that prevented the demolition of St Pancras station in London, now the terminus of Eurostar) to the charm of the branch line, using print, radio and television as his tools.

In 1955 the man who later would become Britain's Poet Laureate was writing the City and Suburban column in the weekly magazine, *The Spectator,* and on one occasion he wrote about what he saw as the need for the railways to advertise with greater effect and show that trains were more comfortable than buses or motorcars. 'You can read in them, which you can't in a motorcar or bus without feeling sick. You can eat on a train, admittedly not very well, though the Great Western still keeps up the tradition of radishes and watercress with cheese and biscuits', he argued.

Betjeman then warmed to his subject, pointing out the joys of surveying the passing countryside from a carriage window rather than keeping your eyes on the road and watching the backs of lorries ahead of you; you could feel soothed in a train, as opposed to the effect of driving through traffic or looking for a parking space. Then there was the clincher: 'Finally, railways are much safer than roads. This should appeal to those who wish to remain longer on this earth'.

In the 1950s Betjeman was involved with the establishment of the Society for the Reinvigoration of Unremunerative Branch Lines in the United Kingdom, whose members pledged to travel on branch lines being threatened with closure. Nice idea, but hardly world's best practice when it comes to running a railway. (Even Betjeman grasped that; in a letter offering to be vice-president, he suggested the word 'unremunerative' should be dropped because it could suggest the branch lines concerned might be seen as forever remaining in that unfortunate financial state. Shortly thereafter, the word disappeared.)

* * *

FAST FACT: HOW THE WORLD'S RAILWAYS HAVE GROWN

At the end of 1911, Europe and America dominated the world of railways—and many of the lines built in other parts of the globe were a result of imperial ambitions, by means of either colonial possession or foreign investment (out of London in the case of Latin America). So, as of 1911, this is how the world rail picture looked:

The Americas	540,921 km
Europe	338,813 km
Asia	106,599 km
Africa	40,480 km
Australasia	32,393 km

Within Europe

Germany	61,922 km
Russia in Europe	61,142 km (included Finland)
France	50,221 km
Austria-Hungary	44,810 km
UK/Ireland	37,641 km
Italy	17,244 km
Spain	15,094 km

Sweden ranked highest in terms of railways per capita: its network of 14,092 km represented 27.5 km per 10,000 people. At the bottom of the ladder was Turkey with 2.5 km for every 10,000 inhabitants.

In the Americas

United States	396,787 km
Canada	40,860 km

British India was the leader in Asia (52,856 km), although Russia in Asia and in Manchuria (now Siberia and northern China respectively), China and Japan each had laid more than 9,650 km of rail routes. At the bottom was Persia (now Iran) with 54 km. In Africa, South Africa was the dominant rail power, followed by French North Africa (now Algeria, Morocco and Tunisia) and then Egypt.

Author's Note

No one is sure if he really did say it, but George Bernard Shaw would have been right on the money with the advice that 'England and America are two countries separated by a common language'. Oscar Wilde made the same point in 1887 when he wrote in a short story that 'we have really everything in common with America nowadays, except, of course, language'.

And nowhere does this language gulf yawn more widely that when it comes to railways (railroads). Points and switches, caboose and brake van, engineer and driver—those are just items of terminology that differ, and then you add in Australia and New Zealand and they have their own terms (guard's vans for brake van, gangers or lengthsmen—a term picked by Australian railways taken from canal men in Britain—for platelayers).

Then there are the measurements—miles and kilometres, feet and inches or millimetres for gauges.

There really is no smooth way around these obstacles, so I have used one form where appropriate (such as 'railway' when writing about Britain and 'railroad' when dealing with United States trains) or both where needed to save readers any confusion.

All monetary amounts are in U.S. dollars unless indicated otherwise.

1

Steam in the Railway Age

'Steam, which once reigned supreme on Britain's railways, is now officially extinct'
—*Christian Science Monitor*, 22 August 1968

'I really thought of them as beautiful, not monsters—beautiful.'
—Harry Wix Jr. after driving engine 6322 on the last regularly mainline scheduled steam locomotive service in the United States (upon arrival at Durand, Michigan on 27 March 1960).

IF YOU WERE GOING to try and pick a point when what we think of as 'the Great Railway Age' came to an end—today you might call it an inflection point—then 1965 would as good as any. Steam was either gone from railway networks, or was on its last legs; rail travel was no longer the only viable long-distance (land) transport mode; the proliferation of the motor car and the growth in jet passenger aircraft capability (the Boeing 707 for example) offered attractive travel options; and more and more railway stations and lines were being closed in the Western world, meaning that no longer would the bulk of people have regular contact with trains.

The writing was on the wall by 1960 when the Railways Board in Britain announced that 5,000 steam locomotives were to be 'eliminated' rapidly. That year British Railways had 18,000 steam locomotives and just seven main line diesels (as well as 4,500 small diesel locomotives and 4,000 diesel multiple units). By 1967 the number of steamers was lower than 1,000; a year later even those would be gone from service, the last scheduled steam operation run by British Railways taking place in 1968.

The London & North Eastern Railway in Britain had forty-nine Peppercorn A1 class coal burners delivered in 1948 and 1949, only to begin scrapping them in 1962, laying off the last in 1966.

The last revenue run of a mainline steam locomotive in New Zealand was in 1971, with these locomotives kept on in the South Island mainly because of the need, during the cold southern winters, to heat rakes of old carriages still being used on nighttime long distance services. Yet just seventeen years earlier, New Zealand Railway's fleet of 718 locomotives contained only seventy-one diesel or electric machines. The NZR locomotive fleet as at 31 March 1954 covered a

Last days of steam in Australia. Silhouetted against the late afternoon sun, Beyer Garratt locomotives 6020 and 6038 haul an ore freight near Molong, New South Wales. *John Beckhaus.*

wide variety of steam types that today would horrify cost accountants and fleet managers concerned with efficiency and compatibility. In fact, there were thirty-four classes of steam locomotives, if you count as two those types that were either coal or oil burning.

In Ireland, the last scheduled trains hauled by a steam engine had run in 1964. Even the 'colonies' were getting rid of steam: in 1965 the East African Railways and Harbours Corporation (which operated railways in the three by now former British territories, Kenya, Uganda and Tanganyika/Tanzania until 1977) placed an order with the English Electric Company for twelve 2,025-horsepower diesel-electric loco-motives that would replace steam traction on the Kenya-Uganda main line.

The last regularly scheduled mainline steam locomotives in the United States ran (according to the Association of American Railroads at the time) on 27 March 1960 with the arrival of two trains from Detroit at Durand, Michigan, behind steamers No. 6319 and No. 6322, although the reporter from the *Chicago Tribune* allowed that 'there are other steam locomotives still in service in the United States. Some of them sit on sidings awaiting the call that comes when diesels can't do a particular job. Others earn their keep on some of the small roads scattered throughout the nation'. Two thousand rail fans filled the cars on that March 1960 working; so many booked for the historic journey that the timetabled service ran in two divisions, one of twelve carriages behind 6319 and twenty-one cars hauled by 6322.

The speed of steam's decline was astonishing, and no doubt shocked many railwaymen and enthusiasts at the time. After all, Britain had pro-duced its last steam locomotive only in March 1960 when the 2-10-0 *Evening Star* rolled out of the works with the fleet number 92220. It was withdrawn in 1965; five years, until then, had been only a small part of the normal life span of a steam engine.

That year 1965—which we could also perhaps date as the begin-ning of a new, different but possibly more impressive 'second railway age'—saw a feature published in the monthly British magazine, *Modern Railway*, which described the growing size of freight trains in the United States. By this time trains of between 100 and 200 wagons (or cars, as the Americans termed them) being hauled by multiple diesel-electric units were a common sight.

In this new, post-1965 railway age diesel-electric traction had transformed the rail business. *Modern Railway* had photographs of a train in the U.S. with 233 wagons; that train had three 2,250 horsepower diesel units at its head end and three more (radio-controlled by the head-end crew) cut in at the centre of the train, thus avoiding undue strain on the drawbars. The motive power in total of this train was 13,500 h.p. The train was more than a mile (1.6 km) in length and weighed more than 12,000 tons.

FAST FACT: GOING ELECTRIC

The management at the Chicago, Milwaukee & St Paul Rail Road Company (known as the Milwaukee Road) in the early years of the twentieth century watched (with great interest) the electrification of suburban lines in New York. So impressed was the railroad company that, in 1915, the Milwaukee electrified 440 miles (708 km) of track in its Rocky Mountain and Coast divisions between Harlowton, Montana and Avery, Idaho, including a section where the track rose to 6,300 feet (1,920 metres) above sea level. By 1920 another section, this time in Washington state between Othello and Tacoma, was also electrified.

The news was not good for the future of steam traction: the company found that forty-two electric locomotives could move the tonnage of freight that would have hitherto required the employment of 112 steam engines, the electrics showing their efficiency mainly through allowing increased train lengths but also cutting down running times. This was a boon for anyone operating a single-track railway.

By the early 1920s, the electric locomotives on the Milwaukee were in operation for an average of twenty hours a day. By comparison, the average steam locomotive was hauling freight or passengers for just eight hours a day.

Standing by steam

THE ONLY NOTICEABLE EXCEPTIONS in the 1960s from that decade's global trend away from steam were India and China, countries where these locomotives were still being built. Indeed, in 1960 India's then Union Railway minister Jagjivan Ram announced the country would soon be self-sufficient in steam traction and was looking to build the engines for export (to whom was not specified in the newspaper reports of the time). Yet, just a few years later, India would set 1976 as the target for the elimination of steam. But even that deadline was missed. Manufacturing of steam engines continued until 1970, the last one to roll out of the works being a 2-8-2 broad gauge WG class engine, No. 10560 named *Antim Sitam* (The Last Star). As late as 1990 there were still more than 2,300 steam locomotives being operated by Indian Railways. While dieselisation was eventually completed, Indian Railways retained steam traction for some tourist routes.

In 1996 a reporter working for the *Times of India* wrote that 'the last of India's steam locomotives are hissing and puffing into history, and veteran engine drivers and firemen, and railway mechanics and engineers, are watching them disappear with mixed feelings'. The 1970s steam fleet of around 8,500 locomotives had by then dwindled to just seventy-four working narrow and metre gauge lines in distant corners of India, including the Northeast Frontier. The newspaper predicted it would not be long before the only steam left would be pulling 'toy trains' to tourist resorts such as Darjeeling. In 1996 Indian Railways was auctioning off steam locomotives, with a minimum price tag of the equivalent of £16,000 but there were few bidders, with potential foreign buyers deterred by the cost of transporting the engines from India.

By that same year of 1996, China was still operating around 1,000 steam engines (and would build the last one in 1999) while Indonesia was using some steam to haul sugar; in Zimbabwe shunting operations at several coal mines were still being worked by steam locomotives.

The Battle Between Steam (Britain) and Diesel (Germany)

IN 1932 GERMANY EXPERIMENTED with a new diesel-electric set, called the Flying Hamburger. This new train set was able to make the 286 km trip between Hamburg and Berlin in 2hr 20min, the average speed being 121 km/h. By contrast the Hamburg-Berlin steam-hauled express took 2hr 57min. The new train was called the Flying Hamburger because it consisted of two coaches, each with one blunt and one rounded end—the blunt ends being the ones coupled together, of course. Each coach had a 400 horsepower (298 kilowatt) Mayback diesel engine that operated a dynamo, the power of which was transmitted to the electric motors. The Germans tried to make the train as aerodynamically efficient as possible: projecting surfaces were avoided, with footboards being recessed behind the doors and with the headlights inset. The train set could accommodate one hundred passengers, with space for a small refreshment room. (At the time, there was believed to be only one other passenger service that could match the Hamburger, this being the Cheltenham Flyer running between Swindon and Paddington station in London at an average speed of 115 km/h.)

* * *

However, steam fought back two years later. The London and North Eastern Railway set out on 30 November 1934 to show that steam could compete with the Flying Hamburger. The steam working ran from London to Leeds and return. Four coaches were attached for the first leg, then an additional two for the return. On the London-Leeds trip the average speed was 119 km/h; the return, with the extra weight behind the engine, was only six minutes longer in duration. The railway company argued this trial confirmed that steam was every bit as good in terms of performance as the German Hamburger. LNER used an eleven-year-old Pacific locomotive on a 'ordinary give-and-take road' with gradients in several sections of one-in-a-hundred and other sections having speed restrictions, while the Hamburger ran on a flat track. The steam-hauled train at those speeds could also provide accommodation for a greater number of passengers. The LNER added that its trains ran on domestic coal, while the Hamburger (and Dutch diesels also being experimented with) depended on imported oil.

However, as *The Economist* was quick to point out in its edition of 8 December 1934, 'the English railways have still many problems to solve before timetables based on seventy miles an hour (112.6 km/h) can be introduced. The average main line has to carry express trains, semi-fast trains, local trains, "empties", and goods and mineral trains of every category'.

* * *

By the early 1930s, steam locomotive design had made significant leaps in technology. There was, for example, Beyer, Peacock and Company's Beyer-Garratt locomotive that, by then, was being used on more than fifty large railways systems around the world. During the late 1920 it had been introduced on lines in Argentina, Chile, Peru, Bolivia, Burma, Australia, Ecuador, throughout Africa; in 1930 alone orders came in from Central Railway of Peru, the operators in Uganda and Kenya, Tanganyika, Portuguese Angola, South Africa and Nigeria. The Garratt, an articulated locomotive designed so as to introduce greater power on lines that were laid with light rails and/or had many tight curves, came in various scales, from the 2ft 6in model for Ceylon Government Railways to the 4ft 8½in for Central Railways of Peru.

Manufacturing equipment was big business for Britain's exports. The Metropolitan-Cammell Carriage, Wagon and Finance Company produced 750 passenger carriages and 18,000 freight wagons a year (the latter ranging from narrow gauge mine wagons to those with capacity to carry sixty tons).

Three views of Australian Beyer Garratt locomotives that show their size and their very distinctive articulated nature and wheel arrangement. First, Queensland Railways' Beyer Garratt 1009 sits in Brisbane's Mayne locomotive depot on 2 August 1965. *John Beckhaus.*

In service with South Australian Railways: No. 404 is seen here at Peterborough on 15 August 1969. Peterborough, located 247 km from Adelaide, was noted in Australia for being one of the country's tiny number of triple gauge stations—it could accommodate broad, standard and narrow gauge trains between 1970 and 1988; the preserved roundhouse and turntable also had triple gauge capacity. Peterborough also had the largest South Australian railway workshops outside Adelaide. *John Beckhaus.*

A different view of Queensland's 1009: here it takes on water at Yaamba, just north of Rockhampton on the North Coast line while hauling a rail enthusiasts' special on 12 June 1966. *John Beckhaus.*

In 1931 Armstrong, Whitworth and Company was demonstrating their new engine design, a 4-6-2 three-cylinder express locomotive able to pull trains of 650 tons at up to 50 mph. Steam distribution to the cylinders was effected by poppet valves. Meanwhile, R. and W. Hawthorn Leslie and Company were selling to Argentina tank engines designed to cope with heavy suburban trains.

Coal, not Oil-burners

CECIL J. ALLEN WAS a railway engineer, including a stint working for the Great Eastern Railway, and he was a contributor to *The Railway Magazine* between 1909 and 1958. In a piece for the popular magazine, *Picture Post*, on 3 January 1948, Allen defended the railways. One of his points concerned coal. In the 1930s, when the Germans were developing their diesel-electric technology, the British attitude was that its country had the finest steaming coal and it would be a folly to import oil fuel for running trains. But this no longer applied in 1948: coal was much more expensive after the war and the quality had gone down, and with no grading of coal. 'Much of the present unpunctuality is due to this cause,' Allen argued.

The London, Midland and Scottish Railway and Southern Railway had done what they could by fitting the fireboxes with grates that could be shaken while the engine was in motion, and thus prevent the accumulation of clinker. Locomotives had also been fitted with smoke-boxes designed to rid themselves automatically of ash, so improving steaming. By 1948, not only were diesel locomotives being built for Britain's railways but in 1946 the Great Western Railway had been given permission to convert 1,217 steam locomotives to oil burning; however, eighteen months after approval was received from the Ministry of Fuel and Power, the conversion had been slow and fewer than sixty locomotives had been converted.

Oil burning was clearly a matter of some debate. *The Economist* had weighed in on 31 August 1946. It noted the plan to convert about 1,200 locomotives to oil, thus saving about a million tons of coal a year.

'But what a sorry business it is,' the magazine commented with an undertone of scorn. The magazine pointed out that Britain's greatness had been built on coal and now the authorities had 'urged the railways to abandon the native product and convert their engines to oil which requires, at the least, shipping to import it and probably foreign exchange as well'.

The magazine then went on to question the economics of the proposition with oil then being far more expensive than coal and the fact that capital spending would be needed to convert the locomotives and build oil storage tanks throughout the network. Soon, the journal harrumphed, the government would be telling the country that the age of coal was over 'and that Britain's industrial greatness has gone with it'.

Stanier's Caution on Better Steam

SIR WILLIAM STANIER WAS the chief mechanical engineer for the London, Midland and Scottish Railway and, in that capacity, designed a number of the more modern and powerful steam locomotives for that company. At the beginning of 1947, however, he wrote an article for *The Times* of London that expressed some caution when it came to seeking greater efficiencies for steam traction.

Higher boiler pressures and the extended use of superheaters had lifted efficiency of engines, as had design improvements with piston valves; poppet valves instead of piston valves had brought a high degree of 'steam-tightness'. As a result of these and other improvements, Stanier noted, steam locomotives were by 1947 able to reduce the amount of coal by as much as thirty-five per cent compared with what equivalent older engines consumed. But there was a limit to the potential for further efficiencies.

'Tempting as it is to pursue refinements to give still higher thermal efficiency, their cash value to a railway system is definitely less than arising from keeping the engines at work and reducing the times which must be spent on them in servicing and repairs,' he wrote on 1 January 1947.

He urged that more attention should be given to improving axleboxes (problems with which were the main cause of locomotives needing to go the workshop). Boiler design had made great strides forward, tube fastening and fireboxes in particular.

'Although many attempts have been made with turbine and condensing steam locomotives with various kinds of high pressure water tube boilers, it is doubtful if there is any considerable future for these since, once the straightforward simplicity of the ordinary steam locomotive is departed from, the first costs and maintenance periods affecting availability arise,' Stanier continued.

His comments were made, he said, in view of the new alternative: the diesel locomotive.

Britain's Faith in Steam

BEFORE THE SECOND WORLD War railway opinion in the United Kingdom remained sceptical about the merits of electric and diesel traction. 'Only the Southern Railway gave electrification a favourable reception … The other companies, though not completely hostile, certainly did not welcome it,' wrote Derek H. Alderoft, of the University of Leicester, in his 1969 study of innovation on railways (see bibliography).

As he explained, in the 1930s not too much work had been done on the comparative costs of steam versus electric and diesel. In fact, no thorough study had been done before 1939 by any of the companies or the British Transport Commission.

'But perhaps a more important reason was that the railways continued to maintain their faith in steam,' wrote Alderoft. Almost everyone working in the railway system had been reared with steam traction; moreover, most of the equipment was not considered obsolete and a great of capital had been invested in the country's steam locomotive fleet.

Instead, effort went into improving running times on the main lines, with new express trains such as the *Cheltenham Flyer*, the *Silver Jubilee* and the *Coronation Scot*. By 1938 the London Midland and Scottish Railway had sixty-three passenger trains running at average speeds of 60 mph (96.5 km/h).

Even after the war the senior railway people, all of whom knew nothing apart from steam, showed little interest in other forms of traction. In addition, finance was tight in post-war Britain.

From Wood to Coal

BUT LET'S GO BACK to near the beginning: in 1840 the United States had 2,270 miles (3,653 km) of operating railways and a further 2,346 miles (3,775 km) under construction. Some commentators were already aware that the forests of North America would, at some stage in rail's growth, not be able to provide enough wood to feed the locomotives and provide the wood for the ties (sleepers).

As Edward F Keuchel shows in his study of the introduction of coal-burning locomotives, those engines burned quickly through a load of wood, so frequent stops were required to take on more. A load of coal lasted much longer, and burned more evenly than wood.

After a number of experiments, the breakthrough came in 1856 when Howard Delano, a locomotive mechanic based at Syracuse, New York, designed a grate that enabled bituminous coal to be forced from the bottom up through the bed of fire; it was the first grate that managed to optimise the rate of combustion in the firebox and was simple enough that even the least skilled of firemen could fire the locomotive effectively. The Boston and Worcester Railroad was one of the first to adopt this type of grate; by 1858 the Illinois Central Railroad introduced coal-burning locomotives. The companies found that their fuel costs were slashed.

* * *

There were those who chose to stick with wood. In 1927 *New Zealand Railway Magazine* pointed out that the Wellington and Manawatu Railway Company (WMR) had in the 1880s employed wood instead of coal on their tender engines 'not only because of the economies resulting by its use, but as being an important factor in the disposal of the bush lands owned by the company'.

This private railway company, which operated between New Zealand's capital of Wellington and the provincial city of Palmerston North on its own 135 km line, had acquired substantial areas of virgin timbered country when it began in 1886. The annual saving in firing with the wood-burning machines was estimated at between £300 and £400 per loco. Later, two larger 'consolidation' 2–8–0 type locos were converted to burn wood fuel and the amount of wood required was more than double what was previously necessary. But not only did it save the railway company in terms of fuel cost (compared to using coal), but it created a market for those farmers who had taken land along the rail route and now had a source of revenue from felling their trees. The use of firewood was discontinued in the summer months in order to avoid the risk of sparks causing fires in the bush. (WMR was purchased in 1908 by the New Zealand government, the company's line becoming the southern section of the new North Island Main Trunk line between Wellington and Auckland.)

FAST FACT: COAL'S BURDEN

In the 1920s, figures produced in the United States showed enormous amounts of coal were consumed when a locomotive was not performing any revenue-earning task. When an engine was having its fire banked in the locomotive depot, coal consumption was at the rate of ninety kilograms an hour. Working up steam used 362 kg of coal an hour, while coal still had to be fed into the firebox while the engine was stationary on a siding or passing loop at the rate 227 kg/h.

At that time, the railroads hauled 150 million tons of coal of year on their tracks—just for consumption by their own locomotives. That meant three million wagon-loads a year.

The Noise and Smell of Steam

THE YOUNGER GENERATIONS OF today may still thrill to the sight and sound of a steam engine on a preserved railway, but nothing now can replicate what the steam era was really like. You had to be there.

Recalling Christmas Eve in 1954 at the North Melbourne locomotive depot, engine driver Jim Seletto told how seventy trains were to depart from Spencer Street station (where country and inter-state trains departed the Australian city, with Flinders Street station the hub of the suburban services) between 2.00 p.m. and 7.00 p.m. From 9.00 a.m. that morning the shed staff workers had been going around the locomotives, writing with chalk on the sides of the driving cabins each departure time and destination. By 1.00 p.m. the first crews were clocking on. By 3.00 p.m. all was noise, heat and confusion. Seletto continued:

> Suddenly an engine would whistle for the turntable, a score of watches would be scanned and the great parade would commence. Steam would scream out of a safety valve, usually scaring the crew oiling the engine alongside, then slowly and majestically an engine would move, steam spurting over the shed floor from its open cylinder drain cocks.

Hard to imagine anyone waxing so lyrically about a shed full of diesel locomotives, isn't it? But, of course, for all the practical reasons in the world, steam had to go.

And, for all the romance surrounding steam, it generally was not much fun for passengers. While this writer, as a child, could watch entranced out the window at the wafts of smoke trailing behind the locomotive, it was not so romantic to his mother who had to keep wiping her hands and face, and telling her son not to rest his elbow (in a white shirt) on the sooty windowsill in the carriage.

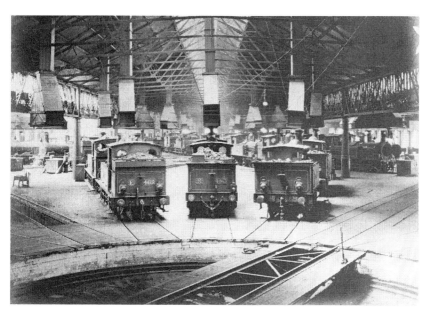

A quieter moment at the North Melbourne locomotive depot. The sheer scale of the place is shown in this 1890 scene. *National Library of Australia.*

Bob Wiedrich, a columnist for the *Chicago Tribune*, recalled in August 1964 what steam meant to those who lived alongside the rails.

> Back in the 1930s, when American railroading was in full flower, we dreamed of living right smack by the railroad track with the pungent smell of soft-coal smoke drifting through the window. Thankfully, more realistic parental heads prevailed and our folks managed to keep their distance from the trains in the night that tantalised us with lonesome whistles from several miles away. There was already enough soot on the window curtains from the coal stove that graced the living room ... Steam locomotives chugging by would have been just too much.

Yet the romance of steam lingers. In an article about Britain's steam preservation groups in an August 1990 edition of the Sunday newspaper *The Observer*, Paul Routledge conjured up the appeal: 'A hiss of steam, a whiff of hot oil and gritty smoke, a clank-clank of connecting rods: the sounds, smells, noises and images of the bygone railways'.

Steam's End in the United States

OF THE MAJOR UNITED States networks, Union Pacific ran its last steam working in July 1959, the Illinois Central in April 1960. Union Pacific Railroad had taken delivery of its last steam locomotive only fifteen years earlier, while the Norfolk & Western Railway of Roanoke, Virginia, had acquired fourteen J Class 4-8-4 engines as late as 1950.

The Americans were generally no slouches in switching to diesel. The New York, New Haven & Hartford Railroad made its decision to switch exclusively to the new technology in 1947 for its through freight service from New Haven, Connecticut, to Maybrook, New York, a 201 km line. This was a full year ahead of Britain scheduling its very first diesel-electric hauled passenger service, and twenty-one years ahead of abolition of steam on British Railways. The New Haven was able to buy fifteen diesel-electric locomotives, which replaced forty-six steam locomotives employed on that run—one of the many practical reasons for getting rid of steam is that it was estimated by the New Haven management that $1.34 million would be saved annually.

* * *

Indeed, steam motive power had been under notice since the mid-1920s at which time, as Thomas G. Marx explains in his review of the American locomotive industry (see bibliography), railway operators needed faster, more economic traction. But the transition to diesel was put off as the main locomotive builders, American Locomotive Company (Alco), Baldwin Locomotive Works and Lima Locomotive Works, opted to improve the efficiency of steam; as Marx points out, while Alco had produced its first switching (shunting) diesel engine in 1924, the wholesale move to this form of motive power was held back by fears that any large such locomotive would be too heavy for existing roadbeds.

In 1930 General Motors got into the business of building the new diesel-electric locomotives, having bought out two locomotive companies, the Electro-Motive Company and Winton Engine Company. By 1934 this new competitor to steam produced the *Burlington Zephyr* for the Burlington Railroad and the *City of Portland* for the Union Pacific Railroad. The performance of these two trains, establishing new time and distance records, demonstrated the viability of diesel traction.

Nevertheless, the steam engine builders fought back. They argued that the cost savings from diesel traction were not sufficient to justify its extra cost (as Marx points out, at that time a new diesel locomotive cost about twice what a steam one did). Naturally, the coal industry threw its weight behind steam, that industry being heavily dependent on their railroad customers needing fuel for the locomotive fleets. As Marx relates, the United Mine Workers even tried in 1947 to block the plans of the Pennsylvania Railroad to buy and put into service twenty-five new diesel-electric engines. The union petitioned the Pennsylvania state legislature to intervene with the railroad company. The contradiction, as *The New York Times* explained, was that coal haulage was the most important revenue source for the Pennsylvania Railroad; and that the union's own actions in pulling frequent strikes and interrupting coal supplies had actually spurred the railroad into hastening its switch to diesel traction. One two-week stoppage by the union saw the Eastern state railroads between them being forced to lay off huge numbers of rail workers due to the sharp decline of coal haulage traffic. The Penn stood down 20,000 workers, the Chesapeake & Ohio 15,000, the New York Central 3,375, the Baltimore & Ohio 85,000, along with layoffs at five other railroad companies.

By January 1947 ninety-five per cent of all locomotives under order by U.S. railroad companies were diesel-electric. The die was well and truly cast.

In 1934, thirty-seven diesel locomotives were delivered to American railroad companies; by 1941, the annual total broke the 1,000 mark for the first time, 1,104 engines being delivered (by which time General Motors had a 62.1 per cent market share). The industry did not break the four-figure total again until 1947, a year in which United States railroads took delivery of 2,149 new locomotives.

FAST FACT

In 1830 more than one hundred independently owned locomotive manufacturers existed in the United States. By 1920 these were down to three still making mainline engines, the oldest of which was Baldwin Locomotive Works, a company founded in 1831. The other surviving makers were the American Locomotive Company of Schenectady, New York, and the Lima Locomotive Works of Lima, Ohio. In the 1920s those three companies between them produced around 15,000 locomotives over the ten years of the decade. (A few other makers were still producing small industrial locomotives.)

By the early 1920s, there were about 59,000 steam locomotives operating in the United States and they seemed unchallengeable as the prime traction for the nation's railroads, there being fewer than 400 electric locomotives and the first mainline diesel engine would not make its appearance for another five years.

As recorded by Edwin P Alexander in his 1950 study of American locomotives, from 1920 until the demise of steam the principal types of locomotives in the United States were (with predominant traffic use):

4-4-2   Atlantic (Passenger)
4-6-0   Ten-wheeler (Passenger)
2-8-0   Consolidation (Freight)
4-6-2   Pacific (Passenger)

2-6-2	Prairie (Passenger)
2-8-2	Mikado (Freight)
4-4-0	American (Passenger)
2-6-6-2	Mallet (Freight)
2-8-8-2	Mallet (Freight)
2-10-2	Sante Fe (Freight)
2-10-4	Texas (Freight)
4-8-2	Mountain (Passenger)
2-8-4	Berkshire (Freight)
4-12-2	Union Pacific (Freight)
4-6-4	Hudson (Passenger)
4-8-4	Northern (Dual)
4-8-8-4	Big Boy (Freight)
2-6-6-2	Allegheny (Freight)
4-6-6-4	Challenger (Dual)

There were also 0-6-0 and 0-8-0 switching (shunting) locomotives.

Diesels at Santa Fe

BY 1949 THE DIESEL-ELECTRIC locomotive had dethroned steam to the degree that the Atchison, Topeka and Santa Fe had found it necessary to establish a huge diesel maintenance depot at Barstow, California. Its locomotives were repaired and checked there and trains running the 2,227 miles (3,584 km) journey between Los Angeles and California frequently underwent a locomotive change at Barstow.

A 1949 profile of the shop noted that passenger train locomotives underwent checks at Barstow approximately every 10,000 miles (16,093 km) while freight-hauling engines were checked each 3,500 miles (5,632 km).

'As soon as it is cut from the train at Barstow, the locomotive is run to the cleaning rack where it is showered, its trucks washed and steam-cleaned, and it is fueled by large suspended hose lines that can "fill 'er up" in two or three minutes,' wrote Art Ryon of the *Los Angeles Times*.

After that, the engine was moved to the repair shop for inspections of wheels, brake shoes, brake levers, bogies and traction motors, the checks taking approximately thirty minutes.

And Ryon adds a point about what he calls the 'imposing noses' on the new diesel locomotives: 'Well, there's nothing in them except a small generator for all the equipment on the engine, the headlight boxes and—in good old No. 58—an old broom'.

Barstow remains an important transportation hub, with the BNSF railroad operating a huge classification (marshalling yard) there.

UNITED STATES HISTORICAL SNAPSHOTS

1898 Snapshot: That year, locomotive passenger and freight car manufacturers in the United States completed:
Locomotives: 1,875—the best year since 1894 when 1,946 had been built.
Freight wagons: 99,809
Passenger carriages: 699
Streetcars (tramcars): 4,650.
(That combined figure of 105,158 from builders was the highest since 1890; that year 103,000 passenger, freight and streetcars had been completed).

1923 snapshot: The rolling stock of all railroads in the United States consisted of (approximately):
65,000 locomotives
53,000 passenger cars
2,348,000 freight wagons

The average freight locomotive in 1923 hauled a 1,300-ton train 56.5 miles (90.9 km) each day. On average, steam locomotives spent about a quarter of their time out of traffic being repaired and maintained.

New Freight Record for Steam

IN 1924 THE *Christian Science Monitor* newspaper ran with the headline 'Longest Freight Train on Record', noting that in May that year the average train in the U.S. consisted of 42.1 freight cars. As the newspaper pointed out, 'a comparatively small increase in the average train load results in many millions of dollars of savings in operational expenses'. But the growth had been—and would continue to be while steam provided the bulk of motive power—very gradual; in 1920 the average size had been 36.6 freight cars.

Meanwhile, 1924 was a strong year for manufacturers of rolling stock. As at 1 February that year, reported the American Railway Association, there were 25,390 freight cars on order, including 8,128 boxcars, 7,663 coal wagons, 5,244 refrigerated wagons, 2,553 livestock wagons and 1,178 flat wagons. In January railroad companies in the U.S. had placed orders for 271 locomotives; as at 1 February, 439 steam locomotives were in various stages of construction.

FAST FACT: THE DAY IN THE LIFE OF A FREIGHT WAGON.

In the early 1920s a study of American railroads showed that freight wagons (cars), on average ran about one-third of their lives empty. In a typical year back then, an average car spent fourteen weeks in sidings being loaded and unloaded; a further six weeks was spent being switched (shunted) on to or off trains; then there five weeks of the year sitting in yards at various stages of its journey and nine weeks being transferred to trains between railroad companies. Five weeks a year were spent in the workshops. Adding in times spent idle in a yard because a wagon arrived on a Sunday or public holiday (three weeks a year equivalent), and allowing two weeks for being idle between consignments, the average wagon was lucky to spend the equivalent of ten weeks a year actually on the move between destinations and some of that time, of course, being empty, a problem exacerbated by the fact that there was much more freight moving eastwards (to the big cities near the Atlantic) than in the other direction.

Incidentally, at that time the American railroads moved many horses and mules—some 80,000 car loads a year.

Austria, Short on Coal, Goes Electric

AUSTRIA EMERGED FROM THE First World War a very different proposition from its status before the conflict. Its defeat led to the break-up of the vast Austro-Hungarian empire, whose had borders had embraced parts of present day Poland, Romania, Ukraine, Italy, Hungary, the Czech Republic, Slovenia and Slovakia.

Austria, by 1919 now reduced to approximately its present-day size, therefore lost much of its imperial railway system. More devastatingly, most of the coal mines that had supplied its railways were now in the territories of the newly independent countries which had once been part of the empire; on top of that, much of central Europe's coal mining had been damaged during the fighting so Austria could not obtain enough imports of the fuel. There was simply not enough coal to keep all the trains running; on two occasions in 1919 all Austria's train services were cancelled for a week. At one stage, Vienna's Western station was seeing only two express trains a day instead of the usual seventeen. Many slow train services were cancelled for the duration.

In September 1920 Austria's National Assembly approved plans to electrify 630 km of track to overcome the lack of coal and also to end the costly operation of steam locomotives in mountainous areas. The sections to be electrified were to be from the Swiss and German borders to Innsbruck including the 1,220 metre (4,000 feet) high Arlberg Pass, part of the line between Salzburg and Innsbruck, and the

The 760 mm (2ft 5$^{15}/_{16}$ in) Murtal railway (Murtalbahn in German) is an example of the possibility of operating a local railway in a low density rural region. It is operated by Steiermärkische Landesbahnen (STLB), a company owned by the province of Styria. It was opened in 1894 with Austrian-built U class 0-6-2T locomotives. Nowadays the service on the line is operated by diesel-electric railcars manufactured in 1981. At 76.1 km, it is the second longest narrow gauge line in Austria, the longest being the 85 km Mariazellerbahn, a line that is electrified and operated by low-floor EMUs.

Murtal runs along the valley of the River Mur, in the state of Styria, and provides a regular service Unzmarkt—Murau—Tamsweg. It carries around 600,000 passengers a year and has freight operations that are vital to its economic viability. This stamp was issued in 2014 to mark the line's 120 years of operation. © Österreichische Post.

line over the Tauern Range. The work was to have been completed by 1925. Electrification had been proposed before the war but the military leadership had then opposed the diversion of funds away from the army's needs. The new post-war plan called for the construction of four hydroelectric plants, new bridges and workshops, a fleet of electric locomotives, and heating equipment to be installed in passenger carriages that could no longer be warmed by steam.

In September 1924 Britain's *The Observer* newspaper reported that some of the electrification had been finished. The completion of work on the Arlberg railway had resulted in a considerable quantity of coal being saved. 'The new big locomotives can carry fast trains with a weight of 360 tons up that mountainous line at a speed of over thirty miles an hour,' the paper reported.

But by December 1927 *The Manchester Guardian* was proclaiming in a headline: 'The Victory Of Coal—No Railway Electrification in Austria'. It said the Austrian federal state railways had decided to abandon the electrification of the main line from Vienna to Salzburg. It had been decided it would be cheaper to remain with steam.

Yet the paper's Vienna correspondent noted that Switzerland had begun electrification during the war and Austria had decided to follow suit but that plan had been based on a 1922 cost to the railways of eighty Austrian schillings a ton for coal suited for use in steam locomotives; but at the of 1927 that same coal was costing just thirty schillings. Technical improvements had also reduced the use of coal per ton hauled by steam. 'The coal bill of the Austrian railways was twice as high in 1923 as it was this year,' the reporter noted.

The End of Firemen

Small diesel locomotives were first used in the United States rail yards during the 1920s. Firemen were not assigned to them.

But it was a different matter in the early 1930s when the then new streamlined diesel passenger train sets came into service. Some rail companies assigned firemen to them, while other operators tried to resist. In 1936 the Brotherhood of Locomotive Firemen and Engineers (BLF&E) started campaigning for a national rule that would have firemen assigned to all locomotives and this came to pass when nine railroad companies signed off on the 1937 National Diesel Agreement; this provided that firemen-helpers would be assigned to all diesel-electric, oil-electric, gas-electric and steam locomotives. The only exceptions were to be multiple electric units used on commuter services and locomotives weighing less than 90,000 pounds (40,823 kg) on the driving wheels. Amazingly, the agreement had no provision setting out what the duty of these firemen would be (only in steam engines, of course, were those duties self-evident).

Here's another twist: of the nine companies that agreed to this, only three owned diesel locomotives, the others having no experience with that type of traction. The ones that signed mostly operated suburban electric multiple units so, therefore, they did not need to assign firemen.

But it was a different matter for those companies switching from steam to mainline diesels. On Class 1 railways in the United States at the time, 43,624 steam locomotives were in use and just 218 diesel engines, and most companies did not expect steam to be supplanted in the foreseeable future. This was illustrated in December 1944 when the *Chicago Tribune* reported that the Pennsylvania Railroad was committing to continue using coal as a locomotive fuel, the company showing off its new S-2, described as a 'turbine driven steam engine'. The company at that stage operated around 4,400 steam locomotives, many of them having been built after the United States entered the war in 1941. By comparison, at that time Pennsylvania Railroad owned just eighteen diesel locomotives. The availability of abundant coal was the main consideration for the retention of steam traction.

By 1959, though, the 1937 agreement was biting hard: steam by then was hauling just 0.3 per cent of the freight task, the fleet numbers having fallen from that 43,624 of 1937 to 754; the diesel numbers had risen over the same period from 281 to 28,163. An effort had been made in 1956 to renegotiate the agreement covering the employment of firemen but even those companies that had managed quietly to do without this extra person in the cab were sometimes found out and hauled back into line. In his history of dieselisation in the United States, Jeffrey W. Schramm recounts the case of the former Washington-based Southern Railway (later part of Norfolk Southern) which operated in many of the states of the Old South and which was running diesels without firemen in the 1950s. The BLF&E fought to have 100 firemen hired for those locomotives, which the railroad company felt forced to agree to—except they issued this statement:

> Since firemen have no duties at all to perform, no skills, no training, physical standards or education are required, in the circumstances it seemed reasonable to employ unskilled elderly people who are having a hard time finding jobs.

In fact, the company was too cunning for the union: it hired elderly African-Americans knowing that the union would not have African-Americans as members.

The matter of firemen had come to a head in 1960 when President Dwight Eisenhower appointed the Presidential Railroad Commission. Its task was to investigate the standoff between the railroad companies and a number of trades unions—the Brotherhood of Locomotive Engineers, the Brotherhood of Locomotive Firemen and Enginemen, the Order of Railway Conductors and Brakemen, the Brotherhood of Railroad Trainmen, and the Switchmen's Union of North America. The operators argued there was no need for firemen; the unions maintained modern diesel locomotives were much too complex to be operated by one engineer and that firemen were necessary to ensure safety.

In 1958 a Canadian royal commission had decided that firemen had to go, but the transition to single crew operation was to be done by attrition. No new hires, and no replacements for those who retired, left the job, or died. The U.S. commission came to the same conclusion but it took the famed arm-twisting skills of President Lyndon B Johnson in 1964 to get both sides to agree to that plan. However, it was not until the 1980s that all the U.S. firemen had gone from railroad service, and in those last years they were aboard locomotives on lines where no steam had been seen for twenty-five years. In delivering the 1962 report to Eisenhower's successor, President John F. Kennedy, commission chairman Judge Simon H. Rifkind said the big mistake had been the 1937 agreement. 'Because that mistake was made, we have something like 40,000 firemen on our hands today who are condemned to a life of doing something which doesn't have to be done and that does not contribute to the human personality,' he added.

* * *

REMEMBERING THE FIREMEN

'Upon the fireman and his efficiency depends the rhythmic swing of the locomotive as it hauls its enormous load over the rails. He has to have knowledge, as the verse goes "of a number of things", and his figure is a familiar one in the glow of the light as the fire doors open and, with deft and easy action, he fills the furnace. He has very little room, and the ordinary strong man would be in physical agony after a few hours of it.'
—O.N. Gillespie, *The New Zealand Railways Magazine*, 1 June 1936

Another Victim of the Modern Era: That Car at the End of the Train

THEN THERE WAS THE matter of the guard, or brakeman, or trainman—the terms varied, but there was a time when the brake van (or caboose or guard's van) was an essential part of locomotive-hauled trains. *The Times* newspaper of London in 1967 did not think much of having a 'rusty little brake van' still being a conspicuous feature of the otherwise sleek new freightliner trains on British lines. "It serves no purpose,' sniffed the newspaper, still known then as The Thunderer. 'It is there merely to give a ride to the guard, whose purpose is equally out of date'.

The cause of the newspaper's sudden interest in brake vans was that the government had just agreed to an increase in pay for guards. This was in recognition of the extra duties these men had assumed after the disappearance of firemen, such as coupling and uncoupling the locomotive to and from their trains, and walking to the signal box when required to check with the signalmen.

But the dispute between the union and government was not just over money. British Railways wanted to do away with guard's vans and, instead, have the guard sit in the rear cab of the locomotive.

Most developed countries would soon do away with the brake van or caboose. In 1986, New Zealand's then Minister of Railways, Richard Prebble, made a robust argument to Parliament for the abolition of the brake van, or the guard's van as it was known there. The vans were costing some NZ$18 million a year and, added Prebble, these had not been needed on trains for twenty years, since the introduction of automatic braking systems. The vans themselves weighed up to thirty-nine tonnes and, on many journeys, the guard's van was frequently the heaviest vehicle being hauled by the locomotive. It was estimated that the fuel needed to haul the vans was costing NZ$3.2 million a year, and repair costs to the vans NZ$3.6 million a year ('and that's without the cost of the guards' salaries,' Prebble added).

Union Pacific had similar grumbles, in 1985 having 12,000 cabooses still in service—and they each weighed thirty-five tons, an added fuel cost that was punishing the company. It was estimated that the need to attach a caboose to trains was adding some $400 million a year to railroad fuel bills in the United States. As the threat to the caboose as a part of every American long-haul train became evident (and with it the threat to jobs of the brake men), the United Transportation Union mounted an all-out campaign to get state legislatures to enact laws requiring a caboose to be attached to trains for safety reasons, this at a time when end-of-train electronic monitors were available to keep the engine crews informed about what was happening at the other end of their trains.

Eight Long Island Rail Road caboose cars parked at Holban yard, Hollis, New York on 1 June 1958. The rail company was based at Jamaica station, New York and had been founded in 1834. The caboose numbers (from left) are Nos. 43, 51, 72, 20, 50, 52, 21 and 74. The carbooses with the raised centre cupolas had been acquired from the New York, Ontario and West Railway, based in New York.
Photo: George E Votavo, David Kellor Archive.

The caboose first came into service about 1850 as trains got longer and the engine crews could not monitor the rear wagons or carriages. The caboose (there is one theory it got its name from the Dutch word 'kabuis', meaning cabin shed) originated as a hut attached to a flat car; it then evolved its now familiar shape, usually with a cupola above the roof for the brake man to see along the train, although extended side windows were also used.

But you can sympathise with the railroad companies: in the 1980s union agreements required them to have five-man crews: engineer, fireman, brake man, flagman and conductor. Union pressure on the states got nowhere, with Virginia in 1988 repealing its law that required cabooses to be included on all trains.

* * *

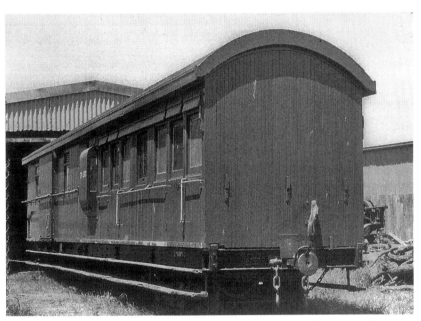

One Australian solution to the weight and space taken up by a brakevan—this is Western Australian Government Railways composite van ZA 200, one section being for the guard, the other for passengers. This photograph was taken before restoration and the van is now held by preservation group based near Geelong, Victoria. *John Beckhaus.*

Not that brake vans are entirely a thing of the past; they are still attached to the rear of trains in various parts of the world, particularly in India and Pakistan. In 2016 the latter country ordered new ones from China and in 2017 Indian Railways unveiled a new brake van with both solar panels (the guards will now have lighting, fans and mobile charging devices) and a biological waste lavatory.

In 2009 *The Hindu* newspaper, under the heading 'It's tough to be a goods train guard', reported that this tail-end workplace was an extremely humid place to be in summer and they leaked during the monsoons. 'There is no water facility inside and one has to stay alone for hours in the dark with just a torch,' the reporters told their readers. The four-wheeler van was known to 'shake vigorously' when their trains were travelling at higher speeds and the guards had to hang on for dear life, and most days they suffered body pain after their shifts. Many of the vans were more than fifty years old and there was no lavatory or light with which to see in the dark, the guards filling their logbooks by torchlight.

Danger: Steam Locomotive

APART FROM THE FACT that steam engine footplates were noisy, dirty and arduous places to work, steam had its dangers—and among those was the fact that boilers could, and did, explode. Late nineteenth century newspapers are littered with stories of such explosions.

In August 1887, for example, the *The Argus* in Melbourne, Australia, reported an explosion at the small country station of Taradale in the then colony (later state) of Victoria. Locomotive No. 51 blew up and 'immense sheets of iron and fragments of the boiler were seen flying through the air in all directions but the train continued its course for more than 300 yards (275 metres) after the explosion before coming to a standstill', the paper reported. Both the fireman and driver had been badly scalded in the face; the coat of one of the injured men was hanging on a telegraph wire.

As the Texas State Library and Archives Division has recorded, railroad work was extremely dangerous. Between 1890 and 1917 in the United States a 'staggering' 72,000 employees were killed and more than two million injured on railroad tracks. An additional 158,000 were killed in repair shops and roundhouses.

Steam boilers were a particular hazard. Since the beginning of the steam era there had been literally thousands of explosions, some with horrific loss of life. (It must be added that the individual railroad incidents due to explosions, however, were far exceeded in losses by similar maritime events: for example, in 1865 the steamboat *Sultana* exploded with the loss of 1,238 lives.) Nevertheless, rail explosions were constantly in the news because of their frequency; as the library states, 'explosions of railroad steam boilers took place on a regular basis'.

In 1911 the United States Congress passed the Locomotive Boiler Inspection Act, after which the Bureau of Locomotive Inspection was established.

The bureau began with circularising all the American railroad companies, big and small. The 2,200 companies were asked to provide copies of their rules for ensuring safe use of boilers. Only 170 operators were, in the event, able to provide such rules. In its first annual report, the bureau said it had inspected 74,000 engines in that year, of which 49,000 were found to have defects; of those, 3,400 had such serious problems they were ordered out of traffic until repairs could be made. Enginemen were found to be using large numbers of plugs to block flues where steam was leaking; not only was that practice unsafe, but it reduced locomotive fuel economy.

Even with the new inspection laws, boiler accidents happened. One of the most dramatic occurred before the new Bureau of Locomotive Inspection had actually come into being. On 18 March 1912 an engine of the Galveston, Harrisburg & San Antonio Railroad was sitting in the Southern Pacific yard at San Antonio, the men testing and firing the locomotive ahead of a day's work. At 8.55 a.m. the boiler exploded, the pressure wave levelling the nearby railroad workshops. The front end of the engine came to earth seven blocks away. The final toll was twenty-six killed, fifty injured and another ten unaccounted for and presumed dead.

Mark Aldrich, in his study of the first twenty-eight years of the new inspection service, cited one case where, in 1925, the cylinder plug on a Pennsylvania Railroad freight locomotive blew out while the engine was passing a passenger train, the blast scalding twelve people in the nearest carriage on the other track. That same year in Britain, a Great Western Railway fireman, a Mr. W. Hulme, was killed at West Acton station when a connecting rod pierced the boiler. Then two men were killed and one badly injured when, in November 1922, the locomotive on a New York Central freight train exploded as it approached the Astor tunnel near Rhinecliff, north of Poughkeepsie. George B. Dugan, the engineer (driver), was blown twelve metres up a hill alongside the track, his clothing torn to ribbons; however, pieces of the boiler were found almost a mile from the explosion point. The firemen and brakeman (who was riding on the locomotive) were killed.

In June 1928 the Munich-Frankfurt express was thundering along at fifty miles an hour (80 km/h) and had just passed the small village of Siegelsdorf (located northwest of Nuremburg) when the locomotive left the rails, the first seven cars crashing ten metres down an embankment and piling one upon the other (the three cars at the rear of the train remaining on the track). The driver was killed instantly and the fireman badly hurt. But it was the passengers in the wreckage who suffered ghastly deaths: scalding steam from the locomotive poured into the wrecked cars. Twenty-two people in all died (some instantly, others succumbing to burns) and more than 100 were injured.

It was not only the train crews and passengers that were in danger. It was estimated in 1911 that, apart from the drivers, firemen and brakemen working on American railroads, also threatened were the 348,000 people who worked at depots. In 1923, for example, two workers were scalded to death in a Pennsylvania Railroad roundhouse when the boiler of an engine exploded through the firebox.

While these accidents continued to occur—but not nearly at the rate applying before the new legislation—the inspection system did result in some dramatic improvements. In 1922 the Missouri, Kansas and Texas Railroad had suffered an engine failure for every 5,200 miles (8,369 km) travelled; by 1925 the failure rate was one for every 57,000 miles of train working.

FAST FACT: THE SLOW CREEP OF ELECTRIFICATION

In mid-1931, the *Manchester Guardian* newspaper published a summary of the electrified sections of railway around the world. These are the figures in descending order of length (in km):

United States	2,928
Switzerland	2,481
France	1,686
Italy	1,659
Germany	1,557
Sweden	1,168
Argentina	875
Great Britain	798
Austria	713
Spain	595
Australia	412
Japan	346
South Africa	312
India	243
Morocco	241
Norway	230
Netherlands	135
Mexico	127
Canada	64
Czechoslovakia	48
Dutch East Indies*	42
China	40
New Zealand	24

* Now Indonesia

The single longest electrified line in the United States in 1931 (about 500 miles or 804 km in length) was owned by the Chicago, Milwaukee and St Paul Railroad. At the time the Pennsylvania Railroad was planning to electrify about 800 route miles (1,287 km) between New York and Philadelphia, what with double track, sidings and yards came to 2,700 track miles (4,345 km). The St Paul, Minnesota-based Great Northern Railroad had electrified 72.7 miles (117 km) in Washington state, including the 7.8 miles-long (12.5 km) Cascade tunnel; the use of electric engines enabled the railroad to retire steam from this mountainous section and increase train sizes to twelve passenger cars travelling at up to 40 km/h and freight trains hauling about 5,000 tons at up to 24 km/h (and increased frequency of trains using the tunnel as there was no longer the necessity of waiting while gases escaped). The Virginia Railway (1907-1959) had electrified 134 miles (215.5 km) of track; this meant one 7,125 horsepower electric locomotive could haul coal trains of up to 9,000 tons; previously three steam engines had been able to haul 5,500-ton trains.

Over the ten years to 1931, Swiss Federal Railways had withdrawn steam traction on about 1,000 route miles (1,609 km) and substituted electric traction. In 1931 Sweden was proceeding to electrify the Stockholm-Malmö line.

Japan's Golden Age of Steam

THE 1920S AND 1930S were one of the golden periods for manufacture of locomotives and rolling stock in Japan, according to a study by Eiichi Aoki (see bibliography).

As Aoki explains, it was in the 1920s and 1930s that more powerful locomotives started to emerge on Japan's railways. The primary locomotive for passenger use was the 4-8-2 Mountain 18900 (renamed the C51 in 1928), of which 289 were produced from 1919 to 1928. For freight operations there was the 9900 (renamed the D50 in 1928), of which 380 were built from 1923 to 1931. Of the 18900, Aoki notes that the drive wheels had a diameter of 1,750 mm. 'At the time, they were the largest wheels in the world on the 1,067-mm gauge track,' he wrote. 'The axles weighed 14.2 tons, about one ton heavier than previous locomotives, but this was made possible because at that time the rails on all trunk railroads in the nation were being changed over to 37 kg rails.'

If there ever was a workhorse of Japan's steam era, it was D51 class. From their introduction in 1936, they would provide the bulk of traction through the war years (those built in the 1940s would be austerity models, with wood rather than steel being used for running boards,

Two shots of the 2-8-2 D51 class: D51 520 (above) and D51 871 taken at unknown locations some time in 1973. *Photographer unknown.*

some deflectors and coal tenders). In all, 1,115 of these engines were built (by five firms: Kawasaki, Kisha, Hitachi, Mitsubishi and Nippon Sharyo)—a greater number than for any other steam locomotive made in Japan; some were exported to Taiwan (until 1945 a Japanese colony) and also shipped to Sakhalin Island (off Siberia). Before 1945, when Japan was defeated, it controlled the southern half of Sakhalin and laid 1,067 mm lines there; when the Soviet Union seized control of that territory the Russians inherited the railway system built to Japan's narrow gauge of 1,067 mm (along with rolling stock, the D51s included). But Japan also exported locomotives of that class after the war to Sakhalin where the Russians kept some running until as late as 1979.

The 2-8-2 D51 weighed 76.8 tons and had a wheel diameter of 1,400 mm.

Germany Stuck With Steam

THE SECOND WORLD WAR left Germany with a shattered railway system. By mid-1959, the locomotive fleet still employed about 8,700 steam engines as compared to about 900 electric locomotives. And things were changing slowly: steam was still main traction because of the lack of capital to modernise after the war, but also because one thing Germany did have in plentiful quantities was coal.

By 1959 only 12.5 per cent of the German rail system was electrified (as compared with forty-three per cent in Italy, Sweden fifty-three per cent, Austria thirty-three per cent, Holland fifty-one per cent and Norway 32.3 per cent at that time), but important steps were being taken in Germany. That year saw the completion of electrification of the Remagen-Dusseldorf section; this meant that the northern and southern electrified systems of Germany were now connected to each other and so the western areas of Germany could send electric trains as far as Vienna.

The other problem was that Germany could not handle electric trains from neighbouring countries, with France, Belgium and Switzerland all having more than one electrification type.

One of the many steamers saved from the scrap yard and the blowtorch. New South Wales Government Railways locomotive M 78 was built at Redfern Workshops in Sydney in 1877. It was constructed on frames supplied by Robert Stephenson and Company and its design follows the style of British locomotives of that era. The engine was declared obsolete in 1896 and sold to a railway contractor and later was used in the building of various other lines. M 78 has been preserved in various states since 1928 and suffered weather damage. It is seen here at the Thirlmere museum south of Sydney in 1983 but was later restored and moved indoors as a static exhibit. *Robin Bromby.*

Country Profile: Bangladesh

(All figures 2015)
Total route length: 2,877 km
Total track length: 4,093 km (including yards, sidings, etc.)
Gauges (route km): 659 km—broad gauge 1,676 mm (5ft 6in)
1,648 km—narrow gauge 1,000 mm (3ft 3⅜in)
570 km—dual gauge
Stations: 458
Bridges: 3,367
Level crossings: 1,546 (207 manned 24 hours)
Passengers: 67.34 millions
Freight: 2.55 million tonnes
Trains per day: 341 passenger (88 inter-city), 37 freight.
Staff: 27,620

TIMES ARE CHANGING FOR railways in Bangladesh with a $30 million program aimed at renovating stations, upgrading workshops and large sections of the permanent way, and the introduction of new train sets on main routes. Much of the money will be coming from China which sees Bangladesh as a vital part of its New Silk Road plan (a resurrection of the old Silk Road trading routes, a modern day belt of ports, railways and roads that will allow Beijing to expand businesses into the heart of Europe and Africa; the railway dream is a connection from Singapore to Istanbul). Chinese President Xi Jinping visited Dhaka in October 2016 to announce $24 billion in loans and aid. Of that sum, $9 billion was earmarked for rail loans.

The government in Dhaka has a strategic plan for modern rail connections linking the capital with the main industrial areas and the Indian network.

The improvements are overdue.

The Bangladeshi rail system was a victim of two political events: first, the partition in 1947 of the former British India into two separate countries, India and Pakistan. The latter was made up of two parts, Eastern Pakistan (now Bangladesh) and Western Pakistan. Then in 1971 what is now Bangladesh seceded from Pakistan and achieved independence after a bloody civil war.

The inherited rail system in Bangladesh does not suit the needs of a separate country; many of the railways of the sub-continent were built as part of the old British India that were in 1947 fractured into three separate systems. Bangladesh has ended up with truncated parts of the old East Bengal Railway and the Bengal Assam Railway. In recent decades many branch lines were closed and the land corridors surrendered after successive governments placed top priority on improving highways. Track maintenance and rolling stock were neglected so that some locomotives in service in 2014 were more than fifty years old.

This is not the first time there have been hopes raised that Bangladesh will gets its railway act together. The country's oldest newspaper *New Nation* reported in 2004 that Bangladesh Railways, over the preceding three years, had improved the overall condition of 'this fragile sector' with a special focus on maintenance, repair, rehabilitation and development. (In that 2004 report, *New Nation* listed Bangladesh Railways as having a total track length of 2,880 km, a fleet of 277 engines, 1,410 passenger carriages and 13,679 four-wheel freight wagons.)

But the dreams of 2004 have yet to be realised. Nevertheless, there has been progress. Over ten years from 2005, annual passenger numbers increased from forty millions to sixty-five millions and there was also a significant increase over that period in numbers of containers moved by rail. Staff numbers have been reduced, and the number of derailments has fallen since 2005.

But Bangladesh Railways ' financial performance is hobbled by its requirement to carry several cargoes at low rates, and is required to provide cheaper rates to remote areas. These cargoes include food grains, fertilizer, jute, cement, coal, iron and steel, salt and sugar.

The seventh five-year plan (2016-2020) requires 856 km of new track to opened, dual-gauging of 1,110km of track and rehabilitation of 775 km of existing track.

Rolling Stock

Locomotives: 282

(274 diesel-electric, 8 diesel hydraulic).

As of 2015, The existing main line locos were all DE type manufactured by ALCO (USA) , MLW/ Bombardier Inc. (Canada) & Hitachi (Japan) for BG and General Motors DLW (India) and Hyundai (South Korea).

Passenger cars: 1,507

324 broad gauge

1,183 metre gauge

(inc. 33 non-revenue vehicles including luggage vans, departmental vehicles)

Freight wagons: 21,781 (inc. 12,602 four-wheelers)

An inland customs depot has been established at Dhaka and containers are now carried between the capital and Chittagong. Bangladesh Railways purchased 130 wagons from China and 100 from India to serve this traffic.

Pahartali and Dhaka Diesel Workshops undertake repairs of metre gauge diesel locomotives while Parbatipur Diesel Workshop undertakes repairs of both broad and metre gauge engines. Heavy repairs and overhauls of diesel locomotives are done at Central Locomotive Workshop, Parbatipur.

* * *

The Asian Development Bank in 2016 announced a $1.5 billion investment—both the largest the bank had ever made in Bangladesh and in any railway project—to build a dual gauge line that would be part of the new Trans-Asian Railway, so providing a continuous rail link between Asia and Europe. This ADB project will connect Cox's Bazar with the existing Bangladesh rail network at Dohazari and will offer an alternative to air and road as a way to get to the country's most popular tourist resort.

There will be nine stations developed along the 102 km route, and the government is rehabilitating the 47 km existing rail corridor that runs south from Chittagong to the present railhead at Dohazari (converting the Dhaka-Chittagong section to dual gauge will be financed through a separate ADB programme). The ADB says demand is expected to be high from the 2.2 million people living in the Cox's Bazar district, and the government is keen to further develop the city as a tourism hub. About 1.9 million tourists visit that resort each year and Bangladesh Railways will operate special trains from Dhaka once the line is built.

The ADB says it expects, at a later stage, to finance extensions to the border with Burma (Myanmar).

The study by the Asian Development Bank confirmed that Bangladesh has a shortage of modern and reliable rolling stock. Of the 2015 fleet of locomotives and passenger carriages, some seventy-six locomotives and 651 passenger carriages had passed their economic life of thirty-five years. The ADB program will finance 264 new passenger cars, ten new locomotives and new equipment to improve maintenance of existing rolling stock.

* * *

Linked at Last. The Bangladesh government in 2016 approved a 172 km line from the capital to the southwestern city of Jessore, thus linking that region by rail with Dhaka for the first time; Jessore has a rail line running to the interconnection with the Indian system. The new line will require a 6.5 km bridge over the Padma River, the main channel of the Ganges.

2
Danger on the Rails

26 December 2004—1,700 dead

Sri Lankan train The Queen of the Sea ran between Colombo Fort station in Sri Lanka and the southern city of Galle. The train was struck by a tsunami while stopped at a signal. Around 1,700 people were on board, the train being heavily overloaded, when a wave from a tsunami (generated after an earthquake off Sumatra, Indonesia, struck the line). The water roared up from the beach 200 metres away, sending the carriages rolling over and over as the twenty metre-high wall of water flooded inside them, drowning the occupants and also claiming those who had been clinging to the train's sides as they were swept away by the water. It was a holiday weekend, so the passenger numbers were much higher than was normal. Fewer than twenty people survived.

6 June 1989—800 dead

A heavily laden train derailed while travelling over a bridge crossing the Baghmati River in Bihar, India, and plunged into the water. It occurred in the monsoon season and the river was running and fast. Various theories were advanced from the driver applying the brakes too hard in order to avoid hitting a cow on the line, to very slippery rails due to the drenching rain.

12 December 1917—700 dead

December 1917 at Saint-Michel-de-Maurienne, France, a heavily overloaded 19-carriage troop train derailed on approaching a bridge, the carriages (some of which had no working brakes) piling into the water one of top of another. The death toll has been estimated at around 700. The train was travelling at excessive speed and suffered brake failure on the Culoz-Modane line. The troops were going on leave after fighting on the Italian front against Austro-Hungarian forces.

2 March 1944—More than 600 dead.

(The official Italian Government figure was 521 dead, including 516 passengers, four engine crew and conductor. More recent accounts have estimated more than 600 were killed, a 2017 report citing 626; there were estimated to have been more than 700 aboard. A 1979 account said only the brake man, whose vehicle remained outside the tunnel, survived but there were others who lived, one of whom told their story in a London newspaper in 2017.)

Mixed train No. 8017 carrying Italian civilians stalled on the steep gradient inside the long, curving Galleria delle Amri tunnel. The passengers, many of who had boarded the train in Naples (others having scrambled to join the train at intermediate stations) were mostly black marketers, regulars on the weekly service to the Lucania region. Their journeys were to buy much needed food supplies (meat, grains, cooking oils, vegetables among them) for resale to their city customers. This day, the train was made of two locomotives, forty-two empty boxcars, four passenger cars and a brake van. The train pulled out after a stop at Balvano-Ricigliano station to travel a few miles to the next stop, Bella-Muro. But this entailed travelling through three tunnels under the Apennines, two quite short and then the long Amri tunnel. The train was estimated to weigh 511 tons, eleven above the maximum weight for a two-locomotive pull. The train stalled on the tunnel gradient. Almost all those on board succumbed, killed by carbon monoxide poisoning from the low-grade coal being burned by the locomotives. The engine crews also died. The deaths were covered up by the Allied forces, then in control of the area, and by the Italian authorities.

22 January 1915—600 dead

During the Mexican Revolution, the government ordered the movement of soldiers' wives and children to the comparative safety of Guadalajara. During a steep descent into that city the train suffered a brake failure (the brakeman at the rear losing control) and the twenty cars plunged into a deep ravine. The train was said to be heavily overloaded with some people travelling on the roof of carriages.

13 January 1917—600 dead
A train of twenty-six carriages was travelling through Ciurea, Romania, carrying wounded troops and also civilians fleeing advancing German troops. The train was negotiating a steep descent and needed to brake before being switched on to a loop line; there was another train standing on the main line. The train derailed and caught on fire after the brakes failed.

4 June 1989—575 dead (and 800 injured)
At Ufa, Russia, on the Adler-Novosibirsk line, two trains were passing each other, a total of almost 1,400 people in total travelling on them. It is thought a spark from a wheel on a rail ignited a large area of liquefied gas that had escaped from a rupture in a nearby pipeline. The explosion destroyed thirty-seven carriages and the two locomotives and flattened trees for up to four kilometres away.

* * *

ON 21 JUNE 2010, a train running between Pointe-Noire and Brazzaville in the Republic of Congo took a bend while travelling too fast and derailed, with four carriages full of passengers cascading into a ravine. Within two days the toll had climbed to seventy-six dead and many hundreds injured. The line had been built by the French colonial government between 1921 and 1934 and largely followed the bank of the Congo River. This accident came nineteen years after another disaster on the track, operated by Chemin de Fer Congo-Ocean.

The 2010 tragedy prompted London's *The Daily Telegraph* to itemise the world's worst railway accidents since 2002. In that first year, 377 people died on 20 February 2002 when a train caught fire south of Cairo, more than 190 died after a derailment in Mozambique, then 288 were killed in Tanzania when a locomotive failed on a steep gradient with the twenty-two carriages careering back down the track and into a following goods train. And 119 were killed when a train plunged into a river in Bihar, India.

Then in 2003 there were fifty deaths when a passenger train in Zimbabwe collided with a goods train. India suffered further fatalities, including fifty-one people dying in yet another derailment.

On to 2004 and an explosion that killed 328 people, none of them rail travellers. On 18 February, at about 4.00 a.m. local time, fifty-one chemical wagons broke free from a train in Iran and derailed at Neyshabur, with chemical leaks and fires breaking out in the city; seventeen of the wagons contained sulphur, six contained petrol, seven contained fertilisers and ten cotton wool. The explosion was recorded by Iran seismologists and registered as a 3.6-magnitude tremor. Also that year, two freight trains carrying fuel collided at Ryongchob, in North Korea, killing more than 150 local residents.

There were three disasters in 2005. In February fifty-three people on a vehicle carrying guests from a wedding died in India when the vehicle was hit by a train, and 107 people died in a Japanese derailment, and then a three-train pile-up in Pakistan resulted in 150 dead and more than one thousand people being injured.

The 2006 toll was lower: fifty-eight killed in an Egyptian train collision and 110 in an Indian derailment. No major accidents in 2007, and only one in 2008 when two trains collided in China and seventy people died. It seems that 2009 was rail disaster-free.

Rail Horrors at Christmas

WHILE IT REMAINS SAFER to travel by rail than by some other forms of transportation—travelling on a road in a car comes to mind—there is no doubt there have been many pretty dreadful trains smashes, some killing in the hundreds.

But, beyond the disasters that took hundreds of lives, there were many other harrowing episodes that have largely been forgotten with the passing of the years. Take, for example, the accidents that occurred in the United States and Canada in the final two weeks of 1934. Several railroad wrecks occurred within the space of just a few days, killing in total forty-six people and injuring 111 others.

The rail horror began at Delaware, Ohio, two days before Christmas. Two trains belonging to New York Central collided, killing three railroad workers (two engineers or drivers, one fireman) and injuring fourteen persons. The Eastern Mail was running on the main line after a short stop at Delaware station, having right of way over the Midnight Express, which ran from Columbus to Cleveland. The latter train was using the cut-off built to save time on the Midnight's route, a cut-off being a supplementary line laid when the old line is inadequate for the traffic, or to bypass a town or station. The Midnight was coming off the cutoff and struck the Eastern Mail as she was going through the points that connected the two lines. The Midnight was running two hours late because of congestion due to the Christmas season.

Then on Christmas Day itself a Canadian National Railways train travelling from Detroit to Toronto was passing through the small station at Dundas, Ontario, and hit an open switch (set of points) and, instead of running along the main line as intended, was diverted into a siding on which stood an excursion train with 397 passengers aboard; this train had stopped due to technical problems with its locomotive. The Maple Leaf crushed the last two carriages of the excursion train, with fifteen people killed and thirty-two injured.

Meanwhile, the train running the other way between Montreal and Chicago that same night, named the International Limited, was delayed by two hours until the main line was re-opened. The crew were, according to one report, travelling at higher than normal speed (presumably trying to make up time) through Harvey, a Chicago suburb, when The International hit an automobile at a level crossing, killing the four women and three men in the car. Later the locomotive engineer, George Henry, said he had reduced speed at Harvey and had blown three blasts on the whistle as he approached the level crossing. The International arrived at Dearborn station four hours later, pulled by a replacement locomotive.

But that train's troubles were not over: two days later, and also in the suburbs of Chicago, the International Limited struck another car driven by a dean of the University of North Dakota, killing the man's wife and daughter.

Then, the day after Christmas in West Virginia, a locomotive was pulling a train carrying miners to the coal pit owned by Elkhorn Piney Coal Co. In all, there were around 300 passengers on board. The train, as usual, stopped at various settlements along the way to pick up men waiting to travel to work; shortly after easing out of a stop at the small mining community of Powelltown the locomotive exploded, tossing the driver and fireman into a creek and the engine cab was sent flying into the air, coming down through the roof of a house, narrowly missing a mother and her two sleeping children. The boiler, also catapulted into the air, crashed down upon the first carriage of its train. The dead and dying were scattered over an area of thirty metres; the body of the fireman was thrown more than eighty metres. Both the crew died; the other fourteen killed, all passengers in the front passenger car, were so badly scalded that identification was difficult. Forty-two men were injured. The company said the top of the firebox buckled, loosening the boiler tubes. The boiler had last been inspected in August.

* * *

IN 1955, AND WITHIN the time frame of forty hours, three British Railways trains ran into the back of others. On 22 December, at 4.45 a.m., the Thames-Clyde Express, running from London to Glasgow, crashed into the rear of an passenger train en route from London to Edinburgh, and which was standing at Hellifield station near Settle, Yorkshire. Fortunately the express was travelling at slow speed and only one person was injured. But there was a fatality (and twenty-four people injured) later that day, at 8.00 p.m., when the express from St Pancras to Derby, while travelling through Luton station, ran into the back of a slow train carrying passengers between St Pancras and Leicester. Then, at 8.29 a.m. the following day, the 7.54 a.m. steam-hauled Waterloo to Basingstoke train collided with the rear end of the Waterloo-Portsmouth service at Woking, with fourteen people injured. Just five days later, on the twenty-seventh, the Colne-Euston train ran away backwards, dragging the engine. The train was stopped by safety catch-points; fortunately no one was injured but it was yet another incident that added to the growing concern about rail safety.

In fact, 1955 was a wretched year for British railways and there were newspaper reports saying that the public were shocked by the number of accidents. On 28 May of that year, a picnic train taking 301 children and their parents to Dundee (along with 238 other passengers) derailed at Wormit station. Two men and a boy of ten were killed; a church elder and the boy had requested to ride on the footplate, the other death being that of the fireman (the driver lost an arm). An enquiry found that the train emerged tender-first from a tunnel near the station, travelling at least 50 mph (when the speed limit was 25 mph); a report stated that the driver might have been showing off to the unauthorised people in the locomotive cab.

Earlier that year, on 23 January, the York-Bristol express derailed at Sutton Coalfield after being diverted into a passing loop as a track gang worked on the main line. Seventeen were killed and forty-five injured.

The popular illustrated weekly, *Picture Post*, in a report on the spate of accidents in 1955, drew attention to what it described as plunging morale on the railways.

'The *really* surprising thing about British trains accidents is that there aren't more,' the magazine said. 'After seven overworked war years, when almost no ordinary replacement and maintenance work was done; after nine years post-war years during which once-proud railwaymen have seen their job sink lower and lower in public esteem, and their living standards get progressively and apparently inescapably worse compared with those of almost everybody outside; in face of a staff shortage of twenty thousand men; in spite of overtime too often carried to lengths that *must* impair alertness; with skilled, long-service key men leaving in a steady stream; with a lowering of quality amongst recruits and over-quick promotion to key safety posts.' The magazine concluded that the numbers of deaths on the track were still surprisingly low: between 1945 and 1950, just thirty-five people had lost their lives due to a railway accident, far fewer than people killed in British homes in that same period.

However, the magazine continued, the events of 1955 did disturb the public because of the nature of the accidents: four of the smashes were caused by a train running into the back of a preceding train ('the last kind of accident that *should* happen', the writer added parenthetically) and, in one case, a signalman admitted he left his one-man box before his duty was finished.

* * *

Tangiwai, New Zealand, Christmas Eve 1953. The 3.00 p.m. Wellington-Auckland express hauled by Ka 949 and consisting of nine carriages and two vans plunged into the Whangaehu River near Tangiwai, killing 151 of the 285 people aboard. A passing local motorist Cyril Ellis, realising the rail bridge had been damaged and knowing the express was due, ran down the line waving a torch; the driver saw the light and applied the brakes but it was too late; the train was travelling at such speed to the missing part of the bridge that the locomotive hit the banks on the other side of the river. The accident was the result of a rush of water (known as a lahar) from a breached crater lake on Mt Ruapehu (a dormant volcano) hurtling down the river, the combination of water, mud and rocks severely damaging the railway bridge.

Tangiwai was a small station (closed in 1986) about one kilometre south of the Whangaehu River. The express approached the bridge just after 10.20 pm, the crew unaware that the structure had been damaged by a six-metre-high wall of water just thirty minutes earlier.

The horror of that Christmas morning is evident from these two destroyed second class carriages, the torrential water having subsided. *Bob Stott collection.*

All but the last second-class and three first-class carriages and the two vans plunged into the riverbed. That last second-class carriage teetered on the edge of the bridge. Ellis and the guard, William Inglis, entered the carriage and managed to get some passengers out before the coupling snapped and it, too, plunged to the riverbed. Ellis then scrambled down and broke windows to help other passengers escape. He was awarded the George Cross (the highest award for bravery by a civilian in the then British Empire; the award was created by King George VI to recognise heroic acts during the Blitz).

The tragedy threw a pall over Christmas that year both for New Zealanders and for Queen Elizabeth II and Prince Philip who had just begun their first royal tour of the country.

In 2017 there was a ceremony near the site of the disaster to remember the bravery of the locomotive crew, driver Charles Parker and fireman Lance Redman. Rather than leap from the footplate and save their own lives when they saw that the bridge had collapsed, Parker kept applying the emergency brake while Redman sanded the last 200 metres of track to assist the braking. Their bravery is thought to have saved the last three carriages, the guard's van and the postal van from following the rest of the train into the torrent of water.

Only in Russia (Or how one drunk caused three trains to be wrecked, sixty-eight people to die and another 130 to be injured)

A REUTERS REPORT FROM Moscow on 18 January 1932, filed sixteen days after the event (when the Russians got around to making it public), said a man drunk on vodka seemingly decided to commit suicide by throwing himself under a train speeding between Kossino and Ukhtomskaia, a section of line on the eastern outskirts of Moscow.

The driver of the train saw the man and applied the brakes, but then a second train, described as following behind, crashed into the rear of the stationary train. (No explanation of this breach of safe working was proffered in the report.) But then a third train enters the story: 'While the screams of the injured and the moans of the dying were rising piteously from the wreckage, a locomotive travelling in the opposite direction dashed into the wreckage, running amok into the debris of the two (other) trains and killing several persons who had been fortunate enough to have escaped unharmed,' the report continued. A *fourth* train on the line managed to stop in time. There was no word on the fate of the drunk, but it was noted that eleven people had been arrested 'in connection with the affair'. The report, as noted, does not address the issue of safe working, but it is clear that there were some failings in that regard.

Another glimpse into the problems with the Soviet rail system was given four months later in a brief report in *The Times* of London. Speaking in Riga, Latvia, the Soviet Commissar for Land Transport, M. Andreyeff, was quoted as saying that grain had not been delivered to famine districts because of the unsatisfactory condition of lines and that 'the chief obstacle was the disgraceful quality of rails supplied by the Soviet works in Ukraine and elsewhere'. Many rails cracked before they were laid, while in February 1932 some 300 rails broke on the line between Moscow and Leningrad. The commissar said grain was sitting in around 24,000 railway wagons 'somewhere en route' to the famine areas in the Urals, Bashkiria, Kazakhstan, Western Siberia and parts of the Ukraine while the intended recipients 'waited in vain'.

Drunk in Charge of a Locomotive

TRAINS RARELY RUN WELL *ahead* of schedule but the Trans-Australian Express managed that in 1950, and by a considerable margin. The train, which ran on the standard gauge transcontinental line between Port Pirie (where it met the South Australian broad gauge) and Kalgoorlie (where it met the West Australian narrow gauge), managed the extraordinary beating of the schedule through failing to stop at scheduled stops and by travelling at almost double the regulation speed. The cause: the driver and guard were found to be drunk.

The guard was on the footplate with the driver and there was a relief guard in the brake van. The first sign of trouble was when the train over-ran two stops, and had to reverse back to the stations; then it failed to stop at all at Deakin, on the border of South Australian and Western Australia, to exchange staffs (as in, the device that—in the absence of signalling—gives a train driver exclusive use of a section of track) and just carried on without the correct staff. The man in the brake van used a stopwatch to calculate the speed according to the mileposts, noting that one mile's distance was clocked at forty-eight seconds. Thus he estimated the train was travelling through Deakin at about 75 mph (120.7 km/h), although the designated maximum speed on that section was 40 mph. He also noted, after having leaned out and looked along the train, the presence of two young women whose heads were showing out from the driving cab window. It was a rough ride for the passengers; accounts at the time say those people in the carriages could barely stand or move about due to the violent swaying.

The Trans-Australian finally came to a halt at a passing loop named 639-Mile. The court, at the eventual trial at Port Pirie, was told that upon stopping the driver got down from the locomotive and was swaying and staggering; then he fell over and lay on the loop line with his neck on one rail and his legs dangling over the other. The guard was also unsteady on his feet and was carried by two passengers back to the brake van where he was placed on one of the crew bunks and promptly went to sleep.

The two men were convicted, fined and sentenced to one month in gaol at Port Augusta, South Australia. Charges against the fireman were dropped.

Danger for Rail Workers

Working on the lines and in marshalling yards required men to keep their wits about them, no more so than those in gangs that repaired the tracks. Typical of the dangers was an incident in 1936 when four workmen were killed on the London, Midland and Scottish track between Preston and Blackpool. They were caught by two trains running in the same direction on parallel tracks: the Fylde coast express on the up fast line and, on the other track, the 8.30 a.m. Blackpool North to Liverpool Exchange service. The flagman who was there to warn the track workers of any approaching train sounded his horn and said later he believed, because no one moved, that the men could not hear him; the Fylde express had just passed and the noise from that train drowned out the warning horn sound. One survivor said 'we had just got out of the way (of the express) and did not notice that another one was approaching'.

In another accident that day, a guard on the Great Western Railway was knocked down and killed by a train at Three Cocks Station in Wales.

In August 1928 a reader in Truro, Cornwall, wrote to *The Times* newspaper to complain about careless passengers on trains. A. E. Gardiner was most concerned for the platelayers, pointing out passengers often threw items out of the windows of moving trains without regard to the safety of anyone standing beside the tracks. This was just one more danger faced by the 'poor platelayer', without whom the railways could not exist.

> Upon him we depend for smooth running—the very acme of comfort on our journeys, enabling us to read, sleep, eat and talk with ease. We only remember him if the oscillation is bad—a rare event in this country. We forget the dangers that beset him in his work on a busy track, his life endangered through the smoke from passing trains obscuring vision of the line to which he is attending; a second's delay in withdrawing to the side of the rail when the ganger's whistle has blown, and all will be over. Or, again, injury may be inflicted by small stones or dust cast up by the speed of the express carrying us on business or pleasure spent. He is willing to risk all these perils. But he does not expect the occupant of the trains to add to them.

At around the time A. E. Gardiner was writing his plea on behalf of the platelayers, the everyday perils of working on the trains filled newspaper columns. Railways were a danger everywhere. In the United States, deaths on 'steam roads' totalled 1,451 in just the three months ending 30 June 1920 (with another 14,367 people injured).

The most frequently reported rail-related accidents in 1928 in the United States were collisions between trains and automobiles. In September 1928 *The Wall Street Journal* reported that grade crossing ('level crossing' in British parlance) deaths were increasing. 'During the past ten years 20,427 persons have been killed and 57,625 seriously injured in highway grade crossing accidents on major steam railroads,' the paper reported (and these statistics did not include grade crossings on the smaller steam railways or on electric lines). In 1927 238 people

There would not have been much time to jump clear from an approaching train. Here a New Zealand track worker checks part of a main line. *Bob Stott collection.*

were killed driving into the side of moving trains—that is, they did not cross the tracks *ahead* of the train and be hit by the locomotive, but actually proceeded to cross the lines while trains were actually passing in front of them. There was plenty of opportunity for foolish motorists who wanted to take a risk: at the beginning of 1927, there were 206,533 unprotected crossings in the United States. By comparison, only 6,148 of all crossings were protected with gates, while a further 7,760 grade crossings were manned by watchmen; another 6,421 had both audible and visual signals, 5,308 had audible signals only and 2,204 had vertical signals only. That totalled 27,841 with some form of protection out of a total 234,374 grade crossings across the country.

But even the protected crossings were dangerous. In July 1928 two elderly women travelling in an Oakland sedan (three years later General Motors would rebrand these cars as Pontiacs) drove on to the tracks at the Swamp Hollow crossing of the Central Railroad of New Jersey. The crossing was protected by a bell signal but the eighty-year-old driver must not have heard it, with the southbound Atlantic City express smashing into her car, the locomotive scattering wreckage for half a mile before the engineer could bring the train to a halt.

But there were plenty of other types of rail accidents in the news columns. Joseph Allgire, aged twenty-five, received a few column inches when he fell from a freight train and was killed. Allgire was a brakeman for the Baltimore & Ohio Railroad.

Slight driver error and now famous photograph: on 22 October 1895 at Paris Montparnasse 2-4-0 locomotive 721 from Granville on the Atlantic overran the buffers and plunged through the wall of the station. The only fatality was the death of the woman running the newsstand on the street, killed by falling masonry rather than the train itself. Two of the 131 passengers were injured. The locomotive was hauling six carriages, three luggage vans and one postal van.

Country Profile: Burma (Myanmar)

Total route length: 6,106 km
(7,932 km with yards, sidings)
Double track: 705 km double-tracked (Yangon-Mandalay)
Gauge: Narrow gauge 1,000 mm (3ft 3⅜in)
Bridges: 11,818

A 2016 STUDY BY the Asian Development Bank concluded that, if the then present rate of decline persisted, the Burmese rail system (operated by state-owned Myanmar Railways) could disappear by 2025. In 1995, the system had a forty-four per cent market share of passenger traffic; in 2015 that was down to ten per cent. Insofar as freight was concerned, the drop had been from fourteen per cent of the national freight task to 1.5 per cent (and a quarter of that was accounted for by movement of ballast). There was almost no back-loading of wagons, and there were no wagons capable of hauling containers.

In terms of passenger trains, in 2013 the system carried fifty-three million passengers, thirty-one million being on the Yangon Circular Railway, a suburban system carrying 215 trains a day and where line congestion is such that the average speed is 17 km/h.

In long-distance travel, 198 trains offer intercity services, but seventy-four per cent of business is earned on just four of the thirty-four routes (some country lines carrying fewer than 50,000 people a year). Again, speeds are slow: the ADB calculated that a bus journey from Yangon to Mandalay took on average nine hours but the rail trip could be anywhere between fourteen and twenty-five hours, with trains being slow, overcrowded and without air-conditioning.

Freight train speeds are typically about 20 km/h.

The bank quotes a Japanese aid agency study that estimated a third of the rail bridges in Burma needed either major repairs or replacement. Signalling equipment throughout the system was mainly more than sixty years old.

Myanmar Railways locomotive DF 1246 seen here running light through a typical section of the country's rail network. *Photo courtesy Pixabay.*

Myanmar Railways announced in December 2016 that bidding had opened for new carriages to be used on services between Yangon and Mandalay. It was reported that several Japanese rolling stock manufacturers were keenly interested in bidding. In all, the state-owned railway wanted to buy twenty-four new carriages, paid for mainly from a $390 million loan that Japan was to make to Burma. The new rolling stock is part of a comprehensive upgrade of the line between the two main cities, which includes track refurbishment and new signalling.

Rolling stock
(As of 2014)
Locomotives: 405 (mix of French, Indian, Chinese makes)
Railcars: 166
Passenger carriages: 1,331
Wagons: 3,374
The state of rolling stock is summarized thus by the Asian Development Bank:
Diesel locomotives more than thirty years old—56 per cent
Hydraulic locomotives more than thirty years old—74 per cent
Wagons more than forty years old—48 per cent
Carriages more than thirty years old—30 per cent
Breakdowns of locomotives or railcars—average one a day

Historical Snapshot

The first railway in Burma was laid between Rangoon (now Yangon) and the important frontier town on the Irrawaddy River, Prome (now Pyay). The 161-mile (259 km) route was opened to traffic on 1 May 1877. It was operated by what was then called the Irrawaddy State Railway. Between that date and 1895, the government laid a further 886.25 miles (1,426.3 km) of track. Unlike with British rail construction in the then neighbouring India, there were no variations in gauge, all lines being laid to 1,000 mm. The original locomotives and rolling stock were bought from the Karachi-based Indus and Sutlej State Railway; that company had intended to build its line to the metre gauge and bought rolling stock but then made a last-minute switch to broad gauge.

In 1896 the Burmese government railway system was transferred to the Burma Railway Company backed by N. M. Rothschild & Son. During its tenure, that company laid a further 1,970 miles (3,170 km) of routes, with 205 miles (330 km) double-tracked.

The largest bridges were the Gokteik Viaduct, 2,260 feet (689 metres) long and 320 ft (97.5 metres) above the water, the Pittang Bridge of 1,815 ft (553 metres) in length and Ava Bridge at 3,940 ft (1,201 metres) long.

On 24 December 1929 the railway system was taken over by the Government of India and that situation continued until 1937 when Burma was made a separate colony and no longer controlled from India. In 1928 the Burmese system carried twenty-seven million passengers (mostly in third class) and freight was dominated by consignments of rice, timber and cotton.

In 1937 the top speed on the main Rangoon-Mandalay line was 45 mph (72.5 km/h), the mail train taking 13hr 20 min to cover the 386 miles (621 km), including a half-hour stop for lunch. The private owners had, apart from expanding the network, upgraded many of the lines. The original tracks had bridges that could bear axle loads of eight tons, but by 1937 bridges on the main lines could cope with axle loads of seventeen tons and those on branch lines handling ten tons.

3

The Gauge Question

Gauge	Total world length (km)
1,435 mm Standard	720,000
1,520 mm Broad (Russian)	227,678
1,067 mm Narrow (Cape gauge)	112,000
1,676 mm Broad (Indian)	98,487
1,000 mm Narrow (Metre)	83,665
1,668 mm Broad (Iberian)	14,312
1,600 mm Broad (Irish)	11,724

1,676 mm leaders

India	58,404 km
Argentina	26,391 km
Pakistan	11,492 km
Chile	3,428 km
Sri Lanka	1,447 km

1,600 mm (all lines)

Brazil	5,822 km
Australia	3,727 km*
Ireland	1,872 km
UK (Nth Ireland)	303 km

* As of time of writing, several broad gauge lines in Victoria state were being converted to standard gauge

1,520 mm leaders

Russia	86,200 km
Ukraine	21,684 km*
Kazakhstan	14,184 km
Finland	5,923 km
Uzbekistan	4,304 km

* Before Russian annexations

1,435 mm leaders

United States	293,565 km
China	124,000 km
Canada	77,932 km
Germany	43,209 km
France	29,463 km
Poland	18,836 km
Italy	18,770 km

1,067 mm leaders

South Africa	20,968 km
Japan	22.207 km
Australia	14,513 km
Indonesia	4,816 km (active)
Mozambique	4,787 km
New Zealand	4,128 km

1,000 mm leaders

Brazil	23,341 km
Francophone Africa	10,700 km
India	9,500 km
Argentina	7,523 km
Thailand	4,042 km

(All figures 2014)

IN 1924 THE BULLETIN of the International Railway Congress Association published a survey of the world's railways and found that sixty-seven per cent of lines were of the standard gauge of 1,435 mm (4ft 8½in). The use of this gauge was particularly dominant in Europe and North America.

Broad gauge covered three slightly different gauges at the time. There was 5ft 6in (1,676 mm), 5ft 3in (1,600 mm) and 4ft 11²⁷⁄₃₂in (1,520 mm). Between them, these broad gauges represented twelve per cent of world track length.

With narrow gauge, there were many variants ranging from 3ft 6in (1,067 mm) to 2ft 0in (610 mm). Those lines accounted for twenty-one per cent of track length.

In 1935, the British magazine *Railway Wonders of the World* described the situation thus:

> The traveller probably will not realise, until he is one day bundled out of his large compartment into one of about half the size at some unearthly hour of the night, that the Indian railways are built in three different gauges—broad, metre, and narrow. On a broad-gauge line he will find trains having much larger carriages than those to which he is accustomed in Great Britain; but when he enters a metre-gauge train he discovers that the difference between 5ft 6in and 3 ft 3⅜in is very considerable; while, if he is so unlucky as to be compelled to travel by narrow gauge, he will imagine that he is riding in a box on wheels as he bowls along on rails 2ft 6in apart.

Such an experience would have been common in British India. In 1921 when India's rail system extended over 37,029 miles (59,5892 km), the broad (5ft 6in) gauge consisted of 18,195 route miles (29,282 km); the metre gauge (3ft 3⅜in) was used for 15,248 miles (24,539 km); the narrow gauge of 2ft 6in (762 mm) ruled on 2,948 miles (4,744 km) of track; and there was another narrow gauge of 2ft (610 mm) used on only 638 miles (1,027 km) of line.

North America: Gauge Maze

IN THE EARLY DAYS of railroad construction in North America, it had been up to individual railroad companies to choose what gauge they would select—and they seem to have taken full advantage of such freedom so that, by the 1830s, North America had four different rail gauges, and then subsequent bursts of railroad fever added more so that, by the 1870s, it was quite a mishmash: 6ft 0in (1,829 mm), 4ft 8½in (1,435 mm), 4ft 9in (1,448 mm), 4ft 10in (1,473 mm), 5ft 0in (1,524 mm), 5ft 6in (1,676 mm) and 5ft 4in (1,626 mm), as well as narrow gauges: 3ft 6in (1,067 mm) in Canada and 3ft 0in (914 mm) in the United States. It was quite a task to rectify this situation, but by 1890 the task was pretty well completed.

The problem was that, even where several different railroads used a particular gauge, there was often no connectivity between the systems using that gauge. For example, 4ft 10in was adopted in New Jersey, Ohio and Mississippi, while 5ft 6in was used in Ontario, Missouri, Texas, Louisiana, Arkansas, Maine, and Quebec.

As Douglas J. Puffert explains in his sweeping account of the confusion (see bibliography), the first moves towards adoption of what we now call standard gauge were taking place, in respect to both new lines and conversions of gauge. Between 1865 and 1869 some 1,000 miles of track was converted. But then the pace stepped up with 10,000 miles converted in the 1870s and 20,000 miles in the 1880s.

Fortunately, the weight of numbers of those railroads that had chosen standard gauge was sufficient to make the other companies come into line. Even by 1839 the 4ft 8½in gauge had been laid in New York, Maryland, Louisiana, Delaware, Pennsylvania, Virginia, Massachusetts, Alabama, Kentucky, Quebec, Maine, Ohio, Michigan, North Caroline, Indiana and Illinois because the builders saw no reason not adopt the standard set in Britain (although some of those states also had lines built to other gauges). It was the weight of numbers plus, of course, the growing realisation that railroads were not forever going to be isolated operations but would have to provide connections right across the country.

The Great Gauge Change

THE FIRST OF JUNE 1886 was the date set for changing the gauge in the U.S. state of Georgia—from 5ft 0in (1,524 mm) to standard gauge. The route length to be changed was almost 3,000 miles (4,828 km), the lines being variously owned by Central Railroad; East Tennessee, Virginia and Georgia Railroad; the Western & Atlantic Railroad; the Georgia Railroad; the Atlanta & West Point Railroad; the Richmond & Danville Railroad; the Georgia Pacific Railroad; the Savannah, Florida & Western Railroad and the Brunswick & Western Railroad.

As *The Washington Post* reported, 'the change was begun at daybreak this morning and by noon was finished. By 6 o'clock this afternoon nearly all regular schedules were resumed … The change was the subject of general interest, and it is regarded as of great benefit to commerce in the South'. (The article was published the day after these events but, as was the custom of the time, had the previous day's date under the headline.)

This was part of the 11,500 mile (18,507 km) national 'great gauge change'. The broad gauge was largely adopted in the southern states (those states that would in 1860 become Confederate states) while the northern (Union) states had predominantly laid to the standard gauge. The South came to realise that the break-of-gauge was hurting it economically, especially after North Carolina mandated a change to standard gauge in order to attract northern train companies to run to its ports.

For several years before the days set for the change the southern lines bought or built new rolling stock of standard gauge. But that still required many existing vehicles to be re-engineered so, while thousands upon thousands of trackmen lifted one rail and moved it 3.5 inches inwards, shopmen at terminal workshops got busy converting the last broad gauge locomotives and passenger and freight cars. While the rails were realigned by 1 June, the rolling stock changes took another two weeks. At one depot on the Louisville & Nashville Railroad workers in the space of a day converted nineteen locomotives, eight passenger cars, eleven cabooses, and 1,710 freight wagons.

Forty years later, celebrating the anniversary in 1926, the *Chicago Daily Tribune* (as it was called in those days) bemoaned the fact that, unlike Chicago of its time, 'they knew how to get things done in those days'. It continued: 'The amount of negotiations, which altered the track gauge and rolling stock over an empire of rails was probably not much more than the negotiating which has already been indulged in over the Chicago subway, which isn't started, and the straightening of the south branch of the Chicago River, which isn't straight yet'.

Latin Mess

SOUTH AMERICA WAS ANOTHER hotchpotch, as *The Wall Street Journal* explained to its readers on 16 May 1908. 'It is not that a certain gauge is the rule in one country and another in another, as in the various states of Australia,' the paper noted. 'That is bad enough, but the complications in South America are worse.' (Australia had been divided into separate British colonies until federation in 1901, each distrustful of their neighbours, hence the gauge fiasco.)

Brazil had several kinds of narrow gauge as well as wider ones and the WSJ correspondent found one particular anomaly. 'The stranger finds it very curious that on the great national line of Brazil, the Estrada De Ferro Central do Brazil, or Brazilian Central—originally the Dom Pedro II Railway, since 1865 owned and operated by the Federal government—the trunk line is broad gauge while nearly all the branches are narrow gauge.' As the correspondent, Sylvester Baxter, went on to explain, the feeder lines were largely built by local interests, and they had limited access to capital so chose to build to the cheapest gauge. At the time of the newspaper report, the government was already engaged on converting these branches to broad gauge.

By 1924 a correspondent for the *Christian Science Monitor* was reporting from Buenos Aires that 'a South American "Berne Convention" to harmonise railroad standards, gauges and customs barriers is becoming daily more necessary' (although it was a stretch to liken standardisation to copyright protection). The Argentinians were concerned that, the longer the problem was ignored as the rail systems grew, the worse it would become. By 1924 there was already one trans-Andean rail line (reaching a height above sea level of 3,204 metres, or 10,512 feet) linking Argentina and Chile and two more lines proposed. In fact that one Andean line, 1,000m (3ft 3⅜in), had been completed in 1910 and was the only railway in South America that linked both coastlines and, to further confuse the gauge issue, was itself a central section between two broad gauge lines in Argentina and Chile respectively.

FAST FACT

George Stephenson adopted the gauge of 4ft 8½in (1,435 mm). There has been considerable debate about this over the years; some argued that this gauge was chosen because it was the distance been the wheels of the carts he converted for use on his colliery railways in England, while others argue that it was designed, not to replicate cart tracks, but to fit on the existing colliery roads that were being used to lay railway. Foreseeing the potential for various new railways to eventually become linked, he insisted that early starters such as the Stockton and Darlington and the Liverpool-Manchester railway companies use the same gauge as he had adopted.

The most famous deviation was that by engineer Isambard Kingdom Brunel who was commissioned to design and construct the Great Western Railway line. He decided upon 7ft ¼in (2,140 mm) on the grounds that it would provide greater stability. So the track was opened in 1838 with the broad gauge and even gauge standardisation legislation passed by Parliament in 1845 did not outlaw the broad gauge, let alone stop it from being extended. The final conversion to standard gauge occurred in 1892.

There were other advocates of much wider gauges than Stephenson's: the Austrian engineer Franz Anton von Gerstner, who convinced Tsar Nicholas I that Russia needed railways, insisted a laying the first section of seventeen miles (27.3 km) between St Petersburg and the tsar's palace at Tsarskoe Selo to the 6ft 0in (1,829 mm) gauge. But when the Russians decided to build a line between Warsaw (Poland then being part of the Russian empire) to Vienna the 4ft 8½in gauge was adopted.

Japan Has Second Thoughts about Narrow Gauge

FROM THE EARLY YEARS of the twentieth century, up until about 1920, there had been almost constant discussion in Japan about converting existing lines (and building new ones) to the standard gauge. By 1927, Japan's railway network had grown to nearly 13,000 km of route laid to 3ft 6in (1,067 mm) and it was considered impractical to convert all the track and rolling stock. It was only when the first high speed Shinkansen (bullet train) line was built in the 1960s that it was practical to start afresh with standard gauge as these lines were a separate entity from the existing rail network. At many places (the line from Tokyo's Narita Airport for example) you will still today see narrow and standard gauge lines running side-by-side.

As Shinichi Kato explained in 1995 in the *Japan Railway and Transport Review*, it was about 1910 that the debate began about converting to standard gauge, a move that was 'persistently advocated by many in the railway industry'. He adds that the government railways tried to make narrow gauge better by adopting the technical standards equivalent to those on standard gauge lines. 'Construction gauge, loading gauge, distance between track centres, bridge specifications, and other standards were established on the basis of standard gauge,' he wrote. Axles were designed so they could be converted to standard gauge when and if the time came.

Narrow gauge in Hokkaido seems to be adequate for hauling ore from mines. Here Kishiro mining locomotive 161 pulls an empty ore train on 25 June 1985. *John Beckhaus.*

FAST FACT: RUSSIA'S NARROW GAUGE IN THE EAST

When the Soviet Union seized the southern half of Sakhalin Island off the Pacific coast of Russia after Japan's defeat in 1945, it also acquired the Japanese 1,067 mm railway network. This railway has remained a narrow gauge system—until now, that is. In September 2016, the Tokyo newspaper *Asahi Shimbun* reported that the Russians were planning converting the system to the Russian broad gauge.

However, the system will be upgraded in the first instance with the retention for an interim period of narrow gauge. The new track was being laid with concrete sleepers (ties) at 1,067 mm, although one side of the sleepers would have an extra space to accommodate the broad gauge when the conversion is implemented by 2020. At that time, the Russians plan to suspend all rail operations for three months while the new gauge is implemented.

Japan gained possession of the southern portion of the island after winning the 1904-05 Russo-Japanese War. When Moscow regained the territory in 1945 it even extended the narrow gauge system rather than convert it. As the newspaper reported, the decision made in the post-war period against re-gauging was that the Japanese structures (tunnels and bridges) had been so well made they required minimal maintenance. War-damaged Russia must have been encouraged to retain the Japanese system that was working well, and Japan-made steam locomotives remained in service until 1979; one engine of the redoubtable D51 class remains on static display outside the system's main station at Yuzhno-Sakaliinsk.

The Russians even imported new narrow gauge rolling stock from their former enemy. *Asahi Shimbun* said it had found a 1950 report of Japan exporting to the island thirty D51 locomotives, twenty passenger cars and 310 freight wagons; later Japanese A-1 and four-car D-2 diesel railcars were bought by the Russians, with two of the latter remaining in service in 2016.

Country Profile: Albania

Total route length: 447 km
Gauge: Standard gauge 1,435 mm (4ft 8½in)

THE RAIL SYSTEM IS administered by Hekurudha Shqiptare sh.a (Albanian Railways SA). In 2011, the World Bank noted that passenger traffic had declined from 125 million passenger kilometres in 2000 to thirty-two million in 2009. The low level of traffic reflected the existence by 2009 of traffic being down to only a few passenger trains per day. The underlying reasons for declining passenger numbers included long-travel times (partly due to the absence of a signalling system on much of the network), unreliability of services, and uncomfortable carriages. Between Durres and Tirana—a 37 km section—track was modernised in 1997, and the speed limit had been lifted to 60 km/hour. However, due to extensive trespassing on the lines, drivers often drove slowly to avoid accidents, suggesting that improved infrastructure would not lead to faster operational speeds if the issue of trespassing (and safety more broadly) was not addressed. There are currently no international passenger services.

'From 1985, Albania used to be connected with the international railway network through the Shkoder-Hani i Hotit-Podgorica-Montenegro line', the report continued. 'This line was damaged and put out of use during the 1997 unrest and was not functional until 2002.

Although the connection with Montenegro was made again in 2002, today there are several damaged sections.'

A 2002 USAid report on rehabilitating the 119.6 km line to Montenegro (it called the line the Vora to Hani-Hoti rail link) noted that the line had been opened in 1986 'to provide Albania with a seamless rail access to the European rail network'. This link was used until the political changes of the early 1990s. The report continued that the primary traffic had consisted of exporting minerals to Eastern European destinations and importing grain and flour to Albania from Hungary and Romania. Immediately following the Yugoslavia embargo of 1997, traffic on the line was reduced significantly. 'Later in 1997, approximately 12 km of rail was removed (stolen) near the Montenegro border, thus interrupting all cargo traffic to the Balkans', USAid reported. It then said that replacement of this 12 km was scheduled for completion later that year (2002) and direct rail service to the Balkans and the rest of Europe should then be restored. It did not turn out that way.

USAid reported that, in 2002, Albanian Railways owned 117 passenger cars and eighteen luggage vans, mostly in poor condition and many 'beyond repair'.

In 2010 *The Economist* magazine published a report from a correspondent who took the train from Tirana to Shkodër in the north of Albania. The article quoted the then infrastructure manager of Albanian Railways, Gramos Gjikolli, who recalled the 'golden age' between 1975 and 1989, when the trains held a sixty per cent share of Albania's passenger traffic; in 1989 there were 10.5 million passenger journeys and 25,000 tonnes of freight was being moved by rail every day. 'In theory they have seventy-eight locomotives but only eighteen or twenty actually work, and the rest are cannibalised to keep the others going,' the correspondent reported.

The European Bank for Reconstruction and Development reported in 2016 it was looking to loan €36.87 million to rehabilitate and upgrade the 34.7 km line between the main passenger terminal in Tirana and the city of Durrës (Albania's second largest city and location of the country's main port), and lay 5 km of new line between the Tirana terminal and Tirana airport. As the bank outlined, the Tirana-Durrës line is the busiest section of the Albanian rail network. Built in 1951 and rehabilitated in 1996, the rail line—which runs through mainly flat terrain although with two hilly sections—has a speed limit of 60 km/h; effectively, though, the speed limit is 40 km/h due to the deteriorating condition of the tracks. There are no working signals on the line. Tenders were called in October 2016.

FAST FACT: ALBANIA'S RAILWAY DECLINE

The decline of Albania's railway services can be seen at a glance at these figures for passenger numbers and freight tonnage.

	Passenger journeys	Freight (tonnes)
1993	3,961,000	539,000
1999	2,270,000	361,000
2008	822,000	355,000
2012	448,000	317,000
2015	189,000	198,000

Source: Instituti I Statistikave, Tirana

Rolling stock

No reliable information is available. But it seems that what services do exist are hauled by Czech-built T-699 class diesel-electric locomotives.

Historical Snapshot

Rail-less in Europe. The Austro-Hungarian Empire built a few narrow gauge light lines during the First World War in what is now Albania and, in the Second World War, the invading Italian forces began work on a rail line in 1943. These schemes were, in both cases, thwarted by the actions of enemy forces.

At the end of the Second World War, Albania was the only European country without a rail system. The first standard gauge line was opened in 1947; other lines were opened over the following two decades (some of which are now out of use). The post-war communist government banned ownership of motor vehicles, and decided to expand the railway system with the assistance of other Soviet-bloc countries; the first rails and steam locomotives were provided by the then Yugoslavia. In 1948 Poland supplied more rolling stock and by the early 1980s main line operations were hauled by diesel-electric locomotives built in the then Czechoslovakia (although steam was still in use for shunting at Durrës). A 1984 study by Derek R. Hall (see bibliography) said passenger trains travelled at a maximum 50 km/h due to track conditions and numerous bends and curves; there were six trains a day between Tirana and Durrës, two between Durrës and Shkodër, Durrës and Fier, and Durrës and Elbasan. 'Only occasional passing loops have been laid in an otherwise single track system,' Hall noted.

4

Railways at War

First World War

THE APPROACH OF WAR in 1914 meant mobilisation of a country's young men to provide the armies, and mobilisation meant trains—lots of them. In 1912 Britain's Committee of Imperial Defence had calculated that some 1,000 train journeys would be needed to move the army around Britain, and transport recruits, should war break out on the Continent. By 1914 the French figured that 10,000 trains would be needed to bring their forces to the battlefields but the Germans (facing the possibility of a two-front war) reckoned on marshalling 20,800 train journeys (that for 2.07 million men and 118,000 horses). According to a study by David Stevenson, the Germans did their calculations based on trains of 110 axles long, weighing 600 tons in all, and travelling on the flat at thirty kilometres an hour.

When the war did begin, 670 trains were needed to move the British Expeditionary Force to the Channel coast; then another 361 trains were required to meet the BEF after that army had crossed the Channel and haul it to the front. It seems that the planning was pretty good: stations in eastern France during that exercise typically had a train passing through every four minutes; the longest delay of a military train was two hours.

Three months after the war began, Herbert Walker, general manager of the London and South Western Railway, addressed the American Luncheon Club in London and gave details of how the railways swung into action upon the declaration of war (on 4 August 1914).

'The government gave the railways a time limit of sixty hours to make ready for dispatch to Southampton, the port of departure for the Expeditionary Force, 350 trains of, roundly, thirty vehicles each,' he told his audience. 'We delivered the goods … in forty-eight hours. At Southampton, for practically every day of the first three weeks of the war, we handled during a period of fourteen hours no fewer than seventy-three trains, including the running of them to the boat-side and the unloading of the full equipment of guns, ammunition and horses.'

The trains arrived, on average, each twelve minutes, some from as far as Wales and Scotland and almost always meeting their scheduled arrival times. (And one has to keep in mind that the war planners were not dealing with just one, national rail operator. The system was divided up into many different operations: in 1911 a count showed there were still 217 companies involved in running railways throughout Britain.)

FAST FACT: THE FIRST TRAINS IN BATTLE

'From the heights of Montebello the Austrians beheld a novelty in the arts of war. Train after train arrived by railway from Voghera, each train disgorging its hundreds of armed men, and immediately hastening back for more. In vain Count Standion endeavoured to crush this force in front of him before it could be increased enough to overpower him'.

Thus *The Times* of London captured, on 28 May 1859, the first significant employment of railways as a weapon of war. The Austro-Hungarian Empire had invaded Piedmont, then an independent country encompassing the cities of Turin, Genoa and Nice. The French sought to push the Austrians out of Piedmont and, to achieve the advantage of numbers, used the railway to transport 600,000 soldiers and 125,000 horses to the front, a mobilisation of transport the Austrians could not match and which decided the battle's outcome.

The importance of the railways was made possible by the building effort of the decades leading up to 'the war to end all wars'. Thanks again to Stevenson, we know that European track length increased from 105,000 km in 1870 to 290,000 km by 1914. Moreover, steel had replaced iron for making rails, so the trains could be a good deal heavier. Block signalling, along with gradient and curvature improvements (more cuttings, more embankments, straighter lines) also helped improve the railway performance. Double-tracking was a major plus, making unnecessary trains having to wait on loops until ones going in the opposite direction had passed: in 1914, fifty-six per cent of British lines had two tracks, with forty-three per cent of French, thirty-eight per cent of German lines—but only twenty-seven per cent of Russia's route length was double-tracked.

On 5 August 1914, the day after Britain went to war, the government took control of all British railway companies. Gradually, excursion and other cheap fares were scrapped to reduce the demand for passenger trains, and clear the lines for the great number of trains running with troops or military equipment. In early 1915 a number of services between England and Scotland were withdrawn, including the 5.00 a.m. train out of Euston, the 10.35 a.m. from Kings Cross and the 1.30 p.m. from St Pancras.

Meanwhile, the exigencies of the war led to railway projects being speeded up. In 1915 the Russians completed the line from Petrograd (the non-German name adopted for St Petersburg once the war began) to Murmansk, the only ice-free port in northern Russia. The line branched off the Petrograd-Vologda line.

Other projects spurred by war needs saw Austria-Hungary in 1916 begin planning a new trans-alpine railway to supplement the existing line through the Brenner Pass (Austria-Hungary was the main protagonist in the fighting with Italy, which had joined with Britain, France and Russia to fight the Central Powers, led by Germany).

That year, too, saw better rail connections between France and Italy with the Swiss building new lines with a tunnel under Mont d'Or; this new line, 24 km in length, provided easier grades and wider curves than the track via Pontalier, saving about fifty minutes for trains travelling between France and Italy. Another new section was a short cut on the route from Paris to Berne, and allowed more freight traffic.

Wartime French Railways

IN THE LAST WEEKS of 1914 a correspondent of *The Times* of London took a long railway journey through France. Anyone who did so 'will learn more by that means and about France than he would by a month's reading of the newspapers', the reporter wrote (which seemed an extraordinary point for a newspaperman to making).

It was not easy to get about France at that time. You could never be quite sure within an hour or so as to when you would arrive at your destination. 'The army may want men or guns or it may want potatoes or flour from your part of the country,' the reporter continued. 'Or again it may be sending you sick or wounded. Whatever it is, you have to wait and kick your heels and talk of the war while the military train rolls by.'

And when you did catch a train, the journeys were much longer than in pre-war times. Calais to Paris, once a three and a half hour journey, now took more than nine hours. The engineers had patched up railway bridges on the Marne Valley line once the British Army had repelled the Germans. The reporter described the traffic: 'Men and guns, trains crammed with eager infantry, guard's vans with burly gunners lounging at their doors, followed by grey guns and their limbers standing alone on trolley-cars, trucks full of ammunition and stores, long trains of nothing but petrol tanks, trains with bridging material and stakes and coils of barbed wire, all sort of munitions of war, but always first and foremost men with guns, men and guns'.

FAST FACT: THE RAILWAY FLYING SQUADS OF 1914

When Russia went to war with Germany in 1914, memories were still fresh of the uprisings in 1905 against the Tsarist government. These had included strikes by railway workers and attacks on the railways.

So the army established railway flying squads whose trains were to carry an infantry company, telegraphists and two machine guns; these would restore any line section that had been disrupted, with priorities being restoration of the stationmaster's office and the telegraph room, as well as any workshops.

But these squads were never needed: railwaymen were enthusiastic supporters of the war and mobilisation proceeded without any strikes.

Cuba's War Windfall

ONE OF THE FEW countries to benefit economically from the 1914-18 Great War (the United States and its manufacturers being another) was Cuba. While in 1915 the tobacco industry had suffered from the reduced demand for cigars, the island produced a good crop of sugar and was able to obtain very high prices, with the spending power of the population consequently increased. That year the British-owned United Railways of Havana reported a profit of £1.69 million, up £80,690 on the previous year. Addressing the company's annual meeting at Winchester House in London, the chairman, Charles Cater Scott, reported that the railway had carried a vastly increased volume of goods, 7.37 million tons that year, and passenger numbers had increased by 642,000 to 7.75 millions.

Cater Scott was also chairman of Cuban Central Railways. That year its profit, too, had seen a sharp increase. The company had, in the past year, added sixteen locomotives to its motive power roster, along with 675 freight wagons. All heavy repair work was transferred to United Railways of Havana's workshops.

War Brings Spanish Rail Manufacturing

THE FIRST WORLD WAR had placed great pressure on the availability of freight wagons; not only was there the factor of destruction of these by enemy forces, but the greatly increased demand for wagon space to move war materiel. So it was a fortuitous time for Spain to get into the business of building wagons; American manufacturers were unable to meet orders from Spain and many other countries, so great was the demand in America itself and from their traditional customers abroad. In May 1917 it had been estimated that U.S. manufacturers had unfulfilled orders for 148,627 freight wagons; it was testament to the American war effort that, by September, the waiting list was down to 31,591. So many companies and countries depended on buying in America that the American entry into the war caused severe disruption in export supplies (in 1916 France was trying to place orders for 2,300 four-wheel boxcars with in U.S. manufacturers)

By mid-1917, the financial journal *El Economista* was reporting that the relatively new manufacturer, Sociedad Auxiliar de Ferrocariles, had already lifted output to two hundred wagons a month. Of the first eight hundred wagons completed by August that year, about half had already been sold with the Northern Railway taking more than two hundred, Carbones Asturianos eighty and the Azecarera rail company also buying new rolling stock.

Destruction and Recovery in Poland

AN IMPRESSIVE RAILWAY REPAIR works, Pruszkow near Warsaw, had been completed just before war broke out in August 1914. When the defeated Russians retreated from Warsaw in 1915, they razed the workshops to the ground. Up until 1914, what is now Poland had been partitioned between Germany, Austria-Hungary and Russia.

Poland gained her independence in November 1918, but then war broke out with Russia in 1919 and it was not until 1921 that peace was restored after fighting with the Ukrainians and the Russian Bolsheviks (Poland using eight wholly or partially armoured trains in that struggle). Rebuilding the railway system of Poland was no small task. Not only had the new country been devastated by years of fighting but the government established to rule had inherited three different railway systems built by the previous occupying powers. It was a mess: there were two gauges, standard and the Russian.

Poland inherited 4,228 km of rail routes from Germany, 2,707 km from Austria-Hungary and 7,362 km from Russia. Inheriting the remains of three different systems meant also being left with a diverse inventory of rolling stock: 4,762 locomotives (of 164 class types), 10,379 passenger carriages and 111,092 freight wagons. There were sixty-six types of rails. Moreover, each of the previous railway operators had different signaling and rules. (This was on top of there being six different currencies in circulation in the new Poland, along with four different languages of command used in the army.)

Not only had the Russians destroyed the workshops, they had blown up bridges and track to prevent the German army using the railway to pursue them. Forty-one per cent of Poland's railway bridges

One of the 1919–built Baldwin locomotives seen here in 1962 at the Lublin depot. *Thomasz Galka collection.*

had been destroyed, along with seventy-seven per cent of the water towers, sixty-three per cent of railway stations and all the workshops.

The permanent way that had not been deliberately destroyed was in poor shape after years of neglect, with worn-out rail and rotting sleepers. Help did come, especially from the Americans. A loan of $40 million enabled Poland to buy a new fleet of Pershing 2-8-0 locomotives from Baldwin Locomotive Works. Since 1919, as many as a third of locomotives inherited from the Central Powers and Russia were still out of service in Poland and new motive power was needed urgently. (A third of carriages were also unable to be used in traffic.) Later more locomotives were bought from France, Germany, Austria and Belgium. From December 1922 new passenger cars began arriving from the United States.

(It was not totally a hopeless situation. In 1922 a reporter from the *Chicago Tribune* wrote from Warsaw that he had travelled in considerable comfort from Paris to Warsaw, the running time being twenty hours with the train have sleeping cars and a restaurant car.)

The Polish government then authorised the development of six new workshops, three for locomotives and the others for carriages and wagons. Indeed by the 1930s Poland was exporting its home built locomotives to Bulgaria, Russia, Latvia and Morocco. The workshops had also turned out steel dining cars for the International Sleeping Car Company.

However, there was still one international problem to be resolved: the dispute with Lithuania (which had become independent after the 1917 revolution that overthrew the Tsar), a dispute that had begun with the Polish seizure of Vilnius in 1921. The Poles had dislodged the Bolsheviks from the city but, when Lithuania gained its independence from what would become the Soviet Union, it wanted Vilnius back; after all, the city was regarded as the Lithuanian capital.

Matters were still very touchy in 1926 when the *Christian Science Monitor* shone a light of what it described as 'the difficulties caused by the fact that railway cars belonging to one country have an inconvenient knack of getting into the territory controlled by the other'. The frontier between Poland and Lithuania was still closed but somehow carriages were ending on the wrong side of the border. However, riding to the rescue was the German Central Railway Board, which

Poland builds its own after the devastation of the First World War. Here an undated scene inside the new workshops showing the assembly of a steam locomotive. *Quixi Media.*

In 1936 Poland developed new locomotive designs. Here the prototype Pm36 is seen in its streamline glory. *Quixi Media.*

offered to mediate and charge a fee for locating all the cars in the wrong country and moving them back to their rightful owners. As the paper said: 'Thus neither country need officially know that its cars have passed through untouchable hands'.

Second World War

IN 1939 GERMANY'S RAILWAY system was not up to the needs of the war effort. As Nicholas Stargardt has so graphically demonstrated in his 2015 magisterial study, *The German War—A Nation Under Arms*, the railways of the Reich in 1939 could not cope with the demands of the invasion of Poland, let alone the expansion of the war to other fronts. German forces had crossed the border on 1 September 1939. The German rail system had been strained not only by the need to supply the Nazi's invasion force in Poland, but also by the evacuation of the Saar as French troops crossed the German border to seize that territory, and by the increased demands made on it generally by the war economy. There was simply not enough rolling stock to shift the required quantities of coal from the mines in the Ruhr. Factories had, as a result, to go on short time, and schools closed because there was no way of heating them. By early 1942 matters had got worse. There was not enough rolling stock to move military supplies and even the Holocaust had to be slowed because there were not sufficient trains available to transport the planned numbers of Jews. And, by late 1943, the demands on the railway system continued to grow: apart from normal passenger traffic and moving war materiel, evacuees from bombed cities had to be taken to other areas; as more and more German men were called to the colours, they had to be replaced by forced labour teams from the occupied countries and that meant more special trains; food was needed to be hauled from Denmark to keep the population from starving; and, of course, there was the Holocaust to be pursued as Jews were rounded up in even greater numbers. As Stargardt reports, commuters in Germany had to endure travelling in converted cattle trucks, fitted with wooden benches, bare light bulbs and pot-bellied stoves.

In 1942 German locomotive factories were still building 119 different types of steam engines, with all the lack of economies of scale and the need to make no doubt thousands of different parts to keep all those classes in operation. In 1938 Germany's railway system was making do with 4,000 fewer locomotives than it had possessed in 1929, and 80,000 fewer railway goods wagons than nine years previously (and those that remained were often in poor condition). To move all the material needed for fortification of the western frontier the railways needed to provide 6,400 rail wagons a day in the lead-up to the war; this was managed only by transferring rolling stock that was desperately needed to haul coal in the Ruhr. In November 1943 *Railway Age* magazine decided that one of Hitler's mistakes had been in sacrificing Germany's excellent railway system (in terms of missed opportunities to prepare it for total war) on the altar of his dreams of the country being crisscrossed by autobahns. This misallocation of transport infrastructure spending more than anything, it was argued, led to the failure of the railways to provide for the country's needs in time of war.

German railways had been in trouble well before the war began. As American economist Gustav Stolper explained in a 1943 paper, railway traffic had fallen dramatically after the financial crash of 1929 and the subsequent trade depression. It was not until 1937 that 1929 freight volumes had been regained, at which time the Reichsbahn was short of some 100,000 freight wagons due to the fleet having been run down. Lack of steel (exacerbated by the demands of the military rearmament) held up manufacture of new locomotives. Then in 1938 Germany's forced unification with Austria, which imposed further strains on the system (Austria's rail network, where seventy-five per cent of routes were single-track, was in worse shape than Germany's), as did the occupation of the Sudetenland, also in 1938.

On the plus side, automatic air brakes had been fitted through the fleet so freight trains were able to travel at faster speeds. But, other than that and a belated speeding-up of locomotive construction once the war began, the lack of attention to the railways (and in contrast to the money lavished on the autobahns and even the development of the Volkswagen people's car) came back to haunt the German war effort. As Stopler wrote,

> The railroads were Hitler's stepchild. He looked down on them, as do some people in this country, rather disdainfully as a means of trans- portation belonging to the past rather than the future. He had to pay dearly for this error in judgement.

The price was paid with the invasion of Poland. This was a country of poor roads, but the Germans destroyed much of the Polish rolling stock and permanent way during their invasion (and the Russians—in the eastern part of Poland they had occupied under the Hitler-Stalin Pact—took much of Poland's railway fleet found in their zone back to the Soviet Union for their own use). The large-scale destruction by the German army of Poland's rail system was a blow to German logistics. As was the British naval blockade of Germany, with much of the Reich's trade with its ally, Italy, having previously gone by sea and now needing to be transported by an already choked alpine railway (as will be detailed in a later section dealing with Italian rail problems). Similarly, as Stopler points out, trade with Romania—crucially wheat and oil—had previously gone by sea to Rotterdam or Hamburg; now those cargoes, too, were another burden for the rail system.

So taxed was the system that even on the important lines no passenger timetables were published as the trains could not be guaranteed
to run. Many services were cancelled permanently.

FAST FACT: THE WARTIME GERMAN NETWORK

The Reichsbahn by the end of 1942 was operating an extraordinary rail
network—85,000 miles (136,794 km) of lines extending from Bordeaux in
the south of France, Amsterdam in occupied Holland, all the way to Odessa
on the Black Sea. There were 1.5 million men and women on its payroll.

Apart from the movement of troops and military units, passenger numbers were swelled by travelling foreign workers, soldiers going on leave (and
returning), and the need to move large numbers of homeless people from
bombed cities.

Meanwhile, on the Russian Front

THE RUSSIANS EFFECTIVELY DENIED the Germans use of much of their
rail system by keeping locomotives well behind the front line and
pulling them deeper back into Russia ahead of the invading German
forces. So while the Nazis might have captured the permanent way in
many areas, they did not have many of the locomotives than could run
on the Russian broad gauge of 1,520 mm. This meant that German
troops and engineers had to be taken off other critical tasks to support
the invasion and assigned to converting the lines to standard gauge.
As Alfred C. Mierzetewski points out in his study of Hitler's railways,
the German transportation effort was also hampered by the inherent
deficiencies of the Soviet rail system, including lightweight track in
many sections, few passing loops and sidings, and inadequate locomotive servicing facilities. 'Worse, the (German) locomotives sent to the
front froze because various pipes and fittings were located outside the
boiler jackets', a problem that did not exist in the milder winters of
Germany. The Soviets, with their locomotives, placed all the appliances
under the boiler jackets or in cabs where they would avoid freezing.)

On top of this, Mierzetewski also points out, army units rather
than railway experts got involved in maintenance of locomotives with
disastrous results: by December 1941, the fifth month of the Eastern

Front war, around seventy per cent of German locomotives were out of service. More engines had to be sent from the Reich to take up the freight job, making even worse the rail transport bottlenecks in Germany and other occupied territories. By January 1942 the Reichsbahn informed Hitler that 3,825 locomotives had been sent to the conquered Soviet territories; at Hitler's insistence, another 1,000 locomotives were moved to Russia and the Ukraine over the following month.

Even then, the task of converting the captured lines to standard gauge was massive. Work teams had to move one rail inward over 25,000 km of Soviet track then under German control—and do so in sometime horrendous weather conditions.

Rail Mistakes

IF YOU ARE GOING to invade another country, then probably one lesson from the Second World War is to choose a victim that can pull its weight, in railway terms, not one with a rail network that you have to rebuild. It makes life so much easier. Czechoslovakia had all that heavy industry (including munitions plants), France all those paved roads and extensive rail network (and rolling stock that could be added to the Reichsbahn, the German railway system, all of western European operating on the same rail gauge), Denmark had all those prosperous farms capable of helping feed Germany. Contrast that the invasion of the Soviet Union: yes, the conquered territories yielded much from oil to manganese to food, but the Russian railways used a different gauge and the distances for haulage back to Germany greatly increased with every forward advance of the German army, exacerbating problems that were owing to an already overstretched railway system. And then there were the roads: those same ones that feature in all of those photographs showing German equipment bogged down in quagmires as the unpaved roads turned to slush.

Japan took on a similar challenge with China. There were railways in the countries and colonies they invaded, but not sufficient with which to mobilise a modern war effort; most Chinese still relied on riverboats, pack animals and human carriers for their transportation needs. In fact, had there been better railways and highways in the remote provinces of Yunnan, Kweichow (now Guizhou), Szechuan, Shensi (now Shaanxi) and Kansu (now Gansu), the Chiang Kai-shek government and its armies (which had retreated to that part of China) may have been overwhelmed in their western China redoubt if the Japanese had been able to use trains.

* * *

Logistics was a term unknown, or at least unused in the 1940s for other than military purposes, but in the transport sense of the term, Germany had more than its share of logistics nightmares. The Germans tried to impose control from Berlin on rail traffic throughout occupied Europe. All rail services were to be made subservient to the German war effort. But, along with the immense cost of the military machine and war materiel, the Germans found themselves having to build new roads and railway lines in places like Poland and Norway and, of course, the conquered parts of the Soviet Union. One such new railway line linked the Crimea via the Perekop Isthmus to Kherson in the Ukraine; this line was constructed after some of the bloodiest battles on the Eastern Front, the Germans taking the isthmus but losing large numbers of men in the process. New lines were needed elsewhere, such as in Bulgaria; then, in addition to building new lines, there was the cost of double-tracking existing routes. As already mentioned, once within the borders of the Soviet Union, German engineering battalions had to convert the captured rail lines from Russian gauge.

Some lines in France were electrified to save coal. The French and Belgian railways were partly denuded as some of their rolling stock was transferred to the Eastern Front where the bulk of the fighting was occurring. Before the war began, Belgian railways owned 3,594 locomotives, 8,299 passenger cars and 114,002 freight wagons. Many of these became part of the German war effort. The Nazis seized 200,000 French freight wagons and sent them to fill gaps in others part of Germany's expanding empire; more than 6,000 locomotives were also harnessed to the war effort. But the Germans found that other parts of their territorial holdings could not handle the demands of their new masters: the Reichsbahn had to send, from its owned stretched operations, freight cars to Denmark and locomotives to Norway.

And, while German designers were coming up with improved models of aircraft and weaponry, little innovation occurred on the rail system: a few railcar prototypes were designed and a few new locomotive types came off the drawing boards, but none was to enter mass production.

To the deterioration in rolling stock through lack of repairs and maintenance was added the losses from air raids with British and American bombers frequently targeting railway depots and marshalling yards. According to the League of Nations (still clinging to life at that time and surviving in neutral Switzerland) French State Railways, because of German seizures, damage and destruction by bombing, had by September 1943 lost the use of about thirty per cent of its locomotive stock, fifty-three per cent of its freight wagons and thirty-six per cent of passenger carriages. Belgian railways by this time had only one-third of its freight wagons still in service. The Germans even ripped up rails in Belgium to be used for desperately needed new lines in the east. By 1942, 598 km of track had been lifted in Belgium and removed.

And, just when Germany needed as many munitions, aircraft, tanks and other equipment, plants that could have been turning these out (as the railway workshops were in Australia, for example) had to step up production of new locomotives. Locomotive production in May 1943 was three times greater than it had been in 1941. Even then the strain on the Nazi rail network was enormous. For example, in May 1944 the Panzer-Lehr Division, considered the elite tank unit of the army, had completed its occupation of Hungary, a move made to ensure that country remained in the war as Germany's ally. It was then assigned to Normandy to reinforce the units there with the expectation of an Allied invasion. The move across Europe required seventy trains to transport the men and equipment.

Meanwhile, the Russians were able to restore their own transport systems once the tide of war had turned. The victory at Stalingrad allowed the Soviets to restart shipping on the Volga (which before the war had carried half the U.S.S.R.'s inland water traffic). And while the Germans were dependent on their own industrial efforts or looting the occupied territories, the Russians had enormous help from the Americans who by the end of 1944 had supplied them with 362,000 motor vehicles, 1,045 railway locomotives and 478,000 tons of other railway equipment.

FAST FACT: HITLER'S RAIL FANTASY

A railway system built to a gauge of 3,000 mm when the standard gauge was, had been and still is 1,435 mm? That was the plan that Adolf Hitler proposed to unite his new empire once the war was won. The locomotives would be huge—more than twice the height of those that were pulling German trains in the early 1940s and would be six metres wide. There were to be dining cars wide enough to accommodate three rows of tables, and two aisles, running lengthwise. One car on each train would be large enough to accommodate a cinema.

The three-metre gauge lines would run from the Urals to Pyrenees (it 'out-Brunel Brunel', as one historian put it). This while Hitler's Minister for Armaments and War Production, Albert Speer, sought to get Nazi bosses away from dreams of travelling across their empire in the super-trains and to focus on the need for an additional 14,000 standard gauge heavy goods locomotives that were required to meet the immediate freight task on an enlarged Reich system that spanned, as Christopher Harvie in his paper on German railway design (see bibliography) noted, was described as running 'from Brittany to the suburbs of Leningrad, and from Trondheim to Thessalonika'.

Italy and its Coal Problem

COAL WAS A REAL problem for the Italians trying to keep their railways operating. Germany was the main source of supply. The problem was that, pre-war, most of the coal purchased from Germany came by sea, the rail system being unable to cope. The effect of the British blockade of Germany was dramatic when the war began: Germany had delivered 670,000 tons in September 1939, but by November deliveries were down to 175,000 tons with the sea lanes closed off. As German author Gerhard Schreiber and his co-authors explain, Italian railways simply did not have the locomotives and wagons available to suddenly have to cope with that seaborne coal traffic being transferred to rail. But there was another complication: Italy had for some time bought coal not only from Germany but also from Poland and Czechoslovakia. After the subjugation of those two countries by the Nazis, all the coal produced in those two occupied territories was diverted to Germany's needs. The shortages of coal also had a devastating impact on Italy's steel production: it fell from 2.3 million tonnes in 1938 to 1.9 million tonnes in 1942.

By 1941 not only was Italy militarily dependent upon Germany, but almost thoroughly dependent on its senior partner for trade as well. Between 1938 and 1941, Italy's trade volumes with Germany had quadrupled. There was a strategic as well as economic cost: the growing trade between the two countries placed a severe strain on the Trans-Alpine railway; apart from coal and other trade items it also had to handle heavy military transport requirements once Italy joined the war. In 1941 alone, Germany shipped twelve million tons of coal to Italy, along with all the latter's steel import requirements. The great Italian plans for increasing coal production had not materialised: in 1939, the intent had been to treble coal output by 1942. They did not manage that, but they did try. In 1938, the mines in Istria and Sardinia had produced a total 1.37 million tons only. By 1939 the country's mines produced 2.02 million tons of hard coal. At least the Germans kept the price of coal stable; however, by June 1941 the coal shipments from the Reich began to fall because sufficient rolling stock was unavailable, so that the Italian mines could still not close the demand gap even with higher output. There were reports, too, of Italian Railways complaining that railway wagons sent to Germany to be loaded with coal, once in the Reich, were being diverted by the Nazis to assist their own war transport needs.

Nazi Trains in Neutral Sweden

ON 5 AUGUST 1943, the Swedish Government announced it had cancelled the arrangements with the German government to allow Nazi troops to cross its territory. This brought to a close a less than proud moment in Sweden's record of neutrality. When the Germans invaded Norway in April 1940, the Swedes initially had (ostensibly) imposed a ban on assistance to both sides in the conflict—no war materiel could be transported across its territory for either the Germans or the Norwegians (although recent evidence indicates that even this was ignored).

Once the invasion was completed and Norway subdued, however, the government in Stockholm announced (on 6 July) it would allow German soldiers 'on leave' to travel across its territory, a move motivated by Sweden's fear that Germany would turn on it if such a concession were not made. Moreover, Sweden was heavily reliant on Germany for its coal supplies. The agreement meant troops returning to Germany and their replacements could avoid transport via the North Sea coast that carried with it the risk of attack by British aircraft and warships. Daily trains travelled between Norway and the Swedish port of Trelleborg, the closest port in southern Sweden to the German coast.

The agreement stipulated that the Nazi troops could not carry weapons other than side-arms while in Sweden, but this was subverted by storing larger weapons in special vans attached to the trains. Moreover, travel by German military personnel across Sweden to and from Finland (a German ally) was specifically prohibited, but by 1943 it had become public knowledge that the Germans were using two passenger carriages attached to trains that travelled between Storlien, close to the Norwegian border, to Haparanda on the Finnish frontier at the northern end of the Gulf of Bathnia. This particularly riled Swedish public opinion because it was seen as allowing Germany the right to move troops between two fighting fronts—Finland being at war with both Britain and the Soviet Union—rather than maintain the fiction that it was merely for soldiers going on or returning from leave. It was reported in British newspapers that heavy artillery and fuel for the Luftwaffe in Norway were also sent over the Swedish railway system. The Swedish Prime Minister Per Albin Hansson could go only so far to describe the arrangement as a 'burden'.

Earlier in the year, newspapers and trades unions in Sweden began a campaign to end the transport of the Germans. They argued that Sweden was in no position to resist German demands in 1940 but, by 1943, the Nazis could not realistically mount an attack on Sweden.

Time magazine reported in May 1943 that the movement of Nazi troops was 'the sorest spot in Sweden'. Thrice weekly, it said, Nazi troops were transported by special train services between Storlien and Haparanda. These 'Reichswehr specials' were guarded by Swedish troops. 'The sight of well-fed Germans hanging out of train windows, yahooing at Swedish girls, and carrying packages of food, butter and herrings out of starving Oslo is almost too much to stomach,' *Time* said.

A 2012 book by Norwegian journalist Espen Eidum, *Blodsporet* (The Blood Trail), noted that 1.04 million passenger journeys by German troops going on leave were made over the Swedish system. But more damning is Eidum's claim that in October 1940, after British and French troops landed at the Norwegian port of Narvik to try and stop the German invaders, Sweden permitted the Nazis to run supply trains through its territory destined for Narvik, carrying not only additional troops but also artillery, anti-aircraft guns, ammunition and communications equipment.

* * *

While Sweden did not end up being a belligerent, the country clearly feared in the late 1930s that it would be drawn into any large-scale European war. The main worry, so far as the railway network was concerned, was that should Swedish power stations be attacked, that would cripple the largely electrified rail system. So it was decided in 1938 to maintain several steam locomotives in a state where they could immediately be returned to traffic.

Then, with the end of the war, the new fear was the Cold War, Sweden being a near neighbour of the Soviet Union. So the steam engines were kept on, again maintained in a serviceable state and, also, scattered around depots or other building close to railway lines across the country. A few remain today as preserved operating locomotives.

FAST FACT: JAPAN'S GAUGE CHALLENGES

Challenge # 1: Northern China, including what became the Japanese puppet state of Manchukuo, was reasonably well endowed with railways, at least by comparison with other parts of Asia. But out west, and in the south, the network was minimal and six inland provinces had no railway lines at all.

When Japan seized part of northern China, then known as Manuchuria and subsequently called Manchukuo by the Japanese, it also gained the Russian-built China Eastern Railway which had been laid by the Tsarist government to run from Russia's border through northern China to the Pacific as an alternative outlet to the Trans-Siberian Railway. In 1934 the Russian line had come under Japanese control and the new masters immediately decided to re-gauge the track from Russia's 1,520 mm to be compatible with the standard gauge network in Manchuria. The first stage conversion was to involve the line between Harbin and Changchun (about 250 km), but in the form of a dual gauge line to allow both broad and standard gauge rolling stock to use the line. As most of the Russian rolling stock was in poor condition, the Japanese decided to gradually replace all of it, although some old American-made locomotives were to be kept in operation. The locomotives, all 2-10-0 Decapods, had previously been seized by the Communist forces fighting Chiang Kai-shek's Nationalist government and never paid for; fifty-three had been manufactured by the American Locomotive Company and seventy-one came from the Baldwin Locomotive Works and assembled in Vladivostok or Harbin. The engines had been ordered by the Kerensky government that took over after the tsar's abdication and which was later overthrown by Lenin and his allies. The new Soviet government claimed the engines as its property.

Challenge # 2: In late 1944 Tokyo began publicising its intention to revive the plan to have a rail corridor stretching from Korea to Burma. Dusting off old plans was a desperate move to overcome Japan's loss of merchant shipping to Allied naval vessels. The Japanese said the completed corridor would involve a seven-day journey from Tokyo to Rangoon; there would be ferry links from Japan to Fusan in Korea and over the Yangtze River. On a map, it did not look too challenging: there were existing railways over most of the route with, ostensibly, only a few gaps to be filled, mainly in southern China and in what is now Cambodia. There was only one major hitch to this seemingly simple solution: apart from the ferry services across the Tsushima Straits which were by this time in range of American bombers, and where the seas were often stormy, there was the rail gauge problem. Japanese freight wagons could not be ferried because, being built to the 3ft 6in gauge (1,067 mm) of Japanese lines, they could not be taken off at the other end in China where the gauge was 4ft 8½in (1,435 mm).

Then once you got to Indochina, the gauge was one metre, or 3ft 3⅜in. There were other problems, too: most of the route was single track, which limited the number of trains being able to use it at any one time. And it was unlikely that Japanese steel mills would have been able to produce the many miles of new rails required for either double-tracking or building the many passing loops that would be required.

Australia's Missing Link

IF THE AXIS POWERS had shortcomings in their rail systems, the Allies in the Pacific had their own problem: the main north-south link in Australia had a gap of almost 1,000 km between the southern section and the northern section, the latter from Darwin which Australian and Americans used as a key strategic post in the fight against Japan. It was too dangerous to send troops, weapons and materiel by sea. But the rail connection to Darwin had never been finished (although having been promised by the Federal government since 1911).

The northward transcontinental line began at Adelaide, with the first section to Port Pirie being laid to the broad gauge of 1,600 mm; thereafter the track, the Central Australia Railway (CAR), was narrow 1,067 mm gauge. But that line by 1941 ended at Alice Springs. Meanwhile the North Australia Railway (NAR) had been laid south as far as Larrimah, a scruffy little place of a few buildings that could hardly be described as a settlement. Between was that aforementioned 1,000km gap.

The attack on Pearl Harbor in December 1941 meant that Australia was now in a theatre of war. American forces began arriving in 1942 and connecting two rail lines was out of the question given the urgency of the new transport task. The Australian army in effect took control of the narrow gauge lines and requisitioned locomotives, wagons and carriages from Queensland Railways, Western Australian Government Railways and South Australian Railways, all of which had substantial narrow gauge systems. The CAR and NAR had been using antiquated stock, wagons being four-wheelers in the main and only manual signalling on the lines. Average speeds were under 25 km/h.

So the decision was made to seal the 'highway' between the two railheads (a task that involved large numbers of black American troops).

As a government statement of August 1942 noted, 'from the railhead at Alice Springs this vital artery of supply daily carries hundreds of tons of stores and equipment to the armed forces stationed on the northern boundaries along a route that hitherto had been followed by occasional herds of cattle from inland stations and where the passing of two motors in one week would have been considered most unusual'. (The use there of 'stations' is the Australian term for large outback farms or ranches.)

The NAR had, in 1939, notched up traffic figures of 52,085 train kilometres. In 1944 the figure was 1,193,372 train kilometres, with up to 147 trains a week.

American Know-how

AMERICAN FORCES LANDED IN Tunisia in November 1942. By mid-May 1943 1,290 km of the country's 1,930 km route length had been restored to operation. Forty bridges had been destroyed by the retreating Axis troops. The man put in charge was Carl R. Gray Jr., by then a brigadier general but (more importantly) a former senior executive of the Chicago, St Paul, Minneapolis and Omaha Railroad. Fortunately, the Germans and Italians did leave behind at least fifty serviceable locomotives and several hundred freight wagons. The army had a company of 350 men who had worked for the American railroads before joining up, with fifty train crews along with line gangs and workshop specialists, all now in uniform.

One former Alabama-based railroad man, now in 1943 Lt. Col. Fred W. Okie (aged thirty-four), was decorated after retrieving thirteen locomotives from one yard (and removing the side rods from those he could not save) while under constant fire by German tanks and a battery. He also hit an Axis ammunition train in a tunnel.

The Americans had also landed rail wagons shipped from the U.S. As the *Chicago Tribune* reported, 'standard gauge locomotives were shipped on the decks of ships ready to be fired up when landed. Narrow gauge engines were shipped knocked down because they had to be moved overland before being set up'. A Mikado 2-8-2 metre gauge locomotive was in operation in ninety-seven hours after it arrived in fourteen crates. The Tunisian narrow gauge system had employed similar locomotives before the war.

* * *

By 1945 America's railways were gearing up for a vast transportation task—the movement of the war supplies needed for the invasion of Japan. Over the previous twelve months, the U.S. railroad companies operating the main lines to the west had spent $200 million on new equipment and upgrading facilities. The war years had seen the railroad operators lay more double trackage to cut down on delays caused by trains having to wait to pass on loops along single track routes; they had also introduced more centralised traffic control and enlarged marshalling yards, not to mention buying new locomotives and freight wagons. It was all necessary: for example, the Atchison, Topeka and Santa Fe Railway—which was handling about thirty-five per cent of all wartime traffic moving between Chicago and California—by 1945 had 206 diesel locomotives in service and was using almost exclusively diesel traction (instead of steam) on the 740 km section between Winslow, Arizona, and Barstow, California. A train arrived or departed Winslow every twelve minutes, according to *The New York Times* in March 1945.

Well, yes, up to a point in terms of American railroad readiness. But the system was not ready for the German surrender in May 1945 and the decision at that point to transfer American forces from the European theatre to the Pacific, where the fighting was continuing against Japan; there would also been troops returning to bases in the United States. By November, it was estimated the railways would have to be prepared to carry 1.5 million troops from the Atlantic to Pacific ports.

Yet by July 1945 the railroad system in the U.S. was already feeling the strain. The American system had hauled more than twice the freight in 1944 than it had in 1939. Union Pacific alone had, between 1941 and 1943, bought 2,270 new freight wagons and 136 additional locomotives; steam locomotives had continued to be manufactured in the war years after a directive from Washington suspending new diesel engine production due to the great amounts of steel and other components required. Passenger car manufacture had been stopped once war with Japan began and resumed only in June 1945, too late to meet the need to carry millions of returning soldiers, sailors and airmen.

Returning servicemen found they were bundled on to trains that did not have enough seats for all those travelling, and many had to sleep on floors in the passenger cars. Then, too, the trains carrying the returning troops were not given top priority and it was common for these trains to wait long periods on sidings to keep lines clear for key freight workings and civilian passenger services. The Office of Defense Transportation ordered the railroad companies to pool passenger cars.

On 17 July 1945 Colonel J. Monroe Johnson, director of the Office of Defence Transportation, ordered that all passenger cars be placed at the disposal of the army. Around 30,000 carriages were subject to the order—15,320 conventional passenger cars, 2,228 baggage and passenger combination cars, and 12,449 baggage cars. The ODT warned civilians to avoid unnecessary rail journeys. 'Persons leaving home on unnecessary rail trips may find themselves unable to return,' the statement noted.

Rails on the Scrap Heap

'We're going to have to get more scrap some place and I know of no more feasible field than unproductive branch lines.'
        —Major E.T. Butler, Army and Navy Munitions Board,
        testimony to a U.S. Senate committee (October 1942).

IN JULY 1942 THE Interstate Commerce Committee (ICC) approved the ripping up of the 102 miles (164 km) line, operated by the Chicago and North Western Railway in Nebraska between the city of Hastings and the small village of Linwood. The reclaimed rails were to be used to lay spurs into war plants, shipyards and army camps.

Even before war broke out for the United States on 7 December 1941 there was an acknowledged shortage of scrap steel as American geared up for the coming conflict. *The Wall Street Journal* reported on 2 August 1941 that defence officials 'are expected to ask the railroads to tear up hundreds, perhaps thousands, of miles of unprofitable track-age to increase the scrap supply. The railroads like the idea'. Many of the lines taken out were carrying little traffic and generally unprofit-able; the railroads were often glad to see the back of them, having been previously unable to overcome local pressure groups dedicated to keeping their local rail lines

One source of metal for the war effort came from rail lines that were no longer needed. The War Production Board in Washington in 1943 set a target to collect 56,000,000 tons of scrap steel. The railroad companies did their bit: the *Washington Post* in June that year reported that one western rail operator ripped up forty-six miles of what it considered unnecessary sidings and 'a Pennsylvania railroad discovered four miles of track it did not know it owned'. The board set out to target, in particular, over-long sidings, level crossings built up with old rails, fences and railroad stops. (This was all on top of long-established scrap practices among the rail companies; Pennsylvania Railroad had been commonly selling up to 35,000 tons a month of scrap steel; the phasing out of streetcar services in American cities also provided a source of disused rails.) Water towers, bridges and trestles were also being fed into the furnaces.

At the Senate committee hearing addressed by Major Butler there were produced ICC statistics showing that Class I railroads totaled 154,217 miles of main lines and 77,644 miles of branch track. The commission had already changed its policies toward lines being abandoned and would no longer stand in the way of closures.

As 1943 approached the demand for scrap grew even larger with several new blast furnaces coming into operation. By November 1942 more than 1,500 miles of branch line railway had already been requi-sitioned by the government and relaid to form spurs where needed. 'Rail that once carried hay, grain and livestock now is serving in moving troops and supplies,' reported one newspaper that month; The War Department had also seized eighty gondola wagons and a number of small locomotives while the Maritime Commission had seized 171 interurban electric cars to transport war workers in California.

Among the lines that had been closed by the end of 1942 were short branches operated by such companies as the Susquehanna & New York Railroad (sixty miles between Marsh Hill Junction and

Towanda, Pennsylvania), Illinois Central (fifty-seven miles from Dodgeville, Wisconsin, to Red Oak, Illinois) and the Atchison, Topeka and Santa Fe (30.7 miles from Florence to Eldorado, Kansas).

Special Rail Duty in China

EVEN AS LATE AS December 1945, with the war over a full four months, 9,000 Japanese troops were still on duty in China as railway guards near the port of Chinwangtao (now Qinhuangdao) working alongside the U.S. Marines. Japanese military and civilians still working for the railways were anxious to ingratiate themselves with the American forces, by then in command of the area. They saw the Americans, according to newspaper accounts, as protectors against the anger of the local Chinese who reportedly beat Japanese and threw rocks at them. But the reporter found the Americans themselves to be angry, not just about having their former enemies as partners, but also about protecting British property in the form of the giant Kailan Mines Administration coal operation, located halfway between Tientsin and Chinwangtao. The mining company argued that, if the U.S. Marines were to leave, the mine operations would have to close.

Nine months on, and the Marines were even less happy. They were reported to be disillusioned with the Kuomintang (Nationalist) government of Chiang Kai-shek. The Americans' sole task by this time was to guard the Chingwangtao to Tientsin railway along with the associated (and 'filthy') settlements that housed the Chinese miners. These American troops had been living in bare shacks along the track but, in the expectation of staying another winter, were erecting barracks complete with electric lighting and bathrooms.

And Post-war?

THE RAILWAY TABLES WERE turned, that's what. While the Americans failed to build on what they had achieved with their own network, the Japanese undertook a total modernisation and overhaul of their antiquated rail system. Just after the Second World War, Japan's railways were not in good shape. Mark Reutter describes them thus: 'Built in narrow gauge and served by archaic steam locomotives, Japan's rail system was an antique assemblage of short lines whose construction had been financed by British traders in the nineteenth century'.

Japan's railway system was hit hard by the war. Less busy lines were closed and some double track sections were singled, with rails being sent elsewhere in Japan or to occupied territories.

In 1949 the United States military government in Tokyo reorganized the structure of the railways. Japan National Railways was created and separated from the Ministry of Transport. The Americans then insisted that about 100,000 staff be dismissed to reduce the losses being made on the railway system. JNR president Sudanori Shinoyama received death threats when the announcement was made and, soon after he had ordered dismissal notices for 37,000 staff, his mangled body was found on the track in a suburb of Tokyo. Communist railwaymen were also believed to be responsible for sending an unmanned train at full throttle into Mitaka station in suburban Tokyo, the crash resulting in six deaths and many injuries. There was also widespread sabotage: rocks were placed on lines, point/switch levers disabled and passing trains stoned.

But, after the occupation, JNR persisted with its modernisation plan and by 1959 work began on a high-speed line between Tokyo and Osaka. The first Shinkansen, or bullet train, ran on October 1964.

* * *

At the end of the war, more than half the passenger cars on Japan's railways were in a state where they could not be used, and 900 of the carriages in best running condition were expropriated by the American Occupation Authority; by 1948 the coaches left for carrying Japanese were in bad shape. 'They were structurally unsound assemblies of wood and steel, with bare seats, loose nails, excessive noise, leaking roofs, and blocked windows that reduced light and air,' writes historian Takashi Nishiyama. And there were not enough of them: peak hour trains could see four times the number of authorised passengers crammed into carriages.

The issue was made more urgent by a string of accidents involving the old and less than sturdy wooden cars. Between the end of the war and 1948 there were seventeen accidents with casualties in the double figures. In 1945 one head-on collision caused the death of 105 passengers; a month after the war ended another collision resulted in sixty deaths. The worst accident occurred on the Hachikō line on 27 February 1947 when a passenger train headed by a C57 class steam locomotive took a curve at excessive speed and the four rear-most carriages overturned. The wooden cars, which were heavily overcrowded, offered no protection and the passengers were crushed. There were 184 killed and 495 injured.

With the backing of the occupation authority, the national railways began on a program of building steel cars.

* * *

'The end of World War II found the Philippines in a sorry state of devastation. Not a single coconut mill was operable. Sugar mills had been destroyed. Inter-island shipping was non-existent. Concrete highways had been broken up for use on military airports in Taiwan, Japan and Korea. Railways were gone. Manila was eighty per cent destroyed as against ninety per cent for Cebu.' So wrote J. L Vellut, a research scholar at the Australian National University in 1963.

But even if the railways had been working, there would have been little business on offer for them.

It was a hard road back: by 1952 it was feared that the government-owned Manila Railroad would have to close; having come back from the wartime devastation, the railroad was still heavily in debt to its bondholders and had not paid interest on the bonds for some years. At that stage the company had ninety-six locomotives and 160 passenger carriages. It operated ten diesel locomotives and also buses to carry passengers on routes where the railway lines had not been restored after the war.

Country Profile: Ethiopia

Total track length: 681 km
Gauge: Standard gauge 1,435 mm (4ft 8½in)
Electrified: 681 km

Description

IN 2016 A NEW line was inaugurated between Djibouti and Addis Ababa, financed by China's Export-Import Bank and costing $3.4 billion. Freight trains were to complete the run between the two capitals in twelve hours, passenger trains in ten hours. Trains are able to run at speeds up to 120 km/h.

Reporting on the new line, *The Washington Post* noted that the French had left behind 'elegant, arcaded stations' in the heart of Addis Ababa and at Dire Dawa, but the line had been defunct for around a decade, a victim of war and neglect. 'The century-old tracks can still be seen in places from the new train but the Chinese elected to build all new stations,' the paper reported. The 100km Djibouti section was built under a separate contract with China Railway Construction Corporation.

The line is the first step in Ethiopia's rail plans: by 2020, the target is to have laid around 5,000 km of track, providing connections to Sudan, South Sudan and Kenya. In 2012 a contract was signed for the construction by 2018 of a line beginning at Wash, a station on the Addis Ababa line, to Hara Gebeya, 389 km to the north (which will be followed by a line from the latter to Djibouti).

* * *

On 1 January 1903 what was then known as the Imperial Ethiopian Railway was opened as far as Addis Harra (now Harar), 308 km from the port at Jibuti, French Somaliland (now Djibouti). But that left a 500 kilometre gap to reach the capital, Addis Ababa. The gauge was 1,000 mm.

In June 1903 a correspondent for *The Times* took the train on the partly competed line, beginning at the terminus in French Somaliland.

He reported that station at Jibutu had sufficient accommodation for any traffic it conveyed at that time 'or is likely to convey for some time to come'. There were spacious offices and waiting rooms, good engine sheds and warehouses 'and are better fitted for the comfort of passengers and the loading and unloading of trucks than the stations on any one of the Egyptian railways, with the exception of the Cairo-Alexandria main line'.

The train on which he travelled consisted of one first class carriage, four open trucks and a van. Two trucks were loaded with iron rails, upon which sat the African passengers

Although the line had been completed as far as Harra, the correspondent wrote, regular trains terminated at Atigala, 80 km short of the railhead. The line crossed a number of gullies, which could become swollen torrents after heavy rain. Up to Atigulla these gullies were crossed using iron bridges supported by stone masonry, but beyond that there were just temporary wooden structures that were liable to be washed away after a downpour. The train stopped every 15 km to 20 km to refill their tenders from wells, as often the wells dug at the various stations had run dry. 'The railway authorities profess to be confident that in a short time this difficulty will be surmounted,' wrote the newspaper's correspondent.

His conclusion: 'Never in any part of the world have I seen a country so utterly devoid of inhabitants, vegetation, crops or culture, as the region in question ... I could see nothing but endless expanse of stones … gorges without water or verdure, vast plains covered with scrub and thorns, but neither trees, nor crops, nor villages, nor signs of animal life'. He concluded that traffic would never be sufficient to make the Imperial Ethiopian Railway a profitable concern.

* * *

Yet in 1937 *The Wall Street Journal* was telling a quite different story about this line, which by that time had reached the capital. Abyssinia, as the country was called then, had been occupied by Italian troops and the invaders had completed a road to offer an alternative land route to Addis Ababa. The paper reported that the railway operator, Chemin-de-Fer Franco-Ethyopien, was proving itself 'a little gold mine'. Despite the problems faced due to the invasion and occupation by Italy, tonnage had increased in 1937, as did the number of passengers (300,000 for the year). The company was shipping 1,000 tons daily by rail and running two passenger trains weekly, covering the distance in less than twenty-four hours.

5

Rails to Nowhere
(or Hardly Anywhere)

'NIGERIAN Railways Corp is once again on the point of collapse, with only 30 of its 200 locomotives in working order, according to Board Chairman Alhaji Waziri Mohammed. What is particularly sad is that the 50 Class 2101 locos, 150 passenger coaches, 20 railcars, 100 guard's vans and 400 wagons supplied in 1998 from China under a deal worth US$529m now need urgent repairs.'

Railway Gazette International, 1 April 2001

THE NEW RAILWAY AGE has passed by quite a few countries. There have a been a handful of successes: building a new railway through Djibouti and Ethiopia, rehabilitating the system in Angola, and the new lines being built in Mozambique to serve mining projects stand out as exceptions. Unfortunately, there are still numerous developing countries whose rail systems are run down or inoperative and are not likely to be given a brand new, modern railway. Here are some of the less fortunate in the global railway fraternity.

Benin

Total route length: 438 km
Gauge: Narrow gauge 1,000 mm (3ft 3⅜in)

In August 2016 a British newspaper reported that Benin's rail system was so run down that only twenty freight trains made the

Cotonou-Parakou trip each month, and each run taking twelve hours to cover the 438 km distance.

In 2014 the French logistics giant Bolloré, which has a dominant position in Francophile Africa, took over the Benin rail network. Then a Benin billionaire went to court to dispute the transaction. Bolloré was prevented from implementing its plans to upgrade the railway and it was reported that a new passenger train set brought from France had been sitting idle and not used.

The Bolloré move into Benin followed the decision by the Benin and Niger governments to renovate the original line (in Benin) and extend it into landlocked Niger. Bolloré was reported to have laid 140 km of new track in Niger before the court decision against it. The newspaper reported that a large quantity of rails had been lying in the Benin capital but Bolloré could not proceed to lay them northward to the Niger border.

Before the court decision, Bolloré paid wage arrears (covering nineteen months) to rail staff and also pension payments to retired railway workers.

In June 2017 it was reported that Bolloré was operating trains in Benin under the name of Benirail, with stakes held by the Benin and Niger governments. The line was in the news that month after a train struck a bus, with several people being killed.

* * *

Railway projects sometimes spend a very, very long time in the development pipeline. The aforementioned extension of the Benin railway to Niger (at the time of writing yet again delayed) has been proposed on several previous occasions. For example, in June 1963—at which time Benin was known by its French colonial title, Dahomey—and while reporting on railway plans in Francophone Africa, *The Economist* noted that 'the French speaking republic of Niger is planning to build a railway to take its produce the long way around through Dahomey; Nigeria is considered "English" and therefore a route through Nigeria, though shorter and far more economic, is thought unreliable'.

Ghana

Total route length: 947 km (134 km operational as of January 2016)
Gauge: Narrow gauge 1,067 mm (3ft 6in)
Axle load: 16 tonnes

THERE ARE THREE MAIN lines: Western Line 340 km, Central Line 240 km, and the Eastern Line 330 km.

The 2013 Ghana Railway Master Plan said that most of the existing rolling stock was 'quite outdated, corresponding to the "state of the art" twenty-five years ago'. Only a few of the locomotives (GM, Henschel and Alstom models) were equipped with six axles, and were less than twenty years old and had sufficient adherent mass for heavy freight trains. GM and Henschel members of the fleet were, however, not very powerful being only around 1,600 horsepower; Astom engines had around 2,500 hp rated power.

Fleet availability was also compromised by lack of spare parts and suitable maintenance tools and equipment. Passenger coaches were in need of 'major maintenance interventions', especially the interiors including lighting, toilets and windows. The goods wagon fleet needed extensive repair and overhaul and at that time could not be used on railway operations.

But maintenance depots and workshops were of a size far in excess of requirements, most of them dating back to a time when rail operations were more flexible and the rolling stock roster much larger.

Guatemala

Total route length: 799 km (closed)
Gauge: Narrow gauge 914 mm (3ft 0in)

NO TRAINS OPERATE. The railway system closed in 1996 due to a number of factors, one being the fact that some stretches of track were no longer usable. Thus ended the long history of the government-owned railway, Ferrocarriles de Guatemala. The following year the government awarded a fifty-year concession to the Pittsburg-based Railway Development Corporation (RDC), which brought in

Guatemala investors as partners to form Ferrovias Guatemala (FVG). The other problems had been loss of traffic, and squatters building on the rail right-of-way, and then further damage was caused in 1998 by Hurricane Mitch. In April 1999, though, RDC was able to introduce its first rail service, a 60 km haul of cement between Guatemala City and El Chile. A few months later train services were extended to Puerto Barrios and Puerto Santo Tomas, two ports on the Atlantic coast.

RDC restored the network to an operational state over a route length of 322 km, using six locomotives and 130 freight wagons, with the main consignments being containers, steel, cement, paper and bananas.

All seemed to be going well when, in 2006, the government decreed that the leasing contract was harmful to the state, and the Americans refused to accept new more onerous conditions. The last train ran in September 2007. The company says that 'since then the railway has literally disappeared with even steel bridges being stolen for scrap'.

A 2012 report in the *Pittsburg Post-Gazette* said the decree was issued after RDC refused to develop the railway system along the western coast of the country on the grounds that it would have lost money. RDC won compensation after appealing to the International Centre for the Settlement of Investment Disputes.

In 2012 Spanish metre-gauge operator FEVE investigated running passenger service from Guatemala City to the international airport.

* * *

Guatemala City was joined to the Pacific Ocean by rail in 1884, the first line being 121.5 km in length. In 1912 the United Fruit Company established International Railways of Central America (IRCA), although the fruit company's own product—bananas—never provided more than ten per cent of the freight carried by the railway. IRCA was listed on the New York Stock Exchange until 1965. The 2007 book, *Encyclopedia of North American Railroads* (see bibliography) noted that, under IRCA, the 'locomotive shops in Guatemala City were extensive and impressive. At more than 500 miles (805 km), the Guatemala network linking Mexico, El Salvador, and the Atlantic

Two scenes from the shortlived revival by Railway Development Corporation of Guatemala's railway network. *Henry Posner III.*

and Pacific oceans with Guatemala City—was the most extensive in Central America'.

The system was entirely steam-hauled until 1954, the Baldwin company having supplied thirty-two 2-8-2 locomotives between 1946 and 1948. The railroad company had obtained some diesel locomotives in 1950 but their introduction was delayed for four years due to union resistance to job losses. Then in the 1950s a new highway was opened between Guatemala City and Puerto Barrios, a development the *Encylopaedia* described as 'a shattering blow' for the railway.

Libya

Total route length: 0 km

LIBYA IS THE LARGEST country, in terms of land area, without a functioning railway. The system built under Italian rule closed in 1966; it consisted of two isolated systems, one based on Tripoli with the line extending from that city both eastwards and westwards to Zwara and Tajiura, with a branch running southwards to Gharian; the other section ran from Benghazi in two directions, to Soluch and Barce. The former was called Tripolitania Railways, the latter Cyrenaica Railways.

When Italy seized Libya from the Ottoman Empire in 1911 it drew up plans for a narrow gauge railway to connect Tripoli and Benghazi across the desert areas south of the Mediterranean coast, and bruited ideas for lines to as far south as Lake Chad through French territory. An 18 km line from Tripoli harbor was completed in early 1912 and handed over to Italian State Railways. Then followed two lines east and west along the coast, with the branch to Gharian also laid. The track was laid to 950 mm (3ft 1⅜in), a gauge chosen by Italians for some lines at home but also in the other colonies of Eritrea and Italian Somaliland.

In 1914 the English traveller Ethel Braun took a train on the line that was, by 1929, to reach Gharian. 'The train travels very smoothly, if not fast, there being several long waits to take in goods of all kinds at the various stations by the way,' she wrote. 'We reached Azizia (now Al-Aziziya) at 10.30, having covered a distance of about thirty miles.

The train is really timed to arrive at 9.30, but much depends on the amount of cargo to be taken in.'

The railway went into decline during the First World War when tribesmen tried to reclaim the area while Italy was preoccupied with fighting the Austrians. Mussolini seized power in 1922 and reactivated railway building in the colony.

But it was hard going. As Stefano Maggi and Rutger Gras explain (see bibliography), oven-type temperatures, wind storms and poor water quality (for locomotive use) made life hellish for those trying to keep the trains running. In the 1920s about thirty locomotives were in operation, a dozen 0-8-0Ts built by Schwartzkopf of Berlin, five 0-4-0T engines from Hannomag of Hanover, several 2-6-0Ts built in Milan. On top of those, four 0-4-4-0T Mallets were shipped from Eritrea along with three 2-8-2+2-8-2 Garratts built by Ansaldo, the industrial giant based in Genoa. All coal was imported and sometimes locomotives ran with an extra tender attached to deliver water to settlements along the line.

In 1938 five Fiat diesel railcars were added to the fleet.

Most of the trains were mixed; that is, hauling both freight wagons and passenger carriages. During World War II the railways were pressed into serving the German and Italian forces, including supply of Axis forces at El Alamein.

Much of the system was destroyed through Allied bombing and other military action, and services were a shadow of their former selves after the war. A railcar from Walker Brothers arrived in 1953 and was used between Benghazi and El Merj (as Barce had been renamed). But the decline went unaddressed, with the Tripoli-based operation out of action by 1962. The last line, to El Merj, was closed in 1966 and signaled the end of Libya's other railway network.

* * *

Under the rule of Moammar Gaddafi, most of the old stations were demolished and the rails either stolen or sold off as scrap. But there was a change of direction in 2008 when Libya signed contracts with foreign companies to rebuild the country's railways to the standard gauge; Chinese companies were to lay track from the Tunisian border to Sirte, 450 km east of Tripoli; the Russians were to complete the new line as far as the Egyptian border, including an 800 km branch line south from Sirte to Sebha. In all, Libya was to have a rail network with a total length of 3,176 km. American-made locomotives were landed in 2008.

The plan was initially to have diesel-electric traction with top speeds of 160 km/h, followed by eventual conversion to electrification and speeds up to 250 km/h. All work stopped in 2011 as a result of unrest in Libya. There has been no progress since.

Paraguay

Total route length: 30 km
Gauge: Standard gauge 1,435 mm (4ft 8½in)

RAILWAY SERVICES IN PARAGUAY shriveled from 1995. The filling of a hydroelectric dam severed the railway at one point, although a short passenger service continued to run from the capital, Asuncion, over a 44 km route for another four years. There was also a tourist train operated for a while. But no trains were able to operate from the capital to connect with the Argentine rail system, even though Paraguay is one of the world's biggest exporters of soybean, and rail is the most economic means of transporting that product.

Since then various proposals have been suggested, including a rail connection with Brazil. A South Korean-funded study looked into a new linkage with Argentina while an Italian team studied the suggestion of an isolated suburban line outwards from Asuncion.

* * *

The Paraguay government built the first section of rail in 1861 but the railway system was taken over and expanded by a British firm, the Paraguay Central Railway Company. That company operated the line until it was nationalised in 1961. The railway, back in government hands, retained wood-powered steam locomotives until the end of operations.

One of the last steam engines left in service, No. 59, passing through San Salvador, located near the halfway mark between Asuncion and the Argentine border. This photograph was taken in 1995. *Patrick Rudin.*

Locomotive 151 passing Luque station on the outskirts of Asuncion in 1995. The state of the wagon on the siding, the state of the permanent way and that of the water tower attest to the decline of Paraguay's rail network in its final years. *Patrick Rudin.*

The original line was built to the 5ft 6in (1,676 mm) gauge.

The Paraguay railway system had two inbuilt weaknesses. One was that the 376 km line between Asuncion and the border with Argentina had no branch lines, so the rail could draw traffic and revenue from only a slice of Paraguay close to that one main line; another was that it was dependent upon the Argentina rail system for access to the world market.

There were other problems, too: in the 1930s Argentina placed an import ban on Paraguay oranges, which in 1936 in particular had serious effects on the freight revenues of the railway company. During the Great Depression there was not only a drop in export freight, but weakening demand for passenger travel to the connection at the border at the town of Encarnación, with most passenger revenue that year coming from suburban services at Asuncion.

In the early years, however, prospects seemed bright for the British railway enterprise. In 1911 *The Economist* was greatly optimistic even though Paraguay had just suffered one of its revolutions; the magazine thought there would be no impact on the railway. 'The Paraguay Central Railway Company reports a handsome increase in its net receipts, and by judicious financial arrangement with the Argentine government, has succeeded in converting the line into the standard (4ft 8½in) gauge,' it noted. 'The new rolling stock has all been bought in the United Kingdom, and when it arrives the company will be able to run their trains over the lines of the line of the Argentine North-Eastern and the Entre Rios railways ... As only twenty-five miles of the line need to be made, and as arrangements have been made for a ferry across the Parana which will connect Encarnacion, the last station in Paraguay, with Posadas, the first in Argentina, this great work will ... be a triumph of British enterprise.'

At the annual meeting in London in 1926, the chairman noted that the best year for timber traffic had been 1919-20 (94,000 tons) and for oranges it was 1925-26, when 33,200 tons were carried on the trains.

* * *

Discussions were held between Bolivia and Paraguay in 2016 regarding a proposed 'bioceanic' railway that would run from the Brazilian

port at Santos, via Paraguay and Bolivia, to Ilo, a port city on
Peru's coastline.

Then in January 2017 Bolivian and Paraguayan officials signed a
bilateral agreement to investigate a rail link connecting the two countries. The investigation will focus on a line from Roboré in eastern
Bolivia, across Paraguay to the border with Brazil at Puerto Carmelo
on the Paraguay River where there are plans to build a new bridge to
link the two countries.

Senegal

DAKAR: A RAIL METROPOLIS that did not happen. In December 1918,
just a month after the end of the First World War, a well-known French
engineer, Henri Bressler, unveiled a scheme for a railway from Paris to
Dakar, the capital of what was then French West Africa (and now the
capital of Senegal). The scheme had backing from influential figures in
Paris and it was given considerable publicity by the world's press, *The
New York Times* according it a large section of a page complete with
detailed maps.

While the proposed route from Tangier to Dakar would run close
to the Atlantic coast, mainly through French-controlled territory and
the Spanish colony of Río de Oro (later Spanish Sahara and now the
disputed Western Sahara) and thus face no great engineering requirements, the most ambitious part of the plan was the need for a tunnel
under the Straits of Gibraltar, where the seabed depth was around
1,000 metres in places. The tunnel was to be 24 km long and equipped
for electric locomotives.

Bressler offered a number of alluring attractions with his scheme.
One was that ships could cross from South America in a fewer number
of days than going all the way to Europe (by steamer from Recife in
Brazil the sea journey would be just four days to Dakar) and freight
and passengers would reach Paris by rail in just a further three days.
Another selling point was that it would connect Spain to the rest of
Europe with a standard gauge line running the length of its territory
and going via Madrid; Spain was then isolated by the fact that its main
lines were laid to the so-called Iberian gauge (1,668 mm or 5ft $5^{21}/_{32}$in).
Yet another was the idea that a separate line could run from Tangier

to the Belgian Congo (now Democratic Republic of Congo) and thus link to the then railhead of the 'Cape to Cairo' line which had been built from South Africa and but which had by then reached only as far as the Belgian territory; it would, it was argued, allowed Belgian business people and colonial officials to travel from Brussels to their territory in Africa in just five days. Bressler also argued that that Russians would be able to travel from Petrograd (St Petersburg's wartime name) to Morocco. Almost one hundred years later, and if proposed today, it would not seem so revolutionary.

Sierra Leone

This country no longer has a common carrier railway. At its greatest extent the former government railway covered 458 km.

THE NATIONAL RAILWAY SYSTEM was closed down in 1974. The first line in this former British colony was opened in 1897, the first section to the cooler hills district so that British colonial officials could escape the heat of the capital. When completed, the main route from Freetown to Pendembu in the northeast of the country covered a distance of 366 km. A long branch was built to Makeni.

The railway was built to the 762 mm gauge (2ft 6in) and in 1920 a correspondent for *The Times* of London reported that, notwithstanding the narrowness of the gauge, the train 'conveys passengers in surprisingly roomy saloon coaches and goods in trucks carrying eight tons or more … In Freetown the railway run through the streets, American style, but the terminal station is quite imposing'. Station names along the included Hastings, Waterloo and Bradford.

That's not quite way Grahame Greene saw it in 1935 when he described the two-day journey upcountry, where the train travelled around 15 mph, or 24 km/h. Greene wrote: 'I had never been so hot and so damp; if we pulled down the blinds in the small dusty compartment we shut out all the air; if we raised them, the sun scorched the wicker, the wooden floor, drenched hands and knees in sweat'.

The line played an important part in the Second World War with aircraft being unloaded at Freetown docks, railed upcountry and then flown to Egypt.

Dieselisation took place in the early 1950s and new goods wagons were installed. In 1961, the year Sierra Leone gained its independence from Britain, there were also photographs in British newspapers of new coaching stock being unloaded from a ship at Freetown. But by the 1970s there were reports that the Sierra Leone government was complaining that the British had not offered any help to keep the railway in operation, and the country did not have the money to convert the lines to standard gauge. In 1968 some section of lines were closed By the early 1970s services were subject to disruption on the remaining line due to locomotive breakdowns.

The closure of the railway was economically devastating for upcountry farmers who had used it to transport fresh produce to the capital.

* * *

There is a fascinating postscript to this story. A group of railwaymen who had lost their jobs upon closure locked away several locomotives and carriages and after the civil war this rolling stock was saved from being sold off to Chinese scrap merchants. The engines, built in Yorkshire, are now safe in the hands of the Friends of Sierra Leone Railway Museum in Freetown. They will form a core of rebuilding Sierra Leone's economy and are intended to become a tourism attraction.

South Sudan

Total route length: 248 km (inoperable)
Gauge: Narrow gauge 1,067 mm (3ft 6in)

IN 2016 AN ARM of the Rome-based World Food Program published this assessment of the railway situation in South Sudan:

> South Sudan does not have an extensive rail system and current rail
> infrastructure, which was constructed between 1959-1962 and what
> has been left over from the previous Sudan government, is in a serious
> state of disrepair. In 2010, the track was rehabilitated ... with the aim

of revitalising the sector and increasing cargo and passenger transport capacity into the area. However current rail operations have been suspended due to border closures, unserviceable equipment, a lack of capacity, and non-operational rolling stock.

The single, 1067 mm (3ft 6in) gauge, 446 km rail connection linking Babanusa in Sudan to Wau in South Sudan forms part of a rail transport corridor that extends up to Port Sudan and which forms an important transportation link into South Sudan's Northern and Western Bar El Ghazal states with a 248 km link from the border to the major towns of Aweil and Wau. Regionally, however, there has been a shift towards road transport due to the relatively high rail tariff costs, unreliable service and unavailability of adequate assets and general poor management.

When reopened, and rail capacity fully realised, the railway line could serve as a key part of the domestic transport system, and even though the government has indicated the desire to revitalize and extend the network, the current emphasis is on the expansion of the road network and any transport costs will, for the foreseeable future, be constrained by road competition.

Sudan

Total route length: 4,578 km
Gauge: Narrow gauge 1,067 mm (3ft 6in)

IN 2016, THE SITUATION in Sudan was summed up thus by the French English-language news channel France 24:

> Prior to 1997, Sudan's railways, then the largest network on the continent, transported millions of tons of goods and passengers annually. But two decades of U.S. sanctions have crippled the railway system. Unable to import spare parts to repair eroding tracks and a long-outdated fleet of locomotives, Sudan has been forced to ground most of its trains.

Sudan once had one of the longest (operational) railway systems in Africa. Before the separation of its southern areas with the creation of South Sudan, the system totalled 5,898 km. The first railways were built by the British to aid their military efforts to subdue the Madhi uprising.

As Reuters noted in 2013, the state railway operator once controlled trade along the Nile, Sudan's ports and the national telegraph network. It owned housing compounds for its 30,000 employees. In 1959 the railway made up fifty-nine per cent of Sudan's gross domestic product. In the 1970s more than two million passenger journeys a year were recorded and freight trains hauled exports to Port Sudan.

A report by Japan's foreign aid agencies (the Institute of Developing Economies and the Japan External Trade Organisation) notes that 'the 1980s saw a steady erosion of tonnage as a result of a combination of inefficient management, union intransigence, the failure of agricultural projects to meet production goals, the dearth of spare parts, and the continuing civil war'. After an Islamist coup in 1989, two-thirds of the work force was laid off as they were seen as supporters of the Communist Party.

The majority of the rail track remains decrepit. Most track dates from pre-1930.

In 2013 Ulf Lassing of Reuters reported that at Atbara, Sudan's most important rail centre (it included the main workshops), was a scene of locomotives and passenger coaches standing still in the scorching heat. 'The trains broke down years ago and many of the coach windows have been smashed, while the tracks they stand on are derelict', he wrote.

Three years later, in November 2016, Britain's *The Guardian* newspaper reported that a passenger service, known as the Nile train, was operating between Khartoum and Atbara using two six-car sets of the CSR Ziyand diesel multiple units supplied from China. The state of the track limited speeds to 60 km/h. The paper noted that only eighteen of the corporation's 106 U.S.-made locomotives remained in service while the 'sprawling workshop at Atbara resembles a graveyard, dotted with numerous train carcasses which have been cannibalised down to the last screw to keep the remaining locomotives on life support'.

Togo

Total route length (2014): 568 km
Gauge: Narrow gauge 1,000 mm (3ft 3⅜in)

THE TOGOLESE RAILWAY SYSTEM is believed to be inactive and that no trains have run in recent years apart from cement trains using a 3km line across the border in Ghana to load shipments from the Diamond cement plant in the Ghanaian border town on Afloa, and then running to the wharves in the Togolese capital, Lomé.

The most recent information found is in a 2014 International Monetary Fund report stating that the country's rail network included 'nearly 519 km of rundown metric gauge lines, 160 km of which are completely out of service and partially dismantled (the Lomé-Kaplimé and Lomé-Aného lines). This means it is no longer possible to meet the level of service quality required by the Union of African Railways'. The central line (Lomé-Blitta, 276 km) should be Togo's main service line to landlocked countries.

The IMF saw the main priorities being the rehabilitation and construction of the Lomé-Cinkassé-Burkina Faso border line and the modernisation of the existing network. The Lomé-Cinkassé rail line was to provide a link to the Burkina Faso border, 'to serve Burkina Faso, Mali, and Niger, and thus encourage the flow of trade between Togo and these countries'.

In a separate section, the IMF noted: 'The rail network, which dates from the colonial era, includes some extremely dilapidated stretches'.

France's Bolloré Group, a large logistics players, has laid out plans for a 2,740 km West African railway loop to include the Abidjan to Ouagadougou line, a proposed new line linking Ouagadougou, Burkina Faso, Niamey in Niger, Benin's northern railhead of Parakou in Benin and Lomé in Togo.

Yemen

YEMEN HAS NO RAILWAY, but ambitions for one have a long history. In 2006 the then government enlisted several foreign countries to help with a feasibility study, and there were plans for a Chinese delegation to look at building such a line. Those rail ambitions have taken various shapes.

Earlier proposals included one in 1908 whereby Turkish authorities planned to lay a line from Hodeida to Sana'a but that involved building through inhospitable high country. The Turks then settled on a more coastal route. But that was not built, either. (Yemen was part of the Ottoman Empire until Turkey's defeat in 1918, the Ottomans having been allies of Germany and Austria-Hungary.)

More recently, in 2010 there were announced plans for a $3.6 billion line to run from the border with Saudi Arabia, along the Yemeni coast (including via the port of Aden) and on to Oman, and in 2012 a refined design for a 2,155 km line costing $1.29 billion was unveiled. Since then war and disorder have destroyed much of Yemen.

Three Lines, Mixed Success

IN THE WESTERN PART of the Australian state of Victoria, there are about 40,000 square kilometres of country described as 'the Mallee', an unwelcoming semi-desert zone typified by 'Mallee scrub', which consists of varieties of stunted eucalypt species, the result of an uncertain and often non-existent rainfall. No place to dream dreams of intensive agriculture, of course—or a railway network, either. But these obvious drawbacks did not deter the good people of Victoria.

There is just one sizeable settlement in the Mallee, the city of Mildura, sitting on the banks of the mighty Murray River and its prosperity based on irrigation and citrus fruit. Mildura was connected to Melbourne by rail on 27 October 1903, and this triggered demands for branch railways to 'open up' the Mallee to farming. The Mallee was, like so many unpopulated areas of Australia at the time, an itch that was waiting to be scratched. Nothing could halt attempts at settlement and a great deal of public money was squandered before the dreamers were done.

The railway dreamers had been encouraged by the recommendations of a royal commission report in 1911; the commisioners asserted the Mallee was ideal for growing wheat. When the surveyors set to work, they had a blank canvas. There were no towns and few roads on some proposed routes. They could decide the route of the railway lines on the assumption that settlement would, of necessity, take place on either side of the railway line once the track was laid.

Three lines would end up being laid from points along the Mildura main line.

There was one from Ouyen to the South Australian border, 129.4 km in all, completed in 1915. The Ouyen-Pinnaroo line (Pinnaroo being just across the border with South Australia) is still in use, at least as far as Murrayville (27 km short of Pinnaroo). This line is, at the time of writing, being converted to standard gauge. It is used for seasonal grain haulage.

Then there was the Red Cliffs to Morkalla line, 97 km long and finished in 1931.

The first, but disregarded, sign of the problems that lay ahead for this line for any settlers was that the Victorian state government was required to provide water tanks, each holding 136,000 litres, as the railway progressed, there being no surface water available to the construction gangs. By April 1923 construction branch trains were operating over a 30 km section although it appears that the primary task of those trains was to haul wagons, each holding 9,000 litres of water. Another sign of the difficulties ahead was the scene at Werrimull, the station that signified the end of the first section to be officially opened. When that station did open for business on 11 April 1924 there was a station all right—but not much else. The station had a crossing loop and a 362-metre siding but no sign existed of other human activity because the land had yet to be opened up for settlement. The first scheduled train carried no freight, there having been no freight consigned.

However, the lack of traffic or passengers for that line did not discourage the demands for further lengthening of the line and, by 1927, there was talk of taking the rails to the South Australian border (and proposals were being bandied about in Melbourne's *The Argus* newspaper for a further *three* rail projects in the Mallee). By that time, Victorian newspapers were reporting that things had not gone well around the line from Red Cliffs (which by now had a 24.5 km extension opened to Meringur). There was one headline that summed it up: 'No Harvest', followed by a second deck of type proclaiming 'Courageous Victorian Settlers'. In 1927 the planting failed to produce

Thurla, the first station on the Red Cliffs–Morkalla line. It illustrates the manner
in which Victorian Railways managed so many small country stations: the husband
was the track repairer and his wife was the stationmistress. Mr. and Mrs. Gettings are
pictured here about 1929. *Museum Victoria.*

The railway's arrived, but where's the business for it? The economics of the
railway to Morkalla in Victoria's Mallee lands is plain to see in this picture. This
photograph was taken in 1932 and shows the Morkallo railway yard a year after the
line's opening—with nary a settler or farmer in sight. *Museum Victoria.*

a harvestable crop, but the newspaper report added that 'settlers interviewed at Werrimull stated they intended staying on the land. They
liked the life in spite of the hardships'.

Not satisfied with the extension to Meringur, there were then cries
from the pro-railway lobby for the line to be taken on to the South
Australian border—and indeed it was, the extra 15.5 km section being
opened on 16 June 1931. Yet there was demand sufficient to justify
only one train a month (the first Thursday of each month). *The Argus*
dubbed it the 'Once-a-Month Line'.

The third project consisted of 39.1 km of track from Nowingi
to a place dubbed 24 Miles (laid in 1929 and 1930) known as the
Nowingi-Millewa South line. It was not officially opened to traffic but
was used for some years by the Brunswick Plaster Company to haul
gypsum mined in the area; the company had its own 'home-made'
diesel engine hauling Victorian Railways wagons between the deposit
and the main line.

The claims from the boosters had been similar to those seeking the
line to the north: a million acres would be opened up by a railway to
Nowingi; there were 800 British migrants expected to take up land
if it were offered and the Federal government could be expected to
provide finance under its development and migration programs. In
December 1927 the Victorian Parliament passed the 'Nowingi to
Millewa South Railway Construction Act' and another railway folly
was unleashed.

By July 1929, this latest rail project was—not surprisingly—facing
problems. One was lack of water; another was the discovery that the
site of one proposed station turned out to be buried under a large
sand ridge.

It saw only one passenger train: a special working carrying Chief
Commissioner for Railways Harold Clapp on an inspection visit.

Before reality hit, the planners in Melbourne were scheduling a
thrice-weekly goods train service with passenger car attached. It was
a telling commentary that the proposed terminus of Millewa South
named in the enabling legislation did not actually exist as a settlement
and was nothing more than a patch of scrub. The proposed stations
along the planned line were given names relating to their distances
from Nowingi, there being no actual places where the stations were

to be located, but this did not deter the planners in Melbourne drawing up lists of where staff would be assigned: while 6 Mile, 18 Mile, 35 Mile and 49 Mile were to be unstaffed sidings, three stations were to have caretakers assigned (11 Mile, 24 Mile, and 42 Mile); but 30 Mile and 56 Mile were seen as potentially important enough to require the appointed at those places of stationmasters.

But, in the end, all it saw was the occasional rake of wagons loaded with gypsum. It closed in 1988.

Ballast is no revenue earner

NEW ZEALAND'S TOPOGRAPHY WAS such a challenge to railway builders that it is not surprising several false starts were made with important rail projects. In the South Island, particularly, a myriad of short branch lines sprang up and almost immediately became a drain on the finances of New Zealand Railways.

But one of the most ill advised projects occurred on the east coast of the North Island—the Ngatapa branch in what was then the Poverty Bay region on the east coast of the North Island, now known as Gisborne province. The line had been authorised as a route between Gisborne and the railhead of Wairoa, from which existing track provided a connection with the capital, Wellington. Such a plan was to be defeated by the topography; the line would be abandoned and, instead, Gisborne's connection to the national rail network would be achieved by a coastal route—but not for a considerable time: work would begin on the Ngatapa line in 1911 but it would be 1942 before the coastal link was completed and opened.

Ngatapa was reached in 1915 but the line would be operated for nine years by the Public Works Department before being handed over to New Zealand Railways in 1924. On 10 December 1915 the Gisborne newspaper, the *Poverty Bay Herald*, reported that if residents along the line wanted to go into the main town of Gisborne, then there was a train on Saturday morning, with passengers having travelled to the main city able to make their return on Monday mornings but 'as the service is being run in conjunction with the goods and ballast service, the Public Works Department will not hold themselves to any stated time of arrival in Ngatapa'.

It was the reality of the country beyond Ngatapa that did for the project. Apart from the need for extensive tunnelling, the formation beyond the terminus would have taken the line through a 180-degree turn and then followed a winding track through hills and valleys.

If it was not going to be connection to the main line, then the Ngatapa branch soon showed it could not justify being kept as a rural branch line. The only significant traffic was gravel, some for use on unsealed roads, mainly for ballast on the 18.51 km line, and passenger services rarely attracted more than a handful of customers.

The decision in 1924 to use a coastal route meant the running down of work on extending the line beyond Ngatapa; much formation work had been carried out beyond the railhead and three short tunnels cut, but rails were never laid beyond Ngatapa. This development robbed the line of its only traffic: ballast. The line was closed on from 1 April 1931. However (and unusually for New Zealand where track was usually ripped up as soon as a line was closed), demolition did not immediately commence. This meant that in 1938 one last revenue earning train could run as far as the station of Patutahi. The New Zealand Petroleum Company briefly explored what was known as the Totangi Dome looking for oil, and on 26 July 1938 a locomotive-hauled four wagons containing drilling equipment as far as Patutahi.

An American Transcontinental Overreach

BUILD A RAIL LINE from Kansas City, Missouri, right across the United States and then through Mexico to a port on the latter's coast as a draw-card for freight travelling from eastern America and the Far East? Why not, thought the promoters of the Kansas City, Mexico and Orient Railroad. In their minds, the project was obviously a goer—a route that would have involved laying or gaining rights to track length of 1,659 miles (2,669 km).

The project was financed by the issuing of $24.53 million of bonds due to be redeemed in 1951, $12.5 million of preferred stock and $12.5 million of common stock. The investors never saw a return.

Construction began in 1901 with the laying of track across largely agricultural and grazing land in Kansas and Oklahoma. The plan was to reach the port of Topolobampo on the Gulf of California, located near the city of Los Mochis. A deal was done to work with the Hamburg-American Line shipping company to provide the oceanic link to Asia.

Work stopped on the project in 1912 when the railroad company ran into financial problems and receivers took over. By that stage 642 miles had been laid between Wichita, Kansas, and Girvin, Texas, and another 237 miles had been constructed over the border in Mexico. The receivers, clearly trying to salvage the project, then built ninety-five miles of line to enable a connection with the Southern Pacific railroad at Abilene, Texas.

A new company was formed in 1914 but by the 22 September 1922 edition of *The Wall Street Journal* things were going from bad to worse. The paper noted that 'the road cannot earn its salt unless the 240 miles from Wichita to Kansas City are built, or until the Mexican mileage is complete'.

In 1923 other newspapers were reporting that Kansas City Southern Railroad Company was taking over a section of 6.5 miles built as the approach to Kansas City complete with terminal facilities.

As for the great plan, the *New York Times* said in 1923 that 'a number of sections of the road were completed but it was never put into operation as a whole'.

Country Profile: Tanzania

Total route length: 3,695 km
Gauges: 2,725 km—1,000 mm (3ft 3⅜in)
970 km—1,067 mm (3ft 6in)

T HE MAIN RAILWAY NETWORK is operated by Tanzania Railways
Limited; until 2011, that network was fifty-one per cent
owned by the Indian engineering conglomerate RITES. It is
now fully owned by the Tanzanian government.

The national system comprises the central line and five secondary
lines, all of metre gauge. Those lines are:

Central line: Runs between Dar es Salaam on the Indian Ocean
coast to Kigoma on Lake Tanganyika. Work began under German
direction (Tanzania then being known as German East Africa) in 1905
and was completed in 1914. The line is 1,245 km in length. Kigoma is
also a transshipment point between trains and lake vessels for freight to
and from Burundi, the Democratic Republic of Congo, and Rwanda.

Travelling westwards from Dar es Salaam, the first junction is at
Ruva with the **Link line**. As suggested by its name, this 118 km line
provides a link between the Central line and forms a junction with
the 473 km **Tanga line** (serving northern Tanzania) at Mruazi. This
latter line is the country's oldest, construction having begun at Tanga
in 1893 and completed to Arusha in 1929. The Link line carries fuel,

maize, millet and timber while the main traffic on the Tanga line is cement and gypsum.

(The next junction is with the privately operated Kidatu line, a 107 km route between the Central line at Kilosa to Kidatu on the TAZARA railway (see below). Completed in 1963, the branch was designed to allow freight to be transferred between the Central line and TAZARA and avoid the congestion at Dar-es-Salaam.)

Moving further west there is the 115 km **Sigida** line, which leaves the Central line at Manyoni. It was built between 1932 and 1934 and then reconstructed between 1985 and 1997. Traffic includes livestock, cotton cake and maize.

The 378 km **Mwanza** line runs from the junction at Tabora to Mwanza on Lake Victoria. It serves the ports of the lake and the dry port at Isaha, opened in 1999 for handling clearances on freight to and from Rwanda and northern DRC; the dry port is equipped with two rail sidings, each able to accommodate eleven wagons at a time.

The **Mpanda** line runs 210 km southwards from the junction at Kaliua. It was completed in 1949 and now carries cement, timber, logs, fuel and livestock.

At the time of writing, Tanzania Railways operated two passenger services a week between Dar es Salaam and Kigoma and three a week between Tabora and Mpanda.

Tazara

Known as a monument to China-Africa friendship, the Tanzania-Zambia Railway Authority (Tazara) is the main rail line connecting East Africa with the central and southern parts of Africa. China financed and built Tazara, a line that covers a total length of 1,860.5 km running from Tanzania's Dar es Salaam to New Kapiri Mposhi in central Zambia where it connects with the Zambian system. The line was primarily intended as a means for Zambia to export copper using the port at Dar es Salaam.

China deployed more than 50,000 workers who worked with Tanzanian and Zambian teams to complete the construction of the project in five years and eight months before its official inauguration in 1976.

In recent years this railway has been hit by problems with ageing rolling stock and poor patronage. In 2016 it was reported that the line, designed to transport five million tonnes of freight a year, was carrying only about 1.3 million tonnes. Passenger numbers were down to 450,000 a year on a system that had been designed to carry three million people a year. However, the company reported that repairs to freight wagons had enabled transit times for freight leaving New Kapiri Mposhi for Dar es Salaam to be reduced from thirty days to six days.

A weekly express is run in each direction, taking forty-six hours between the two railheads. A weekly service each way is also operated by what are called ordinary trains, these stopping at every 'serviceable' station along the route. Trains include dining cars and parcel vans, the latter able to carry 15.7 tonnes. In early 2017, *African Business* magazine reported the company owed $700 million and needed a further $200 million for new rolling stock and track improvements. The magazine noted that the signalling and telecommunications systems were 'currently non-existent' due to vandalism. Moreover, the Tanzanian and Zambian governments have had to help pay staff and fuel bills.

In fact, Zambia has taken the position that Tazara nneds something more like $1.2 billion to bring it up to date.

HISTORICAL SNAPSHOTS

German Rails. On 19 February 1914 the *Christian Science Monitor* reported that the German East African Railway (now Tanzania's Central line) had reached the shores of Lake Tanganyika. 'It is expected that a through train will be able to accomplish the journey in two days,' the newspaper noted. 'As the time taken by caravan is forty-two days, the immense saving of time will, it is expected, greatly increase the trade of the country.'

The first sod had been turned in 1905 by Prince Albert of Prussia at Dar es Salaam and, when completed, the first section would be opened by Germany's Secretary of State for the Colonies, Dr Bernhard Dernburg. 'A German steamship service on Lake Tanganyika is contemplated, and in this way it is hoped to secure for the new line a considerable freight traffic from the Belgian Congo,' the newspaper ended. (The Belgian Congo is now the Democratic Republic of Congo.)

Freight war. In mid-1928 it was reported that a freight war had broken out between two British colonial rail systems. The completion that year of a railway line in British Tanganyika (as the former German territory had become under a League of Nations mandate following the First World War) to Mwanza, a port on the southern shores of Lake Victoria, had provided inland areas of Kenya and all of Uganda with an alternative route to the coast. Until then those areas had relied solely on the Kenya and Uganda Railway to the port of Mombasa. The latter company had clearly thought its business was assured: its line ran through the Uganda cotton belt, and the Kenya and Uganda Railway also maintained a fleet of steamers on Lake Victoria. But in July 1928 the Tanganyika Railway offered Uganda cotton growers a rate of sixty shillings a ton to rail their product to Dar es Salaam, twenty shillings below the price offered for railing to Mombasa (but, of course, the growers would have to use the Kenya steamers to get their cotton to Mwanza).

The authorities in Kenya and Uganda protested at this bit of commercial enterprise.

There were clearly noses out of joint, and in early August the Tanganyika Railway Administration sent the following telegram to the Kenya and Uganda Railway Administration. 'This government has never had any desire to attract the Uganda cotton to Mwanza and has not regarded the rates as competitive, inasmuch as the Kenya and Uganda Railway can obviously neutralise them on the lake as the cotton would have to be conveyed to Mwanza in its steamers. As you were informed in March last, this government is unable to consider now the question of increasing its rates against Tanganyika cotton ... The Governor regrets that there has been a misunderstanding on your part but suggests this would not have occurred if you had adhered to the agreement made at Nairobi with Colonel Maxwell (general manager, Tanganyika Railway) last November to send a representative to Dar es Salaam to discuss any remaining points of difference in the tariffs.'

6

Rail and its Critics

WHILE BRITAIN PRODUCED SUCH renowned railway lovers as John Betjeman, it also begot Richard Beeching. And this newspaper headline: 'Beeching report proposes closing a third of Britain's 7,000 railway stations'. The headline across page eight of *The Times* on the morning of 28 March 1963 shook the railway world. The word 'Beeching' is even today possibly the most reviled name in railway history.

The name is familiar to anyone who has done some reading on railways, but perhaps it is time to just set down exactly who Beeching was, and what he proposed.

Dr Richard Beeching trained as a physicist; he had also been a director of the British giant, Imperial Chemical Industries. The Conservative government under Harold Macmillan was generally unsympathetic to the state-owned British Railways, which was considered old-fashioned. Beeching's remit was to cut, and cut heavily, to drastically reduce the losses being incurred by the railway system.

His report, *Reshaping of British Railways*, proposed closing around 5,000 miles (more than 8,000 km) of track, closing 2,128 stations and reducing staff (*The Times* cited 70,000 jobs to go in the following five years). Reductions in rolling stock would then be possible, with 1,174 steam locomotives being taken out of service, along with fifty-five diesel engines, 1,074 multiple units (DMUs and EMUs, self-propelled diesel and electric units), and 2,957 passenger carriages. The cuts were deep, too, for freight wagons: Beeching's report said it would be possible to scrap 348,000 of them over a three-year period.

But it was the line closures that really got the public's attention.

Beeching recommended no train services north of Inverness, one of many Scottish cuts in the report. Wales was also to lose many lines. Lines that serviced seaside holiday centres in Devon, Cornwall and East Anglia were to be discontinued. The Isle of Wight was to be railway-free. Lines in the northwest and the Lakes District were also to be closed; lines which carried commuter trains in the Midlands, particularly around Leicester and Sheffield, were recommended for closure.

Not that the report was all negativity, which is the impression you get from reading most present day references. Beeching recommended the introduction of Liner trains to carry containers, estimated to have the potential to add 16 million tons a year to the freight carried by British Railways. These Liner trains would run from London to Aberdeen, Exeter and Plymouth, Birmingham, Liverpool, Manchester and Cardiff, among major industrial centres.

Beeching urged his recommendations be implemented as quickly as possible. Up until Beeching began his investigation, the report found that station closures, withdrawals of passenger services and elimination of freight handling at smaller stations had proceeded too slowly; it had taken twelve years to withdraw unprofitable passenger and freight services from 4,236 miles of the system. A year earlier, there was some newspaper coverage of the closure as of 31 December 1961 of the Ullesthorpe station on the line that linked Rugby with Leicester. About fifty people a day travelled from Ullesthorpe to Leicester and about the same number commuted to Rugby. Over the next four years, British Railways calculated, closing the line would save the railways about £165,000.

At beginning of 1959 *The Economist* noted that, over the preceding nine years, 183 lines had been closed in Britain with a total savings of £2.5 million. But British Railways faced major headaches even when closing a minor branch. It cited the line from Abergavenny in Monmouthshire, via Tredegar, to Merthyr Tydfil in South Wales.

What was known as the Merthyr, Tredegar and Abergavenny line was 23.9 miles (38.5 km) in length, and most of the freight had been removed in 1953 because the traffic was not paying its way and it was estimated that the line would lose £58,939 a year. In 1956 it had been calculated that future income would be £5,705 a year (the average of passengers per train was thirty-six) and, in addition, British Railways said £8,550 worth of repairs would be needed over two years. The Branch Lines Committee recommended withdrawal of passenger services, and a single track left in place should goods trains need to use the line as a detour. The closure process took a year and a half: the aforementioned committee submitted its report and recommendations to the Western Area Board of British Railways. These then it had to be considered by the Transport Users' Consultative Committee for Wales and Monmouthshire. Objections were received from all the local councils and from 1,125 members of the public. The matter was also raised in the House of Commons by the local member of Parliament. The issue in the end went to the Minister of Transport, who decided the line would close on 6 January 1958.

* * *

In December 1975 British railway unions kicked off a real scare campaign after they began to fear that the Labour government under Prime Minister Harold Wilson was going to make substantial cuts to rail services at a time of economic difficulty in the country. The National Union of Railwaymen produced a map purporting to predict what the system, then run by the state-owned British Rail, could look like within six years. The map showed the disappearance of everything except London commuter lines and the main inter-city long distance services. There would be no Scottish services north of Edinburgh or Glasgow, and none west of Plymouth. Only two lines would survive in Wales: the Swansea and Holyhead routes. In East Anglia, only the Norwich line would still be there by 1981. Places to lose railway services altogether would include Blackpool, Aberdeen, Inverness, Worcester, Harrogate and Stratford-on-Avon. The unions warned that the 11,500 miles of track in 1975 could soon be down to just 4,000 miles. As we now know, it never got as bad as that. But, with memories still fresh of the Beeching cuts in the 1960s resulting in the loss of about 4,000 miles of railways (far less than Richard Beeching, as chairman of British Railways, had wanted shut down) it was not hard to start a fear campaign about line closures.

But, while the railway survived, this was not the last threat.

Beeching wasn't rail's only enemy in Britain

'In Memory of the late Brigadier Thomas Ifan Lloyd CBE DSO MC who was the first to realise that a railway route is merely a road which is being misused and wasted'.

— Dedication in a 1982 think tank report
on the future of railways

MODEL TRAIN SETS WERE blamed in the 1980s for the fact that railways still existed.

In what must surely rate as one of the most bizarre attacks on rail transport—bizarre because it came under the guise of a seemingly expert report—a British think tank in 1982 released a report addressing the future of railways in Britain. The problem, as seen by Major Angus Dalgleish, the author of the report, was all those older men and their train sets.

'One must not underrate the influence of the toy train set', he wrote in the report, *The Truth About Transport.* 'There can be few men in positions of responsibility today who have not at some time played with one and surprising numbers of the professional or executive classes keep and expand their train sets into middle age or beyond. For such people maintenance of a real railway is necessary to justify their hobby. Women are far more practical in this matter'.

And no more practical, in his view, could anyone be than Frances Cairncross, the economics correspondent of *The Guardian* newspaper. It was she who in 1974 had first spotted the murky and malign influence of the model railway layouts lurking in spare rooms and basements across the country. Cairncross had attributed the cost of £3 billion (by then spent subsidising the nationalised railways) to the fact that so many heads had been befuddled by the presence of trains in so many nursery rhymes and children's stories.

Dalgleish, a retired transport engineer and having also served in the army, worked on his report following a strike by members of the Associated Society of Engineers and Fireman. His conclusion: there was no future for trains and he proposed turning all the rail corridors into roads. It was not a surprising conclusion given that Dalgleish happened to then concurrently chair the Railway Conversion League, the word 'conversion' denoting the paving over of all railway lines so that motor vehicles could use them instead of trains (that organisation ceasing operations upon his death in 1994).

Dalgleish's report argued that Britain could make enormous savings in the long term if it converted all rail routes to roads. The author calculated that each British taxpayer would, on average, be paying £1,000 a year less tax (as if that would have happened if the savings had been made!), 2,500 fewer deaths would occur and the new generation of large lorries (trucks) could be removed from the existing road network and diverted on to the converted rail corridors. The potential rail corridor for conversion extended over 11,100 miles and 'if asphalted over would make a magnificent road network,' Dalgleish added.

Railway lines could not go everywhere, his argument continued. Roads, by contrast, could—a true, if somewhat irrelevant point (no rail advocate has ever advocated closing all the roads, universally seeing road and rail as being complementary). Dalgleish was now warming to his argument. He continued that railways had to maintain high average speeds in order to attract passengers. Therefore, stations had to be widely spaced or delays from frequent stops would make for a very slow journey. But that, in his mind, just presented another argument against trains: high speed ones brought with them their own problems of noise, vibration and track and vehicle maintenance and, with all that, were nowhere near as fast as air travel. (Fast or slow, trains could not win with him.)

Then there was 'batch-type' transport. A train needed two hundred or three hundred people to make it economic. Therefore the rail traveller could not travel when he or she wanted to; they had to join with others to form a large group. 'This group then makes a trip which is only an approximation to the travel desires of its members and does not accord precisely with the wishes of many of them'.

Then there were points (switches) to go wrong; road signaling was simple compared with that used on railway systems. Seemingly exasperated by the inability of others to see this point, Dalgleish asks: 'How does this expensive, clumsy and ineffective mode of transport manage to survive?'

They Didn't Like the Food—or No Food at All

RAILWAYS HAVE ALWAYS HAD their critics and enemies. Peter Fleming, brother of James Bond creator Ian, was a highly regarded non-fiction author in his day, his titles including such classics as *Bayonets to Lhasa* (an account of the British invasion of Tibet in 1904) and *News from Tartary*, the story of his horseback ride across China and into India in the 1930s. He worked as a journalist, most notably as a correspondent in China for *The Times*; by the 1950s he was writing A Spectator's Notebook in the weekly magazine, *The Spectator*. One such item in May 1950 protested at recent increases in charges for meals on British Railways.

His patrician tastes were evident, the Notebook item comparing the cost of five shillings on trains to the 1s 6d (one shilling and sixpence) at his former college at Cambridge University for breakfast 'fully equal in quality to the railway full breakfast'. And that railway impost contrasted with the 2s 3d (two shillings and three pence) charged by a London restaurant ('which I frequent') for an excellent, three-course hot lunch. British Railways ought to do better, argued Fleming. 'The alternative, and a distasteful one, will be snack-boxes or home-made sandwiches in the carriage—as pre-1900'.

Two years earlier, Donald Nield of Flixton, a village on the edge of Manchester, had written to *The Manchester Guardian* regarding restaurant cars. 'I would like to point out the unusual position regarding the distribution of restaurant cars on the British Railways,' he complained. 'It appears that most if not all the boat trains running between London and the Channel ports are provided with restaurant or buffet cars. The length of the journey is approximately two hours. Yet on no train running between Manchester and Penzance is there any provision made for obtaining a meal. The whole situation is made more ironic by the fact that any traveller to the Continent can obtain a meal on the boat if required and yet on a journey taking in the region of twelve hours one has to starve or pack sandwiches.'

And then there were those who were difficult to please. At the end of 1929, Mr D.G. Kerridge was interviewed upon his retirement from the London, Midland and Scottish Railway. He was termed the 'father' of the dining cars, having been in charge of the company's first such car, having been introduced in 1889. In those early days, he noted, passengers were usually very satisfied due, he thought, to the novelty of being able to sit and eat on a train. But after the Great War people had been 'nervy and difficult to please and, in spite of the fact that the plain food of the nineties has given place to an abundance of dishes and plenty of variety, the tendency to complain and demand all sorts of impossible things seems to have increased'.

By the 1920s, diners became very possessive of their privacy while taking food. 'People make for the corner seats, hate to have strangers sitting opposite, and frequently behave in a cantankerous manner if another person comes to the same table,' said Kerridge.

* * *

At least they had a dining car. 'Passengers who came to Kalgoorlie by the second division of the express were a hungry lot by the time of their arrival at 2.50 p.m.,' reported the *Westralian Worker* newspaper, published weekly from that West Australian mining town. The 9 May 1924 report continued: 'For some reason or other, the dining car was unattached to the train; and no attempt was made to inform intending passengers that this would be the case and then give them the opportunity of providing a little refreshment on a long and tedious journey.

'Tea and scones at Southern Cross was procurable but many, expecting a dining car to be attached to the train at some point of the journey, did not even avail themselves of this opportunity to appease the demands of the inner man and consequently went without refreshments during Sunday until sometime after 3.00 p.m. It's up to the railway authority to notify passengers when they intend to depart from the normal procedures.'

Mind you, they might not have been missing much—unless things had improved on the Kalgoorlie Express since January 1910. At that time, *Truth* newspaper reported complaints about the poor quality of food in the dining car and the attitude of the waiters who, it was said, seemed to serve food at times that suited them. But the cook came in for special mention: 'Also, goes on our own informant, the cook might pay a little more attention to his personal appearance and comb his hair and whiskers occasionally, and if it isn't too much trouble,

You could not call the larger Victoria, Australia, refreshment rooms 'hash foundries'— at least after measures were taken to improve them. In 1898 Victorian Railways decided to end the policy of awarding refreshment room contracts to the highest tenderer. As the *Albury Banner and Wodonga Express* noted at the time, 'the result of this method of course has been that the rooms have been secured by the person who can run them the most cheaply, cheapness involving necessarily stinting the public in the quality of its purchases'. After 1900, Bendigo was one of thirteen Victorian stations offering a set-table menu. Typically the menu would allow passengers to choose from soup, fish, meats (beef, lamb, mutton or pork); there was also a selection of vegetables (potatoes, parsnips, carrots and beans). Bread, butter, cheese and marmalade were provided, and you could wash it all down with tea, coffee or South Australian wine. Even at those lesser stations that provided only a counter service you could order Irish stew, sausages, claret and beer, along with 'Havannah' cigars. By 1920 more than 500 women were employed in Victoria's refreshment service. This Bendigo staff photograph was taken in 1929. *Museum Australia.*

the public would appreciate him more if he would don a clean shirt now and then'. The paper referred to the dining car as a 'travelling hash foundry'.

China's Rail Reluctance

THERE WAS A TIME when some commentators in China doubted the wisdom of building railways and running trains on them.

The first railway line built in China was a 19.2 km track of 762 mm (2ft 6in) built in 1876 by a British company from Shanghai to the port of Woosung (now Wosung) on the Yangtze River. But it operated for only a few weeks before local officials forced its closure. The Chinese wanted no part of the railway age.

Indeed, on 4 August 1928 a writer in *The China Weekly Review* posed the question: 'Are Railways Necessary for China?' Harry Paxton Howard was of the opinion that indications suggested 'the steam locomotive and the railway are on the decline'. He pointed to the United States where, he said, railways were finding it harder to make money and a number of railroad companies had gone into liquidation. 'While industry in the United States continues to expand and the population to increase, the building of railways has slowed down practically to a standstill, and the new question is to how many thousand miles of track will have to be scrapped'. Americans were embracing what Howard called the Autobus.

For one thing, he continued, China should not buy steam locomotives as 'gas-electric' and 'oil-electric' engines were much cheaper to operate.

Given the cost of labour in China, it would much cheaper to build highways than railroads. 'And whenever a highway is built as they are already being built, autobuses at once spring out of the ground and get busy,' he continued. What is more, buses were cheaper to build than second-class railway carriages, more comfortable than third-class ones and usually more convenient to catch. 'Give the people highways, and see how quickly they will take care of transport problems for themselves,' he concluded.

But the railways did prove useful in many ways to China. In 1918 the first agricultural demonstration and lecture train departed Peking (now Beijing) 'loaded with the best seeds for grains, cotton and other plants, other agricultural products and farming implements and easy-reading pamphlets for distribution to farmers along the Peking-Hankow Railway,' reported the periodical, *Millard's Review of the Far East*. The agricultural train was to stop at thirty-five railway stations during its tour.

And the rail system served another agricultural product. In 1931 *The China Press* reported that Order No. 12567 from the Commander-in-Chief's office to the Ministry of Railways allowed for open transportation of opium on government lines. On the Peking-Hankow line opium would be carried at three Chinese dollars per 100 ounces for any distance beyond 300 km.

Any doubts that existed in China regarding the need for railways disappeared when the Communist Party took power in 1949. A rail line construction policy was enacted. But, like much of the headlong rush into modernity ordered by the Communists, the rail enthusiasm was not matched by proper planning—so much so that by 1959 construction on new lines was halted to allow engineers to patch problems on existing track (work having begun in 1958 on fifty new routes). Trains could simply not cope with the additional traffic generated due to industrialisation and the drive to lift farm output. The *Christian Science Monitor* reported from the capital that coal stocks needed in industry were piled up at pitheads, and food and consumer goods lay at stations while cities ran short of these items due to the shortcomings of the ill-planned railway network.

One of the top priorities in 1959 was to double-track the Peking-Canton (Beijing-Guangdong) and Tientsin (Tianjin)-Shanghai lines. 'More than one million workers are reported to have been put on this job', the newspaper said.

Wordsworth and a Railway Line

IN 1844 WILLIAM WORDSWORTH, having just been created Poet Laureate, was aghast at a plan to build a railway line through his beloved, and then still largely untouched, Lakes District. He was driven to submit the following poem that was published in *The Morning Post*:

On The Projected Kendal & Windermere Railway

Is then no nook of English ground secure
From rash assault? Schemes of retirement sown
In youth, and 'mid the busy world kept pure
As when their earliest flowers of hope were blown,
Must perish; how can they this blight endure?
And must he too the ruthless change bemoan
Who scorns a false utilitarian lure
'Mid his paternal fields at random thrown?
Baffle the threat, bright Scene, from Orresthead
Given to the pausing traveler's rapturous glance:
Plead for thy peace, thou beautiful romance
Of nature; and, if human hearts be dead,
Speak, passing winds; ye torrents, with your strong
And constant voice, protest against the wrong.

It was no use: they built the line and the first train ran in 1847 on this new Windermere branch of the Lancaster & Carlisle Railway.

Country Profile: Canada

Total route length: 77,932 km
Gauge: Standard gauge 1,435 mm (4ft 8½in)

IN THE 1960S THE Canadian rail system was in a bad way. The then
Canadian National Railways, a government-owned operation, was
seen as inefficient and was deeply in debt. Things were not much
better at the privately owned carrier, Canadian Pacific Railways. Road
carriers were taking away large quantities of freight that would, in
earlier times, have been consigned to rail.

The Canadian government then moved to remove most economic
regulations from the rail carriers, following up with subsidies for services operated by railways in the public interest. The long distance
passenger business was moved into a new carrier, VIA Rail Canada.
Meanwhile, the railway companies were encouraged to sell branch
lines to short line operators.

What follows is the situation today.

Canadian Pacific

Total route length: 12,402 miles (19,959 km)
(17,381 km owned, 2,575 km access rights)
Also owns 1,770 km operated by short-line railroads
Double track: 1,929 km

Sidings and yards: 6,902 km
Industrial spurs: 1,275 km

Canadian Pacific's network is made up of three main corridors—
Western (Vancouver to Thunder Bay on Lake Superior), *Central*
(Moose Jaw and Winnipeg to Chicago and Kansas City), and *Eastern*
(Thunder Bay to Montreal, Detroit and Albany). Of the total route
length operated, 7,725 km are located within the United States. (In
1923, by contrast, the only incursion into the United States by the
Canadian Pacific was a line in the state of Maine.)

Western is the main corridor for transport of bulk commodities
for export through Vancouver, and includes four feeder lines for coal,
grain and potash traffic.

Central also serves the twin cities of St Paul and Minneapolis and
Milwaukee, Wisconsin. This allows Canadian Pacific to provide a
single carrier route between western Canada and the U.S. Midwest,
connecting to the ports on the Great Lakes and Mississippi River.
Trains on this corridor carry containers from the Port of Vancouver,
along with fertilisers, chemicals, crude oil, vehicles, grain and other
agricultural products. The company's central corridor also connects
with other railroad operations at Chicago and has operating rights
over BNSF (formerly Burlington Northern Santa Fe) lines to the twin
ports of Duluth, Minnesota, and Superior, Wisconsin.

The Eastern Corridor provides a direct service across Canada by
linking with the western corridor and to the U.S. by connecting with
the central corridor. The freight traffic on this corridor is dominated
by forest products, chemicals and plastics, along with crude oil, ethanol,
minerals, containers, automotive and general freight.

Rolling Stock
Freight locomotives: 1,081
Switchers (shunters): 366
Freight wagons:
Box cars 2,944
Covered hoppers: 19,152
Open top hoppers 376
Flat cars 2,249

Gondola wagons* 5,283
Intermodal 1,331
Autoracks** 3,520
Tankers 202
Service cars 2,372
*Open wagon with low sides
** Multi-level wagons for transporting cars
Repair depots: Golden, Vancouver, Calgary, Moose Jaw and Winnipeg
(on western corridor), St Paul and Chicago (on central corridor) and
Montreal, Toronto and Thunder Bay (eastern).

* * *

When Canadian Pacific built its line across the Rocky Mountains (the Canadian part) it initially chose to take on what became known as Big Hill. In the vicinity of Kicking Horse River, trains faced a 4.5 per cent gradient, and between four and six engines were required on each train—not just to get the consists up but to control them on the descent. In regard to the latter, CP built short sections with a reverse grade to halt runaway trains which made the passage even more time-consuming and arduous.

In 1909 the problem was solved by the construction of two spiral tunnels, the first such in North America. The first, a 975 metre bore under Cathedral Mountain, meant the train turned around 180 degrees, crossed Kicking Horse River then headed into the second tunnel, inside which the train curved around to emerge facing in the direction it was originally travelling. It allowed for two locomotives to do the work of the previous five or six.

Canadian National

Total network length: 19,600 miles (31,543 km)
Staff: 22,250
Wagon loads (2016): 5.2 millions
Major loads: Coal (24 per cent of tonnage)
Minerals (9 per cent)
Petrochemicals and chemicals (6 per cent)

Canadian National Railways was created in 1919 as a Federal government corporation to avoid the collapse of several rail operations. The Canadian government had no great enthusiasm for the task. But through various moves, the new railway body took control of the Grand Trunk Railway (3,948 miles), the Canadian Northern Railway (9,259 miles), the Grand Trunk Pacific (2,840 miles), the National Transcontinental (2,007 miles), and the Intercolonial Railway (1,593 miles). It also inherited the Prince Edward Island system of 279 miles and an unfinished line to Hudson's Bay of 334 miles.

The initial problem was how to bring all those lines into a coherent national system. As one academic, Leslie Fournier, remarked in 1931 (see bibliography), 'it is important to remember that the Canadian Pacific constitutes a network of lines complementary to one another and to the entire system, whereas the Canadian National operates many lines that were built to compete with one another. The necessity of maintaining these duplicate main lines has been a great handicap. Moreover, the routes of certain parts of the Canadian National, such as the Intercolonial, were determined largely by political circumstances, to the detriment of economical operations'.

It has since made several acquisitions, starting with that of the Central Vermont Railway in 1927 and with the absorption of the Newfoundland Railway in 1949 when that Dominion became a province of Canada; later acquisitions include the Illinois Central Railway in 1998 and Wisconsin Central in 2001.

The corporation was privatised in 1995 through a public share offering.

Its network is extensive through Canada and there is a continuous rail corridor to the Gulf of Mexico and the ports of New Orleans, Louisiana, and Mobile, Alabama.

* * *

The company has long been innovative. Diesel-electric locomotives were hauling passenger services by 1929. In 1919, the year of its creation, Canadian National received the first batch of steel cars (it had ordered 100—twenty tourist class cars, eighteen sleeping cars, nine dining cars, twenty mail vans, twenty first class cars and thirteen observation cars). But also that year the new company ran into union trouble when it decided to buy its coal from mines in West Virginia, the locomotive fuel from there being much cheaper that the mines of Nova Scotia which had until then supplied Canadian railways.

VIA Rail

Route network: 12,500 km
Stations served: 121

VIA Rail was established in 1977, inspired by the creation of Amtrak south of the border. As early as 1967 both Canadian Pacific and Canadian National had indicated they wanted out of the passenger business. Initially the federal government subsidised these operators to continue running passenger trains, but the rail companies in turn stopped all investment in passenger rolling stock.

VIA offers passenger destinations from east coast (Halifax, Nova Scotia) to west (Prince Rupert and Vancouver in British Columbia), and to the Hudson's Bay terminus of Churchill (although that last service was halted in May 2017 until a flooded section of the line could be repaired).

Rolling Stock
Locomotives: 76
53 units of Class F40PH-2
21 units of Class P42DC
Two units Class SW 1000 (switcher/shunting engines based in Montreal)
Diesel railcars: 5
Passenger carriage stock: 426 (including baggage cars)

FAST FACT: NORTH AMERICA'S
LONGEST NARROW GAUGE LINE

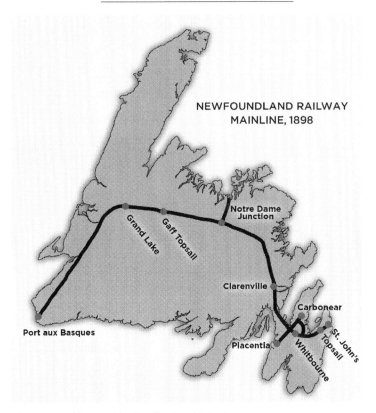

Map courtesy Heritage Newfoundland and Labrador.

The Newfoundland railway had reached 906 miles (1,458 km) of route mileage at its greatest length. It was closed in September 1988. The main line of 548 miles (882 km) was completed in 1897; it had sixty-eight years of its life without any serious road competition; it was not until the Trans-Canada Highway's completion in 1965 that the railway's near monopoly on land transport in the Canadian province was ended. The line was built to the 1,067 mm (3ft 6in) gauge, the longest narrow gauge system in North America. This main line was built by a company owned by Robert Gillespie Reid; the Reid family owned the railway until 1923, the operation then being taken over by the Newfoundland government after the private operator had got into financial difficulties.

Two 1200hp NF210 units 931 and 936 parked in front of the main shops of the former Newfoundland Railway that were opened in St. John's in 1931. No. 931 was delivered by rail to Montreal, Quebec, and shipped to St. John's from General Motors in London, Ontario, in October 1956 as part of Canadian National's first order for twenty-six NF210 units. They followed the successful nine NF110 units of 1953. No. 936 was delivered in March 1958 as part of a three-unit order costing $666,000 to support additional traffic growth. *David Othen, C. Robert Craig Memorial Library collection.*

Passenger trains were withdrawn in 1969 when a bus service between the capital, St John's, to the terminal with the mainland ferries at Port aux Basques cut travel time almost in half. By that time, too, air services were connecting Newfoundland with Canadian mainland cities, particularly Montreal. But the freight business lasted for a while with a bogie exchange to handle standard gauge wagons being shipped to the island and then being returned.

Part of the line's problems once roads were sealed was that its circuitous route left it at immediate disadvantage compared with more direct road connections. That, and the initial decision to save money by building to the narrow gauge, compromised the economics and efficiency of the railway.

Newfoundland had rejected confederation with Canada in 1896, remaining a British colony until 1907 and then being an independent Dominion until merger with Canada in 1949.

With the merging into Canada in 1949, the line (along with 2,600 employees) became the responsibility of Canadian National Railways. The new owner set about investing in upgrading the Newfoundland railway, including introducing diesel locomotives, new passenger carriages and freight wagons. The new first class coaches had seats for fifty passengers (some reclining) along with separate saloons (one at each end) for men and women, the latter including a mirror, a swivel stool, a shelf for accessories and a metal washbasin.

Train 207 had departed the St. John's Station at 9.00 a.m. on Monday, 20 September 1976. It would travel to Argentia via Placentia Junction, 61.6 miles from St. John's, and return as far as Whitbourne, mileage 54.5, as Train 208. The following day it would travel as Train 232 to Brigus Jct. (mileage 41.0) and traverse the 38.5 mile Carbonear Sub to Carbonear first as Train 211 and returning as Train 212. It would then conclude its journey at Train 232 to St. John's. (Argentia was 20.7 miles from Placentia Junction and the former site of a major American WWII naval base.)
David Othen, C. Robert Craig Memorial Library collection.

The main train, official name Caribou but known to Newfoundlanders in its later years as 'the Newfie Bullet', took twenty-two hours for its journey. A seat in 1969 cost $12.10 one way, and that included three meals. The train ran three days a week in each direction, connecting on some services with a mixed train (one coach, up to twenty freight wagons) at Whitbourne for a run down the branch line that involved many stops for shunting the wagons on to sidings. Meanwhile, 'the Bullet' was limited to 35 mph for much of its journey due to the winding nature of the track, and was frequently stopped in sidings to let freight trains pass.

While the main line closed for good in 1988, branches were shut down earlier—Bonavista and Carbonear in 1983, Argentia in 1984 (and thirty-two main line stations closed in the latter year also).

Country Profile: Vietnam

Total track length: 2,600 km
Gauges 178 km—standard gauge 1,435 mm (4ft 8½)
2,169 km—narrow gauge 1,000 mm (3ft 3⅜in)
253 km—mixed gauge

THE FIRST RAILWAY IN what was then known as French Indochina, built by French colonial authorities, was opened in 1881. It was 71 km long and connected Saigon with My Tho. By 1936 the railway network of 2,600 km was completed. The Japanese effectively moved to control this territory after the German victory over France in 1940; a full invasion took placed in 1941 and Japanese forces remained in the colony until their defeat in August 1945.

So far as railways were concerned, it was Tokyo's plan to include Indochina's rail system in its planned Korea-Singapore route. That route was seen as vital after the sinking of large numbers of Japanese naval and merchant ships by U.S. aircraft and submarines. The main line in Indochina was severed after 1945 when what is now Vietnam was divided into two countries and it was not until 1976, following the Vietnam War won by the North, that the line between Hanoi and Saigon was reconnected (the main express train is still known as the Reunification Express).

All routes are single track with the main line being the 1,726 km
link connecting Hanoi to Ho Chi Minh City. Standard gauge mass
transit systems are being built in Ho Chi Minh City (formerly Saigon)
and Hanoi. Hanoi's first urban railway, 12 km with twelve stations,
from Nhon to Hanoi Railway Station received €783 million from the
French government. It was scheduled to be completed in 2016 but
delays and spiralling costs have seen project completion pushed out
to 2019.

Regarding main line operations, a 2014 report by Thai consulting firm UMI stated that freight and passenger transport in Vietnam
were dominated by road providers due to the minimal rail network
(few branch lines) and the long travelling time between the two
main cities (the journey takes more than thirty hours). In addition,
the metre gauge track did not support high-speed, high-stability or
double-stacked container trains. UMI said major investment would be
required to convert the lines to standard gauge. However, investment
is now targeted at upgrading the existing metre gauge line to improve
travel times although there are plans for new lines with dual gauge
capability. In addition, Vietnam is part of the Trans-Asian network
plan with Ho Chi Minh City to be connected by rail to Phnom Penh.

At present, the Vietnam Railways system comprises seven lines and,
in the north where the system connects to that of China, there are
standard and dual gauge lines.

The lines are

Hanoi-Ho Chi Minh: 1,726 km; metre gauge; 191 stations.
Hanoi—Lao Cai: 296 km; metre gauge; 40 stations. (Sleeper train
twice weekly.)
Hanoi-Dong Dang: 163 km; dual gauge; 23 stations. (Passengers
change to Chinese standard gauge sleeper train at border.)
Kep-Ha Long: 106 km; standard gauge; 12 stations.
Hanoi-Haiphong: 102 km, metre gauge, 18 stations.
Hanoi-Quan Trieu: 75 km; dual gauge: 14 stations.
Thai Nguyen-Kep: 57 km; standard gauge; six stations.

Rolling Stock

Locomotives: 383

(Includes engines made in the former Czechoslovakia, Belgium, Romania, United States, India and Australia)

Passenger carriages: 1,063

1,055 metre gauge

8 standard gauge

(*Includes 323 sleeper carriages, 551 sitting carriages, 61 dining cars, 50 baggage cars and 70 postal vans on metre gauge; seven sitting cars and one baggage car on standard gauge*)

Freight wagons: 4,986

4,632 metre gauge

354 standard gauge (*includes 140 brake vans*)

7

Where Did the Passengers Go?

The direct cause of the death of these trains, and dozens of others around the nation, is economic; they lost money heavily. The indirect causes are, perhaps in this order, automobiles, airplanes, bad management and outdated labour rules

—*Washington Post*, 23 February 1970

WHEN IT COMES TO passenger trains, the Old World surely triumphs over the New (at least so far as the developed world is concerned). While long distance passenger services have faded in North American and Australasia, trains rule supreme in Europe. Is it just the distances involved? Why would you spend days in a train to get from side of the United States or Australia to the other when, in a matter of hours, an aircraft can cover the same distance?

Not that the rail operators did not try. In 1929, for example, Central Railroad of New Jersey introduced the Blue Comet, travelling from New York to Atlantic City in three hours. One newspaper account described it as 'a symphony in blue. Coaches, observation cars, and diner are finished in ultramarine tints, cream and nickel. The diner's chairs are upholstered in blue linen'. It was seen as being up there with such trains at the Twentieth Century Limited, the Broadway Limited

(New York-Chicago), and the Super Chief (Chicago-Los Angeles), the last mentioned being one famed for carrying many Hollywood stars on one part of their journeys to and from the New York.

The Europeans had the Golden Arrow (Calais-Paris), the Orient Express (English Channel ports to Vienna and the Balkans and the Blue Train (Channel ports to the Riviera). The Golden Arrow had armchairs covered in dull red leather (covered in warm weather by chintz slips).

Every crack American train included in its staff maids, valets and stenographers; the club cars had magazines, bridge tables, soda water and ginger ale; you could ask for a telephone while at the departing station to make any last minute calls from your club car chair. The American deluxe trains typically provided bathtubs and a barbershop. The Daylight Limited (Los Angeles-San Francisco) was thought to be the only train in the world equipped with a lunch counter where you could buy sandwiches, coffee, pies, doughnuts and cakes.

Trains had speeded up, too: in the 1870s it took 144 hours (six days) to go from New York to San Francisco; by 1930 it was down to eighty-one hours (just over three days).

One politician knew whose fault was the passenger decline: the railroad companies. In 1961 Senator Stephen M. Young of Ohio said the officials of the lines should blame themselves for lost business because of the way they had treated passengers. He told the Senate he had just travelled between Washington and New York on a train

INTERCITY PASSENGER TRAFFIC IN THE UNITED STATES

(Passenger miles)

1929	33,965,000,000
1939	23,669,000,000
1944	97,705,000,000
1950	32,481,000,000
1960	21,574,000,000
1970	10,900,000,000

(Source: American Association of Railroads 1972)

on which 'every coach was a candidate for the junk heap'. He contrasted this with another trip he had done recently between Milan
and Rome, in a carriage that was beautifully decorated and in which
espresso coffee was served to passengers. But in the United States?
'Four hours of travelling on a dirty, crowded, poorly ventilated coach
gave convincing evidence that railroad officials regard passengers as
necessary evils and make their money carrying freight,' he said.

Find More Passengers

BY THE 1930S THE British railway companies were looking for new
sources of revenue as private motor use and expansion of bus services
ate into their passenger traffic. One avenue was to promote rail travel
for leisure and holidays. Stations were plastered with posters extol-
ling excursions to the seaside or holiday resorts. In 1936 the Great
Western Railway, for example, produced three booklets describing
regional attractions, including *Rambles Around the Cambrian Coast*;
for sixpence, you could buy this booklet giving detailed accounts of
twenty different rambles. From that developed the Ramblers' Train
run by Southern Railways.

In 1939 the Artists' Train was introduced to attract people who
wanted to go to the country to sketch and paint. Each Sunday a special
coach was attached to the Ramblers' Train, the amateurs accompanied
by professional artists to tutor them. The charge was one shilling over
the normal fare. The train travelled up to 112 km from London but,
with the long summer days, the artists could have as long as six hours
to draw and paint.

That said, passenger traffic even in the difficult times of the 1930s
did not decrease significantly, there being 1.8 billion passenger journeys on Britain's railways in 1938. Nevertheless, as Juliet Gardiner
notes in her magisterial social history of the 1930s in Britain, 'there
was a sense of decline, a feeling that the terms of transportation had
changed, that roads could meander wherever demand lay, and planes
had the freedom of the skies, while trains were confined to Victorian-
built tracks, laid out in a grid that no longer accorded with newer,
flexible demands of work and leisure, and the railways were restrained
by costs and regulations that made them uncompetitive'.

Gardiner argues that there was an opportunity missed after 1923 when 121 railway companies were 'grouped' in the Big Four operations—Great Western Railway (GWR), London and North Eastern Railway (LNER), London, Midland and Scottish Railway (LMS), and the Southern Railway. That is, they could have engaged in a pre-Beeching cull of uneconomic branch lines and services. Moreover, the big four did not push on with electrification because of opposition from the number of owners of coal mines who sat on railway boards and did not want to lose the lucrative business of supplying the railways.

But trains did improve. The LNR, under its new Chief Mechanical Engineer Nigel Gresley, upgraded the standard of sleeping cars and produced more efficient and powerful locomotives (including the famed Flying Scotsman).

Europe's Answer: Faster Trains

WESTERN EUROPE'S RAILWAYS HAD no sooner completed the process of rebuilding after the destruction of the Second World War than they faced new competition: air and private car travel (albeit both initially beyond the pockets of most people but decreasingly so as years wore on and living standards improved).

New, faster trains and innovative marketing were the responses to these new challenges as the 1960s unfolded. France, for example, had the Sud-Express to the Spanish border; it made the 580 km section between Paris and Bordeaux in 4hr 43min, travelling non-stop at an average speed of 124 km/h.

The French, as did other national carriers, came up with excursions, one such being a day outing from Paris to Brussels, the cost of which included lunch in the Belgian capital, a bus tour and dinner on the return train journey. France in 1957 had been the first European rail operator to attach wagons to long distance sleeper trains to transport passengers' cars.

If you wanted to go from Brussels to Antwerp in 1966 it was said that you did not need to consult a timetable, just turn up at the station and it would not be long before an Antwerp-bound train pulled into the platform.

The Dutch had trains running between Rotterdam and Amsterdam every twenty minutes. The Netherlands system offered some thirty destinations served by excursion trains including two in Belgium (Bruges and Ostend).

Italy in 1966 had trains travelling the 635 km between Milan and Rome at average speeds of 104 km/h (and that included several intermediate stops), while even Spain—which up until that time had a reputation for particularly slow trains—was introducing faster services, while Germany had a train running the short distance between Munich and Augsburg at up to 200 km/h.

In addition the original members of the European Common Market (as it then was) co-operated in running trains under the Trans European Express brand: the Mistral (Paris-Nice), the Blue Bird (Paris-Brussels), the Rheingold (Hook of Holland-Amsterdam-Munich-Geneva) and the Edelweiss (Zurich-Brussels-Antwerp).

Not that this was the first time any European carrier had to be inventive to hold and build its passenger numbers. The Czech railways in the 1920s had to grapple with many changes: the first lines had been laid when the country was part of the Austro-Hungarian Empire. After that empire was obliterated by defeat in 1918, the newly independent Czechoslovakia took nearly a decade to untangle its own railways from the former imperial system. That done, the Central Board of Czechoslovakia Railways first turned its attention to opening more lines in the neglected the eastern part of the country (now Slovakia); few lines had at that stage been laid there, and none of those few was connected to Prague, the capital.

Coal shortages had been a problem, too, as was the lack of snow ploughs that could be attached to locomotives in the winters.

Czechoslovakia wanted to develop a tourism industry and an attractive rail system was seen as essential to that effort.

A correspondent filing to the *Christian Science Monitor* in May 1929 noted that other proposals 'include third-class sleeping cars on all main lines—a much needed innovation in a country where even the poorest are great travellers' as well as fixing a maximum price at all station restaurants, introducing motor train (railcar) connecting services on branch lines and the ability to buy through-fares to destinations on the

French and Italian coasts, along with tickets that could also be used for boats plying the Moldau, Elbe and Danube rivers.

One Problem: Crime

IN 1977, A CORRESPONDENT in Europe for the *Chicago Tribune* filed a report saying the increase in thefts aboard trains was worrying police in Switzerland, Italy, Germany and France 'and is considerably enriching gangs from Yugoslavia and Latin America'. The gangs were particularly targeting night trains connecting Switzerland, Italy and Austria, but only the slower, cheaper services that did not require an advance reservation and where—unlike with the luxury trains—there were no locks on doors in cars

The previous year, 1976, there had been 8,000 trains thefts in Italy compared with 2,500 in 1972. Also police were not catching most of the offenders: of the 8,000 thefts, only 1,680 had been resolved with an arrest.

FAST FACT: ITALY'S PAMPERED PASSENGERS

In 1959, the list of people was very, very long as to who could travel on cheap fares throughout the Italian railway system.

All state employees—and their families—were entitled to a forty-four per cent reduction in their fares, while archbishops and bishops could travel for a thirty per cent discount. So, too, could pilgrims travelling to certain religious sanctuaries in Italy.

Some degree of fare discounting was also available to
- Employees of lottery offices.
- Employees of the country's research council.
- Employees of the Social Research Institute.
- Retired army officers 'with or without their grooms and horses'.
- Members of central committees of patriotic associations.

The railway employed some 200,000 people, the state railway being the largest economic organization in Italy. Some 4,500 km of lines needed a Treasury subsidy to keep them in operation.

Not that these pampered passengers always travelled in the best of style. In 1963 a correspondent of *The Times* travelled on what he called

Italy's 'number two crack train, the Frecchia del Vesuvio', from Rome to Naples; it was 'fast but bouncy, with litter on the floor and frayed uphol-stery'. And he was not too impressed, either, by the Rome Express; the sleeping and dining cars were antiquated and uncomfortable. 'After this, the Dover to London Pullman seemed spick and span, and the service courteously unruffled'.

Japan's Railways Fight Back

BY THE EARLY 1970S, the automobile had meant an end to many long distance services in North America, especially the more luxurious ones. Not so in Japan. By 1972 there were nineteen million private cars in the country but the Japanese government was determined to keep people travelling by train.

But the battle to preserve rail services had begun long before. At the end of 1929, figures were published showing that private railway companies in Japan were seeing revenues falling due to what was described as the conspicuous growth of the automobile. Freight traffic, however, was growing; in 1929 some 98.3 million tons were carried on Japanese lines, up two per cent on the preceding year. However, the reports qualified this by explaining that the opening of new lines was mainly responsible for this increase. But the Ministry of Railways also announced it would abandon opening new lines and, instead, invest in road passenger services.

In the 1970s it became national policy to discourage and, where necessary, prohibit expressways. Meanwhile, road vehicles were hit with a tax (based on the vehicle's weight) that went to help finance railway construction, including tunnels and bridges linking the four main islands.

In 1972 train speeds were considered the key in to the success of the plan to double passenger numbers on the national network by 1985. Bullet trains were one part of the answer, but so was updating rolling stock on the 21,000 km narrow gauge network at the time, adding sleeping and dining cars and lifting speeds close to 100 km/h where possible.

This effort was being made at a time when Japan National Railways (as it was) was losing money on 238 of its 247 routes; moreover, the

Japan Railway Construction Corporation was in 1972 still planning and building new narrow gauge lines and, under the system at that time, JNR was obligated to operate trains on these new lines.

Australia Does Its Best

IN THE 1930S THE various Australian rail systems* all tried to make improvements to long distance services (although not nearly by enough, as anyone who rode the night mail trains in NSW in the 1950s would testify). Victoria made strides in reducing times, and the Adelaide to Perth trip of 2,600 km had been shortened by nine hours since its inception. New, more powerful steam locomotives were being put on trains across the almost grade-less Nullarbor Plain so that the 1,690 km haul between Kalgoorlie, Western Australia, and Port Augusta, South Australia, was soon to be completed in less than twenty-four hours.

Air-conditioning was introduced on trains in Victoria in 1935 and each state was engaged in building new rolling stock; by the outbreak of war in 1939 NSW also had air-conditioned trains including the Silver City Comet, a steel and aluminium diesel train set that had been introduced between Parkes and Broken Hill, connecting at the former station with overnight trains and hurrying passengers on their 645 km journey through sometimes scorching desert to the famed mining town of Broken Hill. The Trans-Australia trains across the Nullabor were also air-conditioned. Queensland was building new luxury long distance carriages and older cars were being refurbished.

Ireland Blows Hot and Cold—and Then Hot Again

'FASTER, QUIETER PASSENGER TRAINS' was the promise in 1961 by Ireland's rail operator, Córas Iompair Éireann (CIE) in 1961. That was outlined by the then Minister for Transport, Erskine Childers, as he inspected the first two of fifteen diesel-electric 950 horsepower

---

* The government-owned state systems in Western Australia, South Australia, Tasmania, New South Wales, Queensland and Victoria, as well as Commonwealth Railways operating the transcontinental line between South Australia and Western Australia and the isolated North Australia Railway line in the Northern Territory

General Motors locomotives. At the time CIE had also ordered twenty-one locomotives using German engines manufactured by Maybach Motorenbau; the purchases were to replace steam on all but eight per cent of Irish rail services.

CIE was promising new carriages, raising and lengthening of all passenger platforms, and faster trains. Childers said rail needed to improve to compete with modern bus services.

Fast forward to 1976 and there was this headline in *The Irish Times*: 'Whatever CIE may be up to—it's a helluva way to run a railroad'. The Galway County Council was complaining that CIE was slowly going through the process of winding up its entire railway operations west of the Shannon River. The council was questioning the figures used to justify the closure of the Claremorris-Limerick line, the longest line closure to date in Ireland at 93 miles (149.7 km).

One member of the Irish parliament complained about the seeming eagerness of CIE to close lines, an eagerness that has been replicated in many countries. 'More serious (than it being the longest line closed) still is the fact that whereas CIE gave thirteen months' notice of closure in the case of the Mallow-Waterford line, six months' notice of closure for the Cork-Bantry line, which was 58 miles long, and four months' notice of closure in respect of the West Clare railway, they now give a bare two months' notice, the shortest ever, for the closure of the largest and most important line to date.

Fast forward (for a second time) to 2010. In March of that year the Limerick to Galway line had been re-opened, trains travelling between the two cities for the first time in thirty-four years. The line was to have five services each way daily. More important, phases two and three were to see the re-opening extended first to Tuam and then Claremorris (although financial issues later stalled this plan).

Amtrak's Shaky Start

AFTER THE END OF the Second World War (during which Americans had temporarily flocked back to train travel because of petrol shortages and lack of new cars), the passenger business of American railroad companies fell apart, as R. E. H Mellor of the University of Aberdeen notes in his 1973 study of the U.S. passenger network. As a result, many railroad companies gave up running long distance services by the 1960s.

From 31 May 1969 Dallas (population 815,000) became the largest city in the United States where it was impossible to catch a passenger train. The last passenger train from the Dallas Texas Union Terminal, the Texas Eagle, pulled out on that 1969 date, ending ninety-seven years of service. The Missouri Pacific had decided to drop the Dallas-Forth Worth section of the Eagle's run. Nine companies were serving Dallas at the time, but only with freight trains. The state now had only three long distance passenger services, the Eagle running from Forth Worth to San Antonio and Laredo (which by the end of its life was down to one passenger car, whereas it once boosted dining cars and big consists of passenger cars), Southern Pacific's Sunset Limited crossing Texas on its way between New Orleans and Los Angeles, and Santa Fe's Texas Chief between Chicago and Houston. By 1969 only memories remained of such great trains as the Texas Special, Bluebonnet, Katy Flyer, Sunshine Special, Westerner, Argonaut, the Sam Houston Zephyr and the Twin Star Rocket (Minneapolis-Houston).

In his memoir of Texan railroads (see bibliography) Everett L. DeGolyer Jr recalls that the Santa Fe railroad had, by 1967-68, eliminated all but a few passenger trains, those being mainline routes (all branch line services had been axed). The Texas and Pacific Railway in the 1930s had a stable of passenger trains that DeGolyer described as having air-conditioning and full-length lounge cars. But by the mid-1950s that railroad company had lost interest in its passenger operations.

By the end of the 1960s, only twenty-six of the seventy-six railroad companies whose shares were listed on American stock exchanges retained passenger services.

'The transcontinental passenger train which built the American west may become a memory of the past,' reported a correspondent to *The Times* of London in February 1967. Western Pacific had just requested permission from the Interstate Commerce Commission to withdraw passenger services between Salt Lake City and San Francisco. And New York Central wanted to abandon its New York-Chicago service. For the demise of luxury train travel in the United States, the correspondent blamed 'hidebound trade union practices and traditional management thinking'. There was no doubt many of the services were proving a strain on railroad companies: the Rio Grande Zephyr, running between Salt Lake City and Denver and operated by Denver and Rio Grande Western Railroad, lost $280,000 in 1965 (the dining car was losing $10,000 a month). Rio Grande, under labour agreements, had to staff the train between the two cities (a thirteen hour run) with four engine crews, each of two men, as well as two three-man crews (one conductor and two trainmen each).

Washington responded to this nation-wide abandonment of passenger operations. On 1 May 1971 the Rail Passenger Service Act came into effect, giving birth to the National Railroad Passenger Corporation—Amtrak. It took over the passenger services of twenty-two railroad companies.

As Mellor explained, Amtrak was given the job of providing passenger services to 340 American cities and it began with 1,300 trains a week and a fleet of 1,200 coaches. The new company even retained some of the more famous train names, including the Super Chief, El Capitan, the San Francisco Zephyr (even though it now terminated at Oakland) and the Empire Builder.

Arkansas, New Hampshire, Maine, South Dakota and Maine were left without any passenger trains while most states west of the Mississippi had only one passenger route. Outside the Washington-New York-Boston-Philadelphia complex (which was well-serviced by Amtrak) and Chicago (with nine passenger routes from its main station), elsewhere the traditional long distance routes were served by just one or two trains a day.

But, as Mellor adds, by March 1972 Amtrak had run out of money; it needed Congress to vote another $174 million to keep the trains running. 'Failure to stimulate traffic quickly enough after years of neglect and inadequate capitalisation meant that, by the end of 1971, Amtrak had to dip into money earmarked for new rolling in order to pay for day-to-day operations,' he wrote.

There was plenty of publicity about Amtrak's problems. In January 1972 the *Wall Street Journal* headlined 'Amtrak Admits Service is Lousy' but the new operator was blaming the owners of the lines over which its trains had to pass; these private railroad companies, Amtrak said, gave priority to their own freight trains, keeping passenger trains waiting for clearance; but there were problems of the carrier's own making, including 'inconsiderate' treatment of passengers and frequent reservation snafus.

In April *The New York Times* headlined 'Amtrak is Deep in Debt at End of First Year'. In February the *Christian Science Monitor* was reporting that some big cities had been dropped from the Amtrak schedules (Toledo and Cleveland among them) while new services had been introduced that could not be explained except by the desire of Amtrak to curry political favour; hence a thrice-weekly train had been introduced to stop at stations in sparsely populated Montana and North Dakota because of the need to get senators from those states to back its request for money. And there was a new train from Washington D.C. to Parkersville, West Virginia; the latter was the home of the congressman heading the committee which decided on allocating money to Amtrak.

By July 1972 the *Chicago Tribune* was labelling the Miami-Chicago service Amtrak's worst. Under private operation the 1,598 mile (2,572 km) journey had taken thirty-four hours; under Amtrak it took forty-two. But the reporter who took the trip was not totally negative. 'The food is quite acceptable; the dining car is clean and well run. The menu prices are high but not outrageously so,' he commented.

FAST FACTS: AMTRAK TODAY

Rolling Stock
20 Acela Express high-speed train sets
260 diesel locomotives
70 electric locomotives
1,236 passenger carriages
80 baggage cars
80 vehicle-carrying wagons

Destinations	More than 500
States served:	46 plus District of Columbia.
Busiest stations:	1. New York
	2. Washington DC
	3. Philadelphia
	4. Chicago

5. Los Angeles

6. Boston (South station)

7. Sacramento

8. Baltimore

9. Albany, NY

10. San Diego

Average passengers	85,700 per day
Tunnels owned	18
Bridges owned	1,414

Seventy-two per cent of track used by Amtrak trains is owned by other companies. The largest host railways are:

BNFS Railway

Metro North Railroad

Canadian National Railways

Norfolk Southern Railway

CSX Transportation

Union Pacific Railroad

Main services financially supported by states:

Hiawatha Service (Chicago-Milwaukee)

Amtrak Cascades (Eugene-Portland-Seattle-Vancouver)

Lincoln Service (Chicago-St Louis)

Downeaster (Boston-Portland-Brunswick)

What Happened to the Luxury?

'WHEN HENRY N. JOHANSON went to work as Union Pacific dining car steward in 1936, dinner cost thirty-five cents. That was on the Challenger. Today dinner on the Union Pacific costs nothing because the railroad has terminated passenger service'. So reported the *Los Angeles Times* on 24 June 1971.

In fact, writer Barbara Hansen continued, the real end of railroad dining had come thirty years earlier with the Second World War; the railroads never recovered from the stress of wartime operations.

On the City of Los Angeles (Chicago-Los Angeles) before 1941, the passengers could book for any one of three sittings and, when seated at tables spread with Irish linen, waiters in tuxedos would serve from silver platters. The meals would begin with shrimp cocktail, soup and salad. Then there would follow a choice of steak, prime ribs or lamb chops (you took as much as you wanted).

There was a choice of vegetables and two potato dishes, washed down with red or white wine, and then followed by French pastries, coffee, brandy and rum.

When Hansen interviewed Johanson in 1971 he was a member of one of two dining crews retained out west by Amtrak. In 1946 the Los Angeles division of Union Pacific had employed fifty-six such crews.

* * *

New Zealand's railway system, for most of its life, has been dominated if not monopolised, by government control. One of early attempts at private operation was the establishment in 1886 of the private operator, the Wellington and Manawatu Railway Company; it built the 135 km line north of Wellington (the capital) to Longburn, just outside Palmerston North and where it connected with the government railway. Among its many achievements was the introduction of New Zealand's first dining car in 1886. However, the initial lack of end platforms to connect with adjacent carriages meant passengers could access or leave it only at stations rather than en route. In 1890 a conventional dining car with end platforms was built from an existing carriage, thus overcoming the access problem.

But what separated it from most railways operating a dining car is that the WMR took on fresh food along the way: bread at Johnsonville (the first important stop north of Wellington), mushrooms and fruit at Paekakariki, peaches, plums and apples at Paraparaumu, fresh trout at Waikanae, vegetables, eggs and poultry at Otaki, and more fish at Levin.

(WMR was twelve years ahead of the government's New Zealand Railways in this move, but it was thirty years ahead of the state railway when it introduced electric lighting in carriages in 1896, using storage batteries. The company also used telephones along the line, rather than NZR's Morse code system. The railway had a distinctly American look to it, from the style of the locomotives to the U.S.-built bogie wagons and clerestory-roofed carriages.)

Dining cars on New Zealand trains disappeared during the First World War. Thereafter if you needed to eat or drink you had to wait until the train stopped at one of the limited number of stations that had refreshment rooms. That involved a race from the train to jostle your way to the counter on the platform and be served tea in thick railway cups, and then balance that while also carrying a plate with a sandwich or a pie while hurrying back to your seat before the train pulled out. Once seated, you always had to watch the tea while the cup was full, ready for the moment when they re-attached the locomotive after its trip to the water vat and the inevitable jolt that sent down the train. Then the cups and plates (and soft drink bottles) were placed on the floor under seats, rattling with the train until one of the staff came through with a large drum throwing all the crockery into that. No wonder the average New Zealander fled the railway service when long distance buses became more common (and which stopped at cafes and tearooms to allow passengers to go inside, sit at a table and consume their lunch or tea in some comfort).

There were some exceptions to this platform rush; a very few stations had proper dining rooms. One such was Oamaru in the South Island where the expresses between Christchurch and Invercargill stopped for lunch. It was an organisational miracle: in just twenty-two minutes, the dining room could handle up to 250 passengers, seated at several long tables, and provide soup, main course and pudding while the express waited at the platform.

But, overall, New Zealanders had had enough of the railways and preferred road or air travel. In 1971 the government, under an enlightened railways minister, Peter Gordon, tried to turn the tide by refurbishing carriages and providing new smart long distance trains such as the Southerner (Christchurch-Invercargill), the Endeavour (Wellington-Napier) and the Northerner (Wellington-Auckland), complete with more spacious seats and a buffet car; they even bought new, all-sleeper train sets complete with dining cars from Japan to provide a second service on the Auckland-Wellington route, the Silver Star. But it was too late: all those have long gone and now the only long distance trains are essentially tourist services rather than providing point A to point B services for New Zealanders.

Travelling in Style in Upper Volta

EVEN ONE OF THE poorer developing countries managed to have a train that retained some of the trappings of old-style rail travel (at least for the more privileged travellers). In June 1981 Leon Dash of *The Washington Post* travelled on La Gazelle, the daily passenger train from Abidjan in Côte d'Ivoire to Ouagadougou in what is now Burkina Faso. The line was still known as the Abidjan-Niger Railway; in 1903, when the first rails were laid out of the port city of Abidjan the French had intended to build the rail to Ouagadougou, and then head eastwards to Niamey, the capital of Niger. But the capital of Upper Volta (as Burkina Faso was known then) was not reached until 1954—and that is where the rails ended.

In 1981 *La Gazelle*, whose livery was maroon and mustard, was divided into three classes: the 'perpetually hot' third, the air-conditioned sitting cars of second-class and air-conditioned sleepers in first-class. Those passengers who could afford first class could use a well-appointed dining car during the twenty-hour trip. For luncheon on the day of Dash's trip there was shrimp fritters for starters, followed by rabbit in mustard sauce, cheeses and sugared and fried banana. The evening meal, served from 7 00 p.m., began with omelette, followed by roast leg of mutton with buttered spring beans, and followed by cheeses. The wine was all chilled.

But, in Bulgaria, Not So Much Style.

IN 2017 AGENCE FRANCE Presse distributed a news item about a new tourist train Bulgaria, a refurbished consist pulled by steam traction and including the carriage used by the former King Boris III. However, the report continued, 'the success (of the tourist train) belies the dire state of the railways in the European Union's poorest nation'.

The report quoted a 2015 Boston Consulting Group study showing that Bulgarian trains had the worst quality and safety record among the twenty-five European nations surveyed. The number of Bulgarians using trains had halved between 2000 and 2015 and the volume of freight was one-tenth of what had been carried in the 1980s.

'Creaking infrastructure, ageing locomotives and rolling stock mean that the average train speed is just 55 km/h', the report noted. Its fastest 'express' train took eight hours to cover 440 km. In winter, said AFP, the simplest journey could turn into a nightmare. Iron nerves and plenty of food were necessary preparations for a train journey.

SNAPSHOT: BULGARIAN RAILWAYS

Total route length: 5,114 km
Gauges: 4,989 km—standard gauge 1,435 km (4ft 8½in)
         125 km—narrow gauge 760 mm (2ft 5^{15}/$_{16}$in)
Electrified: 2,880 km (standard gauge)
Passenger journeys (2015): 22,510,000

In 2015 Bulgarian Railways (Balgarski darzhavni zheleznitsi or BDZ) recorded the greatest increases in freight volume among the European Union states. Yet the latest reports (at the time of writing) shows that BDZ in mid-2016 was continuing to be seriously short of electric locomotives due to lack of maintenance. There have also been problems keeping sufficient diesel multiple units and electric multiple units in passenger service due, not only to maintenance issues, but to damage incurred at level crossing smashes with road vehicles.

Passenger Health

IN 1913, ARKANSAS ISSUED new sanitation rules for that state, including some that applied to railroad companies operating within its borders. Among the requirements were (with the regulation number):

313: 'Seats, windows and walls of cars must be wiped off with a dampened cloth while standing at division terminals or meal stations where a stop of twenty minutes ore more is scheduled, and the passengers are given an opportunity to leave the cars during that time, and at other times during the run to keep the cars as free as possible from dust'.

314: 'Water coolers must be empty and scalded once each twenty-four hours, and shall be filled with good, wholesome drinking water when in service'.

317: 'The smoking apartments of railway cars used for passengers must be provided with one cuspidor for each two passengers according to seating capacity. Each cuspidor must contain not less than one half-pint of clear water.'

318: 'Every sleeping car operated in the State of Arkansas shall be cleaned at the end of each run, and in no case shall any sleeping car be used for a period of time longer than one week without being thoroughly cleaned. All removeable seats and backs shall be dusted and cleaned outside the car.'

322: Passengers, patrons and employees or others are prohibited from washing their teeth over and expectorating in basins which are used for the bathing of hands and faces in sleeping cars, passenger cars, or railway station buildings. Large cuspidors or dental lavatories must be provided for such purposes.

Countries Where Passenger Patience Required

SRI LANKA RAILWAYS IS a government department and, in the present era, is largely passenger-oriented (although with some freight carried). Formerly Ceylon Government Railways, SLR was described in 2014 by a travel writer as 'one of the most charmingly decrepit railway systems in the world'. While air-conditioned cars are now attached to trains used by tourists, the railway stipulates that to make a reservation on any train the intending passenger must visit a railway station thirty days before departure.

But, on the positive side, SLR services still include functions that have long disappeared from many rail systems: holiday resorts that can be booked, and the acceptance of parcels at every station.

SLR operates 400 trains a day, of which 386 are passenger workings with just twenty-five goods trains. There are 362 stations throughout the island. About a third of sleepers laid are wooden, the remainder being made of concrete. The annual management report specifies how many elephants were hit by trains and killed; in 2014 the total was nine.

FAST FACTS: SIR LANKA RAILWAYS

Total route length: 1,340 km (1,186.1 km is single track)
Gauge: Broad 1,676 mm (5ft 6in)

Rolling stock (2016)

Diesel-electric locomotives	96
Diesel-hydraulic locomotives	42
Diesel multiple units	90
Passenger cars	500
Goods wagons	683
Tanker wagons	128

Signalling

Centralised control	199.13 km
Colour light	450.53 km

The remainder of track is controlled either by electronic relay interlocking or mechanical interlocking.

The Sabah State Railway of Malaysia operates a line laid originally by the British North Borneo Company, a British enterprise that ran what is now Sabah before the British government took over the territory as a Crown colony (called British North Borneo).

The line runs from Tanjung Aru station, on the outskirts of Kota Kinabalu, to Tenom. It has thirteen stations and the line is used for both passenger and freight trains.

A July 2016 report by the Malaysian news agency Bernama stated that an ageing fleet of trains, conditions of the railway track and natural disasters (landslides and floods) has led to regular cancellations of services. In 2015, 762 train services out of 6,942 were cancelled, the disruptions usually affecting the Beaufort-Tenom section. As the Bernama report explained, four of the diesel multiple units were more than thirty-five years old. A new DMU set, financed by the state government, was due to be delivered in November 2016, and another three units by 2018.

Country Profile: Cuba

Total route length: 4,183 km
Gauge: Standard gauge 1,435 mm (4ft 8½in)

B EFORE THE CUBAN REVOLUTION that culminated with the rebel forces under Fidel Castro taking power in January 1959, the country had the most efficient railway system in Latin America. In 1958 some 15,000 km of railway covered much of the island state.

In fact, Cuba was the seventh country in the world to embrace rail travel—it was preceded by Britain, the United States, France, Germany, Belgium and Russia—when a 27 km line was opened in 1837 between Havana and Bejucal, constructed by Compañia de Caminos de Hierro de la Habana.

The Central Railway (835 km) between Havana and Santiago de Cuba (effectively a rail backbone spanning much of the length of Cuba) was completed by 1902. But railways in Cuba, in the early decades, had been driven largely by the needs of the sugar industry. In the period 1840-1870 the industry grew threefold. A large network of narrow gauge railways had been built by mill owners to make it possible for them to export raw brown sugar, refined white sugar, molasses and sugar byproducts to Havana and other ports. These trains, after unloading the sugar, would carry fuel and manufactured goods back to their home districts. Cuban Central's narrow gauge network, while

In the 1990s 2-8-2 Alco No. 1910 was the largest locomotive in operation in Cuba and is shown here in two photographs near Pozo on 2 February 1998.
David Longman—david-longman.com

primarily for sugar transports, provided passenger and general freight services, as did sugar mill lines owned by Ferrocarril de Tunas and the Chaparra Railroad.

At the time of the 1959 revolution the common carrier railway system was dwarfed by the length of the narrow gauge railways (1,067 mm) owned and operated by sugar companies and that comprised nearly two-thirds of the railway route length of Cuba. Since the revolution some forty-five per cent of railway routes have been closed.

Today Cuba's railways are seen largely as antiquated and inefficient; symptomatic of this is the much written about Hershey Electric Railway, the main electrified section on the island and running 96.5 km. The line was built for the chocolate maker Hershey Corporation between 1918 and 1922 to carry sugar to the port of Havana (and also transport its workers). A network of branch lines was laid from the main plant, and the company insisted on being a common carrier with a quality passenger service. It electrified its line to end the problems of sparks from locomotives causing fires in the summer.

The Hershey line is now operated with electric cars made in Spain in the 1940s and 1950s and often breaks down, leaving passengers stranded.

In 2004 a U.S. State Department report noted that 'the collapse of the sugar industry has led to a substantial reduction in rail assets, with more than a third of the rail network—itself antiquated and very poorly maintained—being mothballed. The rail signaling system dates from the middle of the last century, and is in need of substantial improvement'.

The rail system is operated Ferrocarriles Nacionales de Cuba (Cuban Union Railways), a body that came into existence after the revolution when all lines were nationalised.

Cuba has indicated it will spend about $1.3 billion through to 2021 modernising its rail system, starting with a fibre-optic communications system to cost about $40 million.

In July 2016 Cuba signed an agreement for seventy-five new locomotives to be manufactured by the Russian maker Sinara. Later Russia agreed to supply sixty-eight new passenger coaches, the existing rolling stock being in such condition that some services on long distance routes do not run some days of the week.

8

Rail's Resurgence

High-speed track under construction (as of March 2016): 15,970 km
High-speed railway being planned (as of March 2016): 35,061 km
High-speed train market (2014): $112 billion
High-speed train market (estimated 2019): $133 billion
China's 2016 high-speed network: 22,000 km (approximately)
Planned China high-speed network 2020: 30,000 km (approximately)

IN 1970 WORK BEGAN on a new, more direct route (49.9 km shorter than the then existing route) between Florence and Rome with the pouring of the first pillar of the 4,575 metre viaduct across the Paglia River that would, when completed, become Italy's longest rail bridge with 210 arches.

By 1975 trains would run between the two cities in 1hr 25min at an average speed of 185 km/h. This would replace the 2hr 57min trip on the existing rail line via Arezzo and Orte, that line being retained for use by slow local trains and freight movements.

The Italians were able to use Japan's advanced railroad technology. Italy's move to build straight lines and then introduce fast trains on them came a decade after Japan had pioneered the 'bullet train'. It was in the first week of October 1964 (in time for the Tokyo Olympics that began on the tenth of that month) that a trial run had been made on the new Tokaido line (the first standard gauge track in Japan) by the Tokyo-Osaka Ivory Bullet, a train that ran at about an average 200 km/h (top speed was 250 km/h). When Tokyo and Osaka were first joined by rail the journey took 20hr 10min; the new bullet train would get that down to one hour. However, these new trains could not run when visibility fell below twenty-three metres. The Japanese name was, and is, Shinkansen, or "new trunk line".

The World Bank had loaned Japan just over $1 billion for the project. It seems to have been money well spent: by 1969 it was being reported that the bullet trains were making money, with cumulative gross takings in November that year reaching $1.39 billion, with a net profit of $305.6 million (the remainder of the Japanese railway system still running at a loss).

And by 1974 *The Times* of London noted that, almost ten years on, 'European and American railway experts still marvel at the production history of the bullet trains', wrote Michael Reich. More than 20,000

One of the earlier models of Japan's Bullet Train: on 1 June 1985, this EMU O set was captured passing through Ogori station in Fukuoka prefecture. *John Beckhaus.*

Japanese companies had been involved in the project, the trains being designed from scratch.

Since the first run, maximum speeds had risen by 42 km/h.

FAST FACT: RAIL BALTICA

Rail Baltica, as the project's website puts it, is seen as a symbolic return to Europe of the three Baltic states (Estonia, Latvia, Lithuania). Until the Second World War the then three independent countries had standard gauge (1,435 mm) connections to Europe. But, by 1945 (the three states by that time having been forcibly incorporated into the Union of Soviet Socialist Republics) the rail systems were changed to the Russian gauge of 1,520 mm. Rail Baltica will again provide a connection with the German and Polish rail systems with a 1,435 mm line from Tallinn, via Riga and Kaunas, to the Polish border and Warsaw. The line will extend over 729 km, 235 km of that in Latvia, and will allow passenger train speeds of up to 240 km/h, with an average speed of 170 km/h. There are also plans to extend the Baltic standard gauge line to Finland, an underwater tunnel connecting Tallinn and Helsinki. This would allow trains to run between those two capitals in about thirty minutes.

A 2013 research paper by the Helsinki-based Nordic Investment Bank noted that 'the current trickle of rail traffic between the Baltic countries and mainland Europe stops at the Lithuanian railway station Šeštokai to switch to a different gauge … It is little wonder the direct passenger service or freight connection by rail between the region and the rest of the EU is close to non-existent'. At that time, the volume of freight crossing the Polish-Lithuanian border was between twenty-five and twenty-eight million tonnes a year.

In June 2017 the standard gauge reached Kaunus and five trains began operating on that section between that Lithuanian city and Poland. The new line parallels the broad gauge track, the route being quite winding. The line onward to Riga and Tallinn, however, will be laid on a new, much straighter alignment.

* * *

Resurgence Case Study #1: Algeria

Total route length: 4,498 km (3,750 km in use)

Double track: 553 km

Gauges 3,443 km—Standard gauge 1,435 mm (4ft 8½in)

1,085 km—narrow gauge 1,055 mm (3ft 5½in)

Electrified: 323 km (standard gauge)

Trains per day: 242 (12 long-distance, 68 regional, 162 suburban)

Passengers 2015: 36.2 millions (845,708 long-distance, 2.03 millions regional, 33.3 millions suburban)

Freight: 4.2 million tonnes

Stations: 175

Other stops: 215

Tunnels: 139

Level crossings: 1,226 (959 unguarded)

RAILWAYS IN ALGERIA ARE operated by the state agency Société Nationale des Transports Ferroviaires (SNTF). The government has in place a plan to overhaul and expand the system through to 2020 at a cost of $7.5 billion, including extending electrification, building new railway stations and introducing more modern passenger rolling stock. The intended length of the network has been put at 12,500 km.

Algeria has had to catch up lost ground: the 1991-2002 civil war that saw the government struggling to repress Islamic rebels left the nation's rail network in poor shape, much of that network having being destroyed during the conflict. Since then a focus has been on electrifying lines to allow the use of faster trains.

The main railway line, of about 1,200 km in length, runs across the northern section of the country, almost parallel to the coastline on the Mediterranean, and connects at one end with the Tunisian system and, at the other, with the Moroccan (although the latter connection has been closed, along with the border, since 1994 after Algeria was blamed for a terrorist attack in Morocco). The line serves several important cities including Algiers, Annaba and Constantine with a branch line to the port city of Oran.

A 1,160 km line is being built across the Hauts Plateaux, a hot, dry region mostly characterised by elevated ground. This will run

east-west across the country as does the main line to the north. (This
line had first been proposed in 1996 but it was rejected because, one,
it was then estimated to cost $3 billion to construct and, two, at the
time this coincided with SNTF needing to replace 250 carriages and
twenty locomotives that had been destroyed by Islamist guerillas.)

There are also lines to serve the phosphate and iron ore mining
areas.

The system relies, however, about ninety-five per cent of its revenue
on passenger transport with more than thirty-six million passenger
journeys a year.

Rolling Stock (2015)
Diesel locomotives: 261
Electric locomotives: 14
Electric multiple units: 64
Diesel multiple units: 17
Passenger carriages: 416
Freight wagons: 10,873

The National Company of Railway Construction signed a joint venture with China Railway Construction Corporation in February 2016
to manufacture in Algeria track for use by high-speed trains, along with
signalling and telecommunications equipment. Then Alstom formed a
venture to build regional and intercity multiple units at a location in
eastern Algeria. In 2015 that company had delivered seventeen six-car
DMUs with plans to build ninety-eight further diesel sets.

In another recent development, $45 million was allocated to
double-track the 117 km line serving Oued Kebir, Tebessa and Djebel
Ouk and which is used for trains transporting phosphate and iron ore.

A new 21 km line opened to expand the suburban network of
Algiers, with the new route leaving the Algiers-Bilda line. The new
route, which is both electrified and double-track, serves five new
stations. As the end of 2016, work on 2,300 km of new track was in
progress and 1,050 km of line was being double-tracked.

In May 2017 a new line was completed linking the eastern Algerian
city of Annaba with the Tunisian railway system, allowing through

running between the capitals of the two countries. The last major work had involved redeveloping a tunnel on the Tunisian side of the border.

Resurgence Case Study #2: Costa Rica

Total route length: 278 km
Gauge: Narrow gauge 1,067 mm (3ft 6in)

COSTA RICA'S RAILWAY SYSTEM is operated by Instituto Costarricense de Ferrocarriles (INCOFER). But in 2016 a private consortium of construction companies proposed to build a 'dry canal'. This would involve a 320 km dual-tracked railway (and a ten-lane highway) linking new ports on the Caribbean and Pacific coasts. The promoters say they could have a system where freight is unloaded from ships on one coast, railed across the country and re-loaded at the other coast within thirty hours. They say it would complement, rather than compete with, the Panama Canal.

Resurgence Cast Study #3: The Gulf Countries

THE ABU DHABI-BASED Etihad Rail's 1,200 km network will extend across the United Arab Emirates, from the border of Saudi Arabia to the border of Oman. The company's website lays out the plan: 'The network will run from Ghweifat to Abu Dhabi, Dubai and the Northern Emirates with major connecting points in between, including Al Ain and Madinat Zayed. Etihad Rail will have an extensive national network with freight terminals, distribution centres and depots located close to major transport hubs, warehouses, and storage facilities across the UAE, including Mussafah, Khalifa Port, Jebal Ali Free Zone, Port of Fujairah and Saqr Port.

The Etihad Rail network will also connect with the Gulf Co-operation Council (GCC) network and this—once fully established—will cover the six GCC countries of Bahrain, Kuwait, Oman, Qatar, Saudi Arabia and UAE, the company added.

Meanwhile, the Sultanate of Oman has been having an on-again, off-again flirtation with building a railway system. At first there was talk of laying 2,135 km (and even 2,244 km) of standard gauge line stretching to the borders with Yemen and the United Arab Republic and a capital investment bill of $15.5 billion.

As 2017 got under way, the focus seemed to be on building a 625 km (some reports said 337 km) mineral line to open up development of mining and be capable of transporting five millions of (each) limestone and gypsum, along with hauling about one million tonnes a year of oilfield equipment to the interior. In 2014 Oman Rail was founded and a year later it sent engineers to Italy for training in railway construction. The line(s) will be double-track and non-electrified. Some plans have allowed for as many as forty-six railway stations and eight maintenance yards.

As for Kuwait, that state has agreed to be part of the 2,117 km planned Gulf railway network outlined above, this $25 billion project now scheduled to be completed by 2023 (missing its first deadline of 2018). Kuwait's section, which has also been delayed, is intended to be 511 km long, double-tracked running from Kuwait City via its airport and main port to the Saudi Arabian border (and also linked with the Iraqi network to the north). Trains will be able to run at maximum speeds of 120 km/h and 200 km/h depending on the section.

Resurgence Case Study #4: Nigeria

Total route length 3,691 km
Gauges: 186 km—standard gauge 1,435 mm (4ft 8½in)
3,505 km—narrow gauge 1,067 mm (3ft 6in)

IN MID-2016 NIGERIA entered the world of standard gauge with the completion by China Civil Engineering Construction Corporation of a line from the nation's capital of Abuja (which hitherto had no rail connection) to Kaduna. Express trains (complete with bar/café cars) cover the 186 km distance between the two cities in two hours. The line has ten intermediate stations and a designed speed of 150 km per hour.

It is the first stage of Nigeria's plan to have an all-standard gauge network capable of providing high-speed services; in the meantime, however, existing narrow gauge lines will be rehabilitated. The network's main lines are the Lagos-Kaduna-Nguru western line, the Port

Harcourt-Kaduna eastern line together with the main spur line from Kafanchan to Maiduguri. There are other branch lines.

In 2017 a consortium consisting of General Electric, South Africa's Transnet and SinoHydro was chosen as preferred bidder to take over running Nigeria's railway system.

There is no question that something needs to be done. As the *Daily Nation* reported in July 2017, five years earlier Nigerian Railways Corporation had bought new tanker wagons; it also made agreements with oil producers to carry those products. Nothing ever happened and the wagons had remained unused, sitting on weed-covered sidings. One of the reasons for this is that the narrow gauge lines for which they were intended are too derelict, while some of the oil marketing parties had no rail connection.

FAST FACT: NIGERIAN RAILWAYS DURING COLONIAL TIMES

In 1928, Nigerian Railways had the following rolling stock on its roster:
Main line locomotives: 208
Shunting engines: 54
Passenger carriages: 283
Freight wagons: 3,326
This colonial rail system extended for about 1,600 miles (2,575 km) with another 210 miles (338 km) of sidings. In addition, another 300 miles of branches were under construction. A report written by the department's general manager, Mr E M Bland, in 1928 explained that passenger traffic was showing 'remarkable increases', more particularly among the Africans who, he said, were 'inveterate travellers when given the facilities and cheap fares'. By that stage, the railways were booking 2.83 million passenger journeys a year.

The principal goods being consigned to rail were cocoa and other agricultural products, coal, building materials, cotton, ground nuts, palm oil, salt and tin concentrates. Two workshops had been established—at Ebute Metta and Enugu.

Nigeria at the time was the only Crown colony in Africa to have a working coal mine, near port Harcourt. It was owned by the railway and was used to power the locomotives with coal also being provided to the marine department, power companies and to shipping companies. The mine also supplied the railways of the Gold Coast (now Ghana) by sea.

Resurgence Case Study #5: the Philippines

Total route length: 995 km (445 km in operation 2015)
Gauge: Narrow gauge 1,067 mm (3ft 6in)

Philippines National Railways (PNR) was established in 1964. The system essentially consists of heavy rail lines on Luzon, the largest island.

The administration of President Rodrigo Duterte, which took office in June 2016, undertook to spend about $20 billion in what it termed a massive railway-building programme. In 2015 it was assessed that the Philippine economy was being hurt to the tune of $64 million a day because its domestic transport system was so inefficient, with traffic congestion, and poor access to ports and freight terminals.

Apart from new light rail lines in the capital, there were announced several new commuter heavy rail lines and a 73 km line between Tutuban (Manila's main railway station) and Los Baños. A 25 km rail line is proposed for the city of Cebu in the Visayas group and for the southern island of Mindanao (whence the president comes); overall, some 2000 km of railways have been promised to connect the island's major cities.

An assessment in 2015 by the Japan International Co-operation Agency (which clearly had a struggle getting hard facts, saying some of its material was 'culled from the Philippine Statistical Yearbook') found that both patronage and level of service had deteriorated between 2001 and 2008. Services south from Metro Manila to the Bicol region were suspended after a typhoon in 2006. Until then PNR ran three trains a week return from Metro Manila to Bicol; the timetable then allowed thirteen hours for a one-way trip but usually it took between twenty and twenty-four hours due to poor track, many level crossings and old rolling stock.

Resurgence Case Study #6: Poland

Total route length (2016): 18,904 km
(37,470 km including sidings and yards)
Gauges: 18,510 km—standard gauge 1,435 mm (4ft 8½in)

394 km—broad gauge 1,520 mm (4ft $11^{27}/_{32}$in)

Broad gauge connects with Ukraine system

Electrified: 11,795 km

Double track: 7,883 km

Stations and stops: 3,211 (1,353 stations, 1,858 stops)

Bridges: 3,365

Flying junctions: 3,035

Tunnels: 25

Level crossings: 14,889

Passengers (2015): 280.3 millions

IN EARLY 2017 POLAND had begun implementing its largest ever rail modernisation programme, spending €10.5 billion through to 2020. According to a brief for a planned trade mission of rail equipment manufacturers, the Australian government trade agency, Austrade, explained that the modernisation was focused on upgrading rail infrastructure to accommodate high speed trains, to ensure better safety and more efficiency, along with buying more rolling stock and making the freight market more competitive. Austrade said that the late 2014 launch of the Express Intercity premium Pendolino services 'is a taste of what travellers and operators may expect'. These trains were first introduced in 2014 and by mid-2017 had completed some twenty million kilometres of revenue service. Alstom has equipped a depot at Warsaw to service these train sets; it is planned to introduce around 500 hundred of these trains over time.

Meanwhile, Poland's rail network is a key element in Europe's wider transport services. Poland is the most important railway market in Central Europe for both freight and passenger traffic. Polskie Koleje Państwowe (PKP, or Polish National Railways) is the dominant operator. PKP Cargo has 1,250 GPS-equipped locomotives and more than 62,500 freight wagons; total freight on the Polish system is twice that carried on the United Kingdom railway network.

'However, despite visible improvements, rail freight operators still suffer from a shortage of suitable sidings, insufficient terminal facilities for intermodal freight, and even modernised single-track lines lack passing loops suited to modern rail freight movements,' the Australian report added.

FAST FACT: WORLD SUBWAY SYSTEMS 2010

When talking of resurgence of rail, one must include the growth of metro and subway railways, particularly in the case of the developing countries. As of 2017, estimates show there could be about 2,300 km of new subway route length built between 2016 and 2030 (with an additional 1,100 stations). China is expected to be the most active in building, followed by India and South Korea. The Asian Development Bank expects Azerbaijan, Japan, Malaysia, the Philippines, Singapore and Thailand all to be highly active in the field of metro expansions.

The figures here show the state of world metro systems in 2010:

	Cities	Stations	Length (km)
Total	138	7,886	10,670
Africa	1	51	56
Europe	40	2,782	3,558
North America	30	1,598	2,219
South America	14	478	627
Asia	53	2,977	4,210

These figures would have looked quite different just ten years earlier: between 2001 and 2010 almost forty per cent of the new subway construction took place in Asia; of the twenty-five subway systems inaugurated in that period, fourteen were in Asia (half in China).

Country Profile: India

Total route length (2015): 66,083 km. (90,000 km—approx. when including yards, sidings)
Gauges: 58,825 km—broad gauge 1,676 mm (5ft 6in)
4,908 km—metre gauge 1,000 mm (3ft 3⅜in)
2,350 km—narrow gauge 762 mm (2ft 6in)
Double track: 20,633 km
Electrified: 23,654 km
Stations: 7,172
Passenger trains per day: 12,617
Freight carried: 1.1 billion tonnes a year
Level crossings: More than 30,000 (around 11,500 unmanned)

INDIA HAS THE WORLD's third largest (after Russia and China) rail system under a single management structure, and is the fourth largest in route length (the United States has the longest).

But the system is suffering from decades of under-investment. As Morgan Stanley pointed out in a 2014 report, in 1951 (four years after the British had left) India's rail network extended over 53,597 km; yet in the following sixty-three years it grew by just a fifth. In 1951 India's rail network was 2.3 times larger than that of China; today China's rail system is 1.6 times longer than that of India.

Morgan Stanley argued that what size and growth that had been achieved was not due to the way the railway system had been run since independence: in terms of size, that was due to the efforts of the British when they ruled India; as for growth, that was mainly a function of India's economic growth over the ensuring decades. In fact, the railways had seventy-four per cent of passenger traffic in 1951 but only fourteen per cent in 2012. Over the same period, according to Morgan Stanley, Indian Railways' share of freight business fell from eighty-six per cent to thirty-six per cent.

The report noted one significant improvement: manning at level crossings has been improved and the number of unmanned crossings had been reduced, important progress when forty-one per cent of all railway accidents, and sixty-five per cent of all fatalities, occur at such crossings.

FAST FACT: INDIA'S RAILWAY BUDGET

A ninety-two year piece of railway history ended in 2016: the railway budget. India was the only country in the world to have two budgets presented to its parliament each year—the general budget covering all other government finances, and the separate railway budget. In 1921 a British committee recommended the railway budget be separated out because the sector was such a huge element in government spending—more than seventy-five per cent of the budget most years. The first separate budget was presented in 1924. The last was delivered in 2016 when railways accounted for just four per cent of the national government spending.

The first of the railway budgets was tabled in India's Legislative Assembly by the then Railways and Commerce Minister, Sir Charles Innes. Because of the surplus in 1924, Innes had allocated funds for the introduction of automatic couplers and for speeding up the repairs to rolling stock.

In the 1923-24 financial year, India's government rail system recorded a surplus of £4.3 million, more than five times the surplus of the preceding year, a result achieved by having reduced staff numbers, watching fuel consumption, and a focus on preventing losses and damage incurred during goods being transported.

The total number of railway employees in 1924 was 727,093. Of that total, 708,942 members of staff were Indian, 11,509 Anglo-Indian (mixed race), and 6,642 Europeans.

Fares had been increased to address a decline in the number of first, second, and intermediate class passengers, although there had been a rise in patronage in third class.

India's rail system was suffering still from events of the 1914–18 war where lines had been dismantled to send rails to the theatres of war. By 1924 all the lines had been restored except from one 145 km section

Rolling Stock

Locomotives: 10,822

43 Steam★ (metre and narrow gauges)

5,714 Diesel

5,065 Electric

Passenger carriages: 60,308 including 8,475 electric multiple unit cars, 51,833 conventional coaches (and there are approximately 7,000 luggage and mail vans).

Freight wagons: 254,006 including brake vans (250,711 broad gauge, 3,139 metre gauge, 156 narrow gauge).

★ *As late as 1990-91, Indian Railways had operated 2,915 steam locomotives, 1,295 of those being on the broad gauge.*

Recent Developments

Accident record. India in 2016 had the worst rail accident across the world, with the most serious being the 148 dead and more than 200 injured when the Indore-Patna Express was the target of terrorist activity and fourteen passenger cars derailed while the train was at high speed. In addition, there were six serious derailments, with more than fifty injured in one and forty in another.

Freight Corridor. The World Bank announced a $650 million loan for the Eastern Dedicated Freight Corridor that will improve efficiency in moving goods between northern and eastern ports. The rail line will be 1,193 km long and extend from Ludhiana in Punjab to Kolkata (Calcutta) and be built in three sections. Axle loads will initially rise to 25 tonnes, and later to 32.5 tonnes. The lines will allow trains of between 6,000 and 12,000 tonnes to travel at up to 100 km/h.

Foreign players. The government announced plans to modernise 400 major stations and there were suggestions that foreign companies would be allowed to take on some projects. New Delhi's railway station (about 500,000 passengers a day) is one of the chosen stations and there is interest from South Korea in undertaking that task. The stations will get digital signage, luggage screening machines, ticket vending machines, Wi-Fi, executive lounges and shopping areas

Historical Snapshots

First line. India's first commercial railway, built by the Great Indian Peninsula Railway Company, was opened to traffic on 16 April 1853. The 33.8 km line ran from Bombay to what is now called Thane. The train's consist was made up of fourteen passenger carriages and was seen off from Bombay with a twenty-one gun salute. By 1870 the trunk lines running from Karachi, Calcutta, Madras and Bombay had all been completed.

The eight original railway companies that built the bulk of the network were East Indian Railway Company (founded 1845), Great Indian Peninsula (1849), Eastern Bengal Railway Company (1857), Bombay, Baroda and Central Indian Railway (1855), Scinde, Punjab and Delhi Railway Company (1870), Great Southern of India Railway Company (1853, renamed South Indian Railway Company in 1874), Madras Railway Company (1845), and Oudh and Rohilkhand Railway Company (1872). Most of their capital had been raised as equity in the United Kingdom.

These joint stock companies operated under a concession granted by the India Office in London.

Government interference. In March 1903 the office in London of the Secretary of State for India proposed greater government control of the sub-continent's railways. Several of the private railway companies, including the Bombay, Baroda and Central Indian Railway and the Madras Railway Company, complained that their share prices had become depressed in view of the possible purchase of their undertakings by the Indian government. The companies had been badly hit by the terrible famine that ravaged the sub-continent between 1896 and 1902, caused by droughts and monsoon failures. During the worst of the famine they had received business in the form of transporting emergency food supplies to the stricken areas, but in the second half of 1902 there was no further relief work deemed necessary—but the crops had not yet recovered to provide substitute freight business. In 1902 there had also been an outbreak of plague around Bombay. 'Owing to the continued prevalence of plague, there was a general falling off in third-class traffic as the natives were prevented from making pilgrimages and attending fairs, these and religious festivals constituting the chief incentives to the native population to make use of the railways,' one newspaper reported.

By 1903 several other companies were involved in running India's railways, some created by mergers of older operators. These included the Bengal and North Western (1882-1943), Bengal Dooars Railway (1894-1941), the Bengal Nagpur Railway Company (nationalised 1944). In 1908 the Madras Railway was merged with Southern Mahratta Railway Company.

* * *

British money. By 1908 Britain had invested £274 million (£25.9 billion in today's values) in India's railway system, its single largest investment in the British Empire.

One of the works completed included the longest tunnel on Indian Railways when the sub-continent was under British rule. Khojak tunnel measured 12,870 feet (3,923 metres) long. This was located on the North Western Railway between Quetta and Chaman (now in Pakistan), the latter town being on the border with Afghanistan (and now the terminus of the Rohri Junction-Chaman line of 523 km).

Then there was the engineering, between 1856 and 1863, of the Bhor Ghat railway incline through the Western Ghats mountain range in Maharashta state. The 24 km incline had a ruling grade of 1-in-37. There was a daily workforce of about 40,000 people and some 25,000 workers died during the building of the incline. The seven years it took to complete the line was not surprising given that, as one description put it, 'the hills were precipitous, covered with think jungle, lacking water and means of approach, and composed of hard trap rock'. The sharpest curve was fifteen chains (302 metres) radius. There were 3.64 km of tunneling required, along with eight viaducts, the highest standing at 139 feet (42.3 metres) high.

9

Russia's Turbulent
Railway Age

FOR ALL ITS OTHER economic failings, Russia has been no slouch
when it comes to building railways. Between 1861 and 1882
some 22,994 km of track were laid. Then in the period from
1882 until 1914 another 51,456 km were added the Imperial Russia's
railway network, much of the impetus coming from the dynamic Tsarist
finance minister Serge Witte. Just on the eve of the 1917 revolution,
and even after three years of war with Germany and Austria-Hungary,
Russia still managed to complete a link from the western edge of the
Urals to Tashkent (now capital of independent Uzbekistan). Between
1866 and 1870, eighty per cent of capital spending in Russia went
to railway building. By 1870, there were forty-seven privately owned
railway companies (the state would buy many of them out but as late
as 1913 thirty per cent of Russia's railway system was operated by
private enterprise).

Private money dominated early railway construction but eventually
companies invested in projects in the full knowledge that their operations would eventually revert to the state. A good deal of the money
required came from the Netherlands with Russian railway companies
often being listed on the Amsterdam Stock Exchange. Dutch money
became especially critical during the lead up to, and the duration

of, the Crimean War when Russia was unable to obtain French or German financing; but after the recriminations of that conflict faded, money was again available from Paris and Berlin. In 1857, for example, the Grand Société des Chemins de fer Russe—which was granted by the Tsar the right to build main lines across Imperial Russia and own them for twenty years—was managed from Paris and was given the concession of being able to ship rails, locomotives and rolling stock to Russia free of any tariff impost.

Many of the privately built railways were no small projects. Just take the example of the 698 km railway completed in 1872 by the Vladikavkaz Railway Company. The Vladikavkaz railway ran from Rostov, near the eastern extremity of the Black Sea, to Vladikavkaz in what is now Chechnya (a present-day republic of the Russian Federation north of the border with independent Georgia). In 1870 the government called for bids to build the line, the winner being a company headed by a German aristocrat. However, the first twelve years of operations saw the company lose money, so it was decided to build a 271 km branch line to Novorossiysk, then a small village on the Black Sea coast. The branch opened to traffic in 1884.

The arrival of that branch line transformed Novorossiysk into what would become Russia's largest port on the Black Sea and today a globally important grain export loading port. The original single wooden jetty was later superseded by the construction of five parallel wharves, each having four railway tracks. The railway company then built elevators along its lines where farmers could deliver their grain to be collected by trains. Before the line was opened, annual grain shipments from Novorossiysk were running at just over 120 tonnes a year; by 1897 270,000 tonnes a year were being loaded at the port. By 1898, the Vladikavkaz company had extended its main line to Baku on the Caspian Sea; a year after that, it opened what would be its longest branch, the 530 km line to Tsaritsyn, the important river port—better known by its post-1925 name, Stalingrad (now Volgograd). By 1911 the company was so profitable it was paying generous dividends on its shares and the government-guaranteed bonds.

Another great plan, although not successfully implemented, was announced in November 1910 when the St Petersburg correspondent of *The Times* of London filed a report saying that an influential group of Russian financiers and public men was planning to build a railway from the Caucasus (starting from Baku, located on the Caspian Sea and now capital of Azerbaijan) to Baluchistan (now Balochistan, a region of Pakistan but then part of British India). The promoters were seeking a concession from the Persian (now Iranian) government. The big selling point was that, upon completion of this 'missing link', travellers would be able to get from London to Bombay within a week. The company believed that the railway journey would be two and a half days quicker than going by rail to Brindisi in Italy and thence by ship via the Suez Canal, and the railway fares would be four-fifths that paid to travel by sea.

After leaving Baku, it was proposed that the line would skirt the Caspian Sea and then proceed via Teheran to British India, the sections within Russia and India being controlled by the respective governments with the portion within Persia being under the control of the company.

* * *

Then came the 1917 revolution and the establishment of the Union of Soviet Socialist Republics. It was the drive to industrialisation that involved significant extensions of the country's railways.

But this grand railway plan was complicated by events at the birth of the communist regime. The 1917 revolution and its aftermath, particularly as it concerned the civil war between the Red and White armies, involved the destruction of much of the railway system—and railway equipment—of what would become the U.S.S.R. Then came the Second World War: during both the occupation of Soviet territory and then the forced retreat, the German forces disabled twenty-six main lines and partially destroyed another eight. The damage list from the fighting and sabotage (by both sides) totalled just short of 65,000 km of track, along with 13,000 bridges, 15,800 locomotives and 428,000 freight wagons.

The first four decades of the communist era in Russia therefore were dominated by two main rail challenges: the need to overcome the destruction wrought by two great political and military upheavals, and the requirement to build a rail system that would support the

ambitious (and usually draconian) policies of development and industrialisation of the Soviet Union.

In the 1940s Joseph Stalin conceived the idea of building the
Trans-Polar Main Line, a 1,600 km-long railway that would open up
vast tracts of Siberia. Its proposed route would see it arc through the
Siberian wastes linking, at one end, Salekhard and, at the other, Igarka
on the Yenisei River.

Two gulags were created along the route to accommodate political
prisoners and camps were established along the route, spaced between
10 km and 12 km apart. It has been estimated that around 300,000
prisoners were engaged on the project over its lifetime and as many as
a third of those may have died.

There had been proposals made from the nineteenth century for
railways to the north of Russia; however it was not until 1943 that
route surveys began from Salekhard. Four years later the decision was
made to construct a large port at the mouth of the River Ob, one of
three great Siberian rivers flowing northwards to the coastline above
the Arctic Circle.

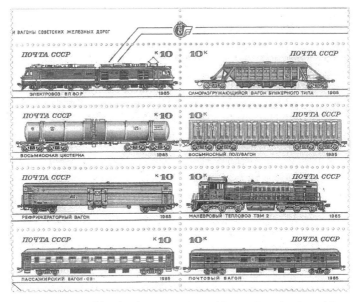

This 1985 stamp set issued by the former Union of Soviet Socialist Republics
shows a variety of rolling stock of the time.

For the railway workers, the worst was (of course) winter with its temperatures falling as low as minus 60°C and frequent, horrific blizzards. But the haste ordered by Stalin resulted in poor engineering, with the result that bridges collapsed and heavy rain washed-out sections of the track. The line was abandoned after Stalin's death in 1953, the 699 km completed track costing many billions of dollar. The more than 100,000 prisoners engaged on the project were released.

FAST FACT: EARLY RUSSIAN DIESELS

Railways were just one of many parts of the Russian economy disrupted by the civil war that raged after the 1917 revolution. While, in the early 1920s, Russian railway planners considered that steam would be the main motive power for decades to come, they nevertheless began to experiment with diesel traction.

The communist leadership was also very keen on electrification, in fact far more keen on finding successors to steam than were the railway men who ruled at the People's Commissariat for Transport. But the latter followed orders, as they did after Stalin assumed control of the new Soviet Union following Lenin's death and, by 1925, the first diesel locomotive prototypes had been built; then in 1926 mainline diesel operations began on the Moscow-Kursk line.

IN 1930 THE SOVIET authorities decided they needed help. Ralph Budd, president of the Great Northern Railway of St Paul, Minnesota, arrived in Moscow accompanied by several of his engineers and other technical people. The team travelled extensively throughout the Soviet Union, including to Siberia where the Americans rode the newly completed 1,458 km-long Turkestan-Siberia Railway, which ran from just north of Tashkent in what is now Uzbekistan, via Almaty, Kazakhstan, to connect at Novosibirsk with the Trans-Siberia Railway.

Budd's recommendations included acquisition of more powerful locomotives, larger freight cars and longer trains, along with the adoption of automatic couplers and air brakes, and upgrading the quality of ties (sleepers) and ballast.

These were taken up by the Second Five Year Plan (1933-37) which, based on Budd's report, set out a plan to double-track about 8,500 km of route, replace light rails with heavier rails on almost 20,000 km of track, and install automatic blocking along 8,300 km. Bridges were to be strengthened, ballast improved and sleepers laid closer together to provide extra support.

The plan called for locomotive numbers to be increased from 19,500 to 24,600; freight wagon numbers were to rise from 552,000 to 803,000. Another 4,990 km of line were to be electrified.

However, plan targets were rarely met, as shown by this table:

Five-Year Plans for New Railways

	Km Planned	Km Built
First Plan 1928–32	17,000	3,900
Second Plan 1933–37	11,000	3,300
Third Plan 1938–45★	11,000	9,000
Fourth Plan 1946–50	7,300	3,200
Fifth Plan 1951–55	5,800	3,200

★ Extended due to war

The Institute of Pacific Relations, in its *Far Eastern Survey* journal in 1939, reported that the Soviet Union was improving its railway network. Correspondent Kathleen Barnes wrote that the Soviets had recognised deficiencies in their rail system at the 1934 seventeenth party congress. At the time of writing, Barnes had just seen a report produced for the 1939 Communist Party congress by Lazar M. Kaganovich, Commissar of Railways.

Any figures produced by the Soviet Union at that time were always considered suspect, but the report states that average freight wagon loadings in 1933 of 51,200 cars had increased in 1938 to a daily 88,000 cars. Over the five years, freight traffic had increased by almost 120 per cent (80 per cent more coal, 130 per cent more metal, 50 per cent more grain, among other items).

Daily running by locomotives, it claimed, had increased on average by 88.5 km and freight wagons were travelling an average 42 km a day. More than 6,000 new locomotives had been placed in service, along with 186,000 new freight wagons (of which 101,000 were bogie wagons rather than the traditional four-wheel wagons), and more than 5,000 more passenger carriages. Barnes continued:

> The most immediate problem which the Soviets face in their railway development is the reconstruction of the permanent way. It is largely laid with old and light rails which must be replaced. New and heavier rails have been laid already on some 25,700 km but all the tracks must be strengthened and the roadbed metalled ... Better mechanisation of loading is urged and lengthening of station sidings to fit the increased length of trains is also considered imperative.

* * *

In 1989, the Soviet Union fell apart—and that meant dividing up a Soviet rail system that had the railways run by thirty-two separate railway organisations. Russian Federal Railways emerged to operate trains in what had been the Russian soviet republic (now the Russian Federation). Fortunately, not too many lines crossed the now international borders between the newly independent republics; where they did, as with Belarus, that new republic found itself not only managing an international crossing with Poland but also (as time went on) with Ukraine, Russia, Latvia and Lithuania. There were also disputes regarding the Trans-Siberian Railway as 188 km of that route ran through the newly independent Kazakhstan. Moreover, Russia's October Railway (St Petersburg-Moscow-Murmansk) had border crossings with Estonia as well as with Finland

The Donetsk, Lvov, Odessa, Dnieper, South-Western and Southern railway bodies were handed over to Ukraine. Byelorussian Railways became the property of Belarus, while Moldova and Azerbaijan now had their own national systems. The Baltic Railway was divided between Estonia, Latvia, Lithuania and the Russian enclave of Kaliningrad. Similarly the Trans-Caucasian Railway was handed over to Armenia and Georgia, while the Central Asian Railway became the property of Uzbekistan (with some parts hived off to Turkmenistan).

The problem for many of the new republics was that they got their share of track, railway stations and rolling stock but not necessarily the means to maintain their locomotives, carriages and wagons if their new homeland was not the site of one of the existing Soviet heavy repair workshops. Moreover, under Soviet rule freight wagons were not the property of any one railway group, a scheme that cut down on empty running to return the wagons; the new republics vied to hold on to the good rolling stock and palm off defective carriages and wagons on to the others.

Following are snapshots of the existing railway systems that were once all part of Soviet Railways. All lines are on the broad gauge 1,520 mm (4ft $11^{27}/_{32}$in).

Armenia

Total route length: 780 km (all electrified)
Double track: 20 km
Stations: 75
Passengers (annual): 5.5 millions
Freight (annual): 50 million tonnes
Axle load: 23.5 tonnes

Armenia's South Caucasia Railway network was placed under the management of Russian Railways in 2008. Most of the Armenian railway system was built during the Soviet era, although the first rails laid in the country had been part of a 180 km track completed in 1899 under the Tsarist government, running from Tbilisi, Georgia, to the city of Alexanderpol (now Gyumri) in northern Armenia.

Before the break up of the Soviet Union, Armenia's rail system was part of the Trans-Caucasus Railway, headquartered in Tbilisi, Georgia, an entity that also oversaw the Azerbaijani and Georgian networks.

As the Asian Development Bank noted in a 2011 report, 'central planning (under the Soviets) dictated that rail would be the primary mode of transport, so little emphasis was placed on costs. The system was designed to handle large traffic volumes, and in some cases it served remote areas. Moreover, without the need to consider competition from road transport, the former Soviet Union rarely updated railway technology after the 1960s'.

The bank noted that track speed in Armenia was often limited to 30 km/h and that some sections had been damaged, firstly, during the 1988–1994 conflict with Azerbaijan and then, secondly, by the 1998 earthquake.

The bank's 2011 report stated: 'About 370 km of the 732 km network are fully operational: the Yerevan–Georgian border line, the Yerevan– Yeraskh passenger line, and sections of the Yerevan–Azerbaijan/Vardenis lines … The railway system has seen its operations shrink ten-fold since independence in 1991, primarily due to the closing of Armenia's borders with Azerbaijan and Turkey'.

In 2014 the Armenian government agreed to Iranian plans for a railway to connect Iran and Armenia, estimated to cost $3.5 billion (including sixty-four bridges, sixty tunnels and twenty-seven stations).

Rolling Stock

Locomotives (electric): 49 (of which 31 are BJI 10 class, 18 are BJI 8 class)*

Locomotives (diesel): 30

Passenger carriages: 135

Freight wagons: 1,839

* *In the 2011 ADB assessment it was noted that most of the electric locomotives were more than thirty years old and that the passenger cars were 'dated'.*

Azerbaijan

Total track length: 2,068 km

Electrified: 1,240 km

Passengers (2014): 2.52 millions

Freight (2014): 21.8 million tonnes

Staff (2014): 22,886

Azərbaycan Dəmir Yollari, or Azerbaijan State Railways, is a joint stock company. Railways had been neglected for many years after the break up of the former Soviet Union, but in 2009 the government in Baku invited the World Bank to help it rehabilitate and upgrade the country's rail system. The bank set out to finance repairs to 503 km of track on the Baku-Boyuyk-Kesik section (running to the border with

Georgia) with the hope of enabling passenger trains to run at speeds up to 100 km/h. The bank said it would change the electrification from 3.3 kV to 25 kV AC.

Azerbaijan Railways said in October 2016 it had built about 200 km of rail line during the year and it was hoped to complete the new Baku-Ganja line in 2017 (trains to operate at 100 km/h). Four new Stadler double-deck electric train sets would be purchased for the line. Azerbaijan is also working with Iran as part of the International North-South Transport Corridor that will connect Europe with Asia.

Two months later Azerbaijan Railways and Stadler Rail AG agreed to expand their co-operation. The Swiss company is to build thirty new sleeping cars for operation on the proposed Baku-Tbilisi-Kars service, which will link Azerbaijan with Georgia and Turkey. That line's construction was completed in 2017.

Belarus

(Statistics are for 2013 except where specified)
Total track length (2016): 5,491 km
Double track: 1,628.5 km
Electrified (2016): 1,128 km
Automatic block: 3,703 km
Semi-automatic block: 1,884.5 km
Stations: 366
Locomotive depots: 17
Level crossings: 1,432
Passengers carried: 88.9 millions
Freight carried: 152.7 million tonnes

According to a 2013 study by the United Nations Economic Commission for Europe, Belarusian Railways is a 'juridical entity with its own balance sheet, bank and foreign currency accounts'. It is a government corporation subordinate to the Ministry of Transport and Communications. Other commentators have noted that Belarusian Railways remains as a legacy of the Soviet era: it puts high priority on its social responsibilities and thus keeps rail fares low. The railway system is run as if were still a government department.

The Belarus rail system is all on the 'Russian' gauge. Belarus Railways took a big step forward in late 2015 when it installed a Talgo automatic gauge-changer at Brest, close to the Polish border. The gauge-changer requires rolling stock to have bogies with variable gauge capability. In about twenty minutes, the train passes slowly through the gauge-changer; the wheels are unlocked and the gauge altered either by moving the wheels closer together or further apart. This renders unnecessary the much longer process of changing bogies at the break-of-gauge. This is significant given that the Belarus rail network is important for transit freight travelling between Russia and Kazakhstan on the one hand, and Latvia, Lithuania and the Russian enclave of Kaliningrad on the other, as well as to Poland and Western Europe.

The main rail centres are Minsk, Brest, Gomel, Orsha, Baranavichy, Zhlobin, Kalinkavichy and Mogilev.

In recent years the system has invested heavily in updating its fleet: in 2012, for example, Belarus bought 3,746 general freight wagons, 1,000 tank wagons, 550 hopper cement wagons, and 116 covered vans.

Some ninety per cent of transit traffic on the Belarus rail system is generated by Russian exports, mainly coal, oil, petrochemicals, chemicals, fertiliser, metals along with liquid and bulk cargoes.

Rolling Stock
Passenger carriages (2013): 1,168
Freight wagons (2013): 37,105

Estonia

Total route length: 1,229 km
Electrified: 132 km
Double track: 94 km
Switches (points) 1,213
Stations: 61 (129 platforms)
Passengers (2015): 6,659,000
Freight (2015) 15.39 million tonnes

Eesti Raudtee (Estonian Railways) is a state-owned rail operator. In 2015, of the 15.39 million tonnes of freight consigned to Estonian Railways roughly two-thirds consisted of goods in transit through Estonia with just 290,000 tonnes of export freight and 1.29 million tonnes destined for Estonian delivery, in addition to which 2.52 million tonnes was freight travelling between domestic points. The largest item was oil and oil products followed by fertiliser.

There are three border stations, two with Russia—Narva-Ivanogrod and Keidula-Pechory—and one with Latvia at Valga-Valka.

Eesti Liinirongid Ltd is a company owned by the Republic of Estonia providing national passenger transport services under the name of Elron with new Stadler FLIRT electric and diesel-engined trains. The great preponderance of passenger traffic was between domestic stations, with just 57,000 passengers travelling between Tallinn and Moscow or St Petersburg in a year.

Estonian Railways was first established in 1918 when the country won its independence from being part of the Tsarist Russian empire following the Bolshevik revolution. This status lasted only until 1940 when Soviet troops invaded all three Baltic republics and incorporated them into the Union of Soviet Socialist Republics. At that stage, Estonia had 1,447 km of railways, mostly of the broad (Russian) gauge and 675 km of narrow 750 mm (2ft 5½in). The Soviet authorities either closed the narrow gauge lines or converted them to the broad gauge. Retirement of steam traction began in 1957.

Estonian Railways was reborn in 1991 upon independence following the collapse of the Soviet Union.

Georgia

Total route length: 1,324 km (2,344 km including sidings, yards)
Other gauges: 29 km—Standard gauge 1,435 km (4ft 8½in) Akhalkalaki-Turkish border
37 km—Narrow gauge 900 mm (2ft 11$^7/_{16}$in) Borjomi-Bakuriani ski resort
Double track: 295 km
Electrified: 1,323 km
Bridges: 1,422

Tunnels: 45
Passengers (2016): 2.3 millions
Stations: 22
Staff (2014): 12,700

Construction of railways in Georgia began in 1865. The first line line (from Poti on the Black Sea to the capital Tbilisi, then known in English as Tiflis) was opened on 10 October 1872. In 1893 traffic increased with transit shipments of oil from Azerbaijan upon the completion of the railway between Tbilisi and Baku on the Caspian Sea. Georgia and Armenia were connected by rail in 1899.

By 1890 the Georgians (then part of Tsarist Russia) had completed the double-track Tsipa tunnel, almost 5 km long and constructed in just four years using rudimentary tools; its opening to traffic made possible fast train journeys between eastern and western Georgia. The highest point in the Georgian Railway network is the Marabda-Akhalkalaki section, 2,200 metres above sea level. The process of electrification was begun in 1932 and completed in 1967, while automatic blocking was introduced through the system between 1946 and 1949.

Georgian Railway has been a joint stock company since 2012. Oil is one of the main loads carried through Georgia by rail to the Black Sea port of Kulevi, mainly from Azerbaijan and Kazakhstan. Ferrous metals and scrap consignments originate in Georgia itself, as well as from Russia and Azerbaijan. Georgian Railway also carries imported sugar unloaded on the Black Sea for transport to neighbouring republics. International passenger services connect Tbilisi to Baku (Azerbaijan) and Yerevan (Armenia). Domestic trains provide daily services from the capital to Poti, Batumi, and Zugdidi. There are also several regional slow train services.

The Georgian railway system is sustained by the fact that it is a transport artery between the Black and Caspian seas and—as the shortest rail route between Central Asia and Europe—it will be a vital part of the New Silk Road linking Europe by rail with the Far East.

To that end, 2017 saw the completion of the 826 km Baku-Tbilisi-Kars railway line. This line is in three sections:

• Baku-Tbilisi: existing operating line (565 km broad gauge).

- Tbilisi-Akhalkalaki: built 1986 and largely unused for many years, now rehabilitated (160 km broad gauge).
- Akhalkalaki–Kars, Turkey: Financed by Turkey, 101 km (of which 29 km in Georgia); twenty-two tunnels (including one on Georgia-Turkey border), two viaducts (standard gauge).

The break-of-gauge is at Akhalkalaki (there will be two stations, one on either side of border) where a bogie exchange station has been built to enable wagons and carriages from broad gauge countries to be converted to standard gauge. However Turkish locomotives will be used in that country's territory and, at Kars, Turkish wagons will be used to move all freight over the remainder of that country's rail system. Kars will become a major rail transshipment point.

Azerbaijan Railways is planning Baku-Istanbul passenger trains, with first and second-class sleepers (257 berths per train, the coaches to be supplied by Stadler), a 2,600 km journey. At Baku passengers can travel to and from Turkmenistan and Kazakhstan by connecting ferries.

(Incidentally, this rail connection has been a long time coming. The three countries agreed to the scheme in 2005, construction began to Kars in 2008 and, in January 2015, the first train ran on the renewed Tbilis- Akhalkalaki section.)

* * *

Tbilisi has a metro system styled on the Russian model. There are two lines totalling 26.3 km with a third line now in development

Rolling Stock
Passenger and freight trains are hauled by various classes of Soviet-designed electric locomotives, several of which having been built in Tbilisi. The electric multiple units are a mixture: there are ones built in Latvia during the Soviet era and three sets bought from China in 2010.

Kazakhstan

Total route length: 14,205 km
Electrified (2014): 4,056 km
Passengers (2014): 20.5 millions

Freight (2014): 275.3 million tonnes
Staff (2014): 76,240

Some narrow gauge 1,000 mm lines were built in what is now Kazakhstan, and then 188 km of the Trans-Siberian Railway was laid through what is now Kazakh territory, but the first significant railway event was the completion of 1,668 km Orenburg-Tashkent line that traversed the country, connecting what are now modern-day Russia and Uzbekistan.

First construction in the Soviet era began in 1920 with a 700 km line to tap the grain bowl of Kazakhstan, and in 1930 the Turksib line was completed, connecting what is now Turkmenistan and Sibirsky in Russia, a route 1,444 km long allowing rail access to Siberia. After the Great Patriotic War of 1941-1945 Soviet engineers built a series of lines into virgin lands. Electrification began in 1964, with the conversion of the Astana-Karaganda line. Connection was made, albeit with a change-of-gauge, with China (in Xinjiang province) at the border town of Druzhba in 1960.

The country's railway system is operated by Kazakhstan Temir Zholy (KTZ), although private operators are active. In 2003 Kazakhstan railways began selling older surplus freight wagons to private operators, who then refurbished them, so that by 2006 about forty per cent of all freight rolling stock in the country was controlled by the private sector. The Asian Development Bank, in a 2014 report, noted that too little progress had been made by the private companies in terms of actually buying locomotives; it seemed they preferred to pay the haulage tariff to KTZ rather than take on the risks of investing in traction.

In a later report, the bank notes that Kazakhstan began its railway reform in 1997 by merging its three regional departments, Almaty, West Kazakhstan and Tselinia administrations to form KTZ, but hiving off some activities of those systems (such as farms and rest resorts).

In March 2002 KTZ was converted into a joint stock company, and by 2006 it was issuing its first euro bonds to raise finance.

But, more recently, KTZ has diversified again, this time into running airports and international trade zones.

Kazakhstan has the advantage of having four potential Europe-Asia rail corridors:

Northern Corridor of Trans-Asian Railway Main line (TARM): Western Europe—China, Korean Peninsula and Japan via Russian and Kazakhstan (section Dostyk–Aktogai-Sayak–Mointy–Astana–Petropavlovsk.

Southern Corridor of TARM: Southeastern Europe–China and southeastern Asia via Turkey, Iran, Central Asian states and Kazakhstan (section Dostyk-Aktogai–Almaty–Shu–Arys–Saryagash).

Transport Corridor Europe-Caucasus-Asia (TRACECA): Eastern Europe– Central Asia via the Black Sea, Caucasus and the Caspian Sea (section Dostyk– Almaty–Aktau).

North-South: Northern Europe–Gulf States via Russia and Iran, with Kazakhstan's participation in the following sections: Aktau–Ural regions of Russia and Aktau–Atyrau.

Kyrgyzstan

Total route length (2016): 424.6 km
Passengers (2014): 320,000
Freight (2014): 7.38 million tonnes
Staff (2014): 5,131

The Kyrgyz railway system consists of two unconnected lines, the southern line of 323.4 km and the northern line of 101.2 km. When the Soviet Union was dissolved Kyrgyzstan inherited fifty locomotives and a number of passenger carriages and freight wagons.

The northern line runs from the border connection with the Kazakhstan railway network (where there are onward passenger services to the Russian cities of Yekaterinburg, Novosibirsk and Moscow) through the capital Bishkek to Bakykchy, the terminus being at Lake Issyk-Kul with connections to lake shipping services. Short distance trains run to and from the capital. There are fourteen major stations on this line.

The southern line connects to Uzbekistan rails at Karasu, Post 38 and Shalmaldysay. There are no connections with China's standard gauge network.

Beijing has long been interested in financing such a connection, especially as it has already built a 129 km line between Angren and Pap in Uzbekistan, and China believes an extension from that line over into Kyrgyzstan and then running in an east-west direction to the Chinese border would provide an attractive shortcut through Central Asia to Europe. But this project has long been stalled, partially by reservations in Bishkek political circles on the one hand, and on the other by the desire that if China is going to build a rail connection through the country then it ought to run north-south, thus connecting two parts of the Kyrgyz rail system—but that would not only be a longer route for Chinese trains to Europe but would involve costly construction through some mountainous terrain.

Latvia

Total route length (2016): 1,860 km
(3,153 km with yards, loops)
33 km—narrow gauge 750 mm (2ft 5½in)
Electrified: 257 km (to be 839 km by 2030)
Stations with loops: 152
Stations with freight: 77
Stations with electrical interlocking: 162
Stations with automatic
block systems: 1,348
Passengers (2015): 17,065,000

Latvijas dzelzceļš (LDZ) or Latvian Railways is the main operator of trains. Some 39.1 per cent of freight carried on Latvia's rail system in 2015 was oil and oil products. The next largest share (34.3 per cent) was coal transportation.

Three routes of container trains were operating in 2015. They were Baltika Transit (freight between the Baltic states and Kazakhstan and other Central Asian countries), Riga-Moscow and Latvia-Belarus-Ukraine/Black Sea ports.

The Latvian passenger operator is Pasažieru Vilciens which operates electric train services from Riga to Aizkraukle, Jelgava, Skulte and Tukums, and diesel trains from the capital to Daugavpils, Madona,

Gulbene, Krustpils, Sigulda-Valga and Rēzekne-Zilupe. In late 2016 the company announced plans to buy new electric multiple units; in all, 42 EMU trains will be brought into service by 2021. It was also reported at the same time that LDZ had updated its plans for the roll-out of 25 kV 50 Hz electrification and the conversion of the routes around Rīga which are currently electrified at 3 kV DC.

Also in November that year, the first pilot container train mutually organized by Latvian and Chinese railways arrived in the Riga railway station, four months after China and Latvia had signed a container traffic agreement. The train had covered the route from the Yiwu city in China (not far from Shanghai), through the town of Zabaykalsk at the Russia-China border and then to Riga. The total length of this route exceeds 11,000 km, and the train covered around 1,200 km per day in some parts of Russia. The train carried textiles, bathroom equipment and household goods.

Rolling Stock (2015)
Locomotives: 204 (all diesel)
Electric train sets: 26
Diesel train sets: 97
Freight wagons: 6,522

Lithuania

Total route length: 1,871 km
1,849 km—broad gauge 1,520 mm (4ft $11^{27}/_{32}$in)
22 km - standard gauge 1,435 km (4ft 8½in)
Electrified: 122 km (broad gauge)
Double track: 428 km
Railway stations: 108
Level crossings: 544
Overpasses/bridges: 383
Passengers (2015): 3,790,000

Two important rail corridors cross Lithuania. Corridor I runs Helsinki-Tallinn-Riga-Kaunas-Warsaw; Corridor IX runs Kiev-Minsk-

Vilnius-Šiaulaia-Klaipèda (with a branch to the Russian enclave of Kaliningrad).

Rolling Stock (2016)
Diesel train sets:
DR1AM sets (12)—maximum speed 120 km/h, built 1988-1995
RA-2 sets (2)—maximum speed 100 km/h, built 2008
620M sets (12)—120 km/h, built 2008-2011
630M sets (3)—140 km/h, built 2013
DR1A sets (2)—120 km/h, built 1989-1991
AR-@ sets (1)—120 km/h, built 1997.
Electric train sets:
ER9M sets (4)—130 km/h, built 1976-1995
EJ575 sets (10)—160 km/h, built 2008-2013
Diesel freight locomotives:
TEP 70 class (5)—160 km/h, built 1990-1994
TEP 70BS class (4)—160 km/h, built 2006
TEP 70M class (1)—160 km/h, built 2014
TEM LTH class (1)—80 km/h, built 2015

In January 2016 AB Lietuvos Geležinkeliai and the European Investment Bank signed a €68 million agreement to upgrade infrastructure and provide new passenger rolling stock. The work includes track duplication, repair and electrification on several sections of the Kena–Vilnius–Kaišiadorys–Radviliškis–Klaipėda line. This will enable 6,000 tonne freight trains to use the line. Seven new three-car diesel multiple units for passenger railway services will join the fleet, replacing obsolete rolling stock. .

In October 2016 Lithuanian Prime Minister Algirdas Butkevicius and European Commissioner for Transport Violeta Bulc, meeting at Kaunas station opened the first completed section of the Rail Baltica 1,435 mm standard gauge line from the Polish border to Kaunas, Lithuania's second largest city.

HISTORICAL SNAPSHOT: LIFTING RAIL

On 6 March 2013 the European Commission issued a press release reveal-
ing that it had opened antitrust proceedings against the Lithuanian railway
company AB Lietuvos geležinkeliai (LG) to investigate whether it limited
competition in the rail markets of Lithuania and Latvia by removing a
railway track.

The release stated that 'in September 2008, LG suspended traffic on a
railway track running between Lithuania and Latvia. One month later LG
dismantled the track. Since then the track has not been rebuilt'.

The Commission was concerned that these actions could have limited
competition on the rail markets in Lithuania and in Latvia, in particular by
obstructing the plans of a major customer of LG from redirecting its railway
freight to Latvia using the services of other rail operators. At the time of
writing, according to the EU website, this matter remains unresolved.

Moldova

Total route length (2014): 1,171 km including 14km standard gauge
1,435 mm (4ft 8½in) near Romanian border.

In August 2016, in his report on his first year of activity in the post,
Director of the National Railroad Company of Moldova (NRC) Iurie
Topala regarded as his main achievement the creation of comfortable conditions for train transit through the territory of Moldova. He
also mentioned that the financial situation of the enterprise had been
stabilised, including partial liquidation of long standing debt.

In the first year of his tenure, more than 8 km of track, several
locomotives and 740 cargo wagons had been repaired. The NRC concluded negotiations with the European Investment Bank by signing
a contract on joint financing of projects with the European Bank for
Reconstruction Development (EBRD) with a total budget of €105
million. At the end of 2016 the EBRD called tenders for fifteen diesel-
electric locomotives for use on Moldova tracks.

A World Bank report of 2001 stated that the Moldova city had
only 138 km of double track and no electrified lines. At that time
there were 159 operational stations. The number of locomotives in

service had declined from 269 in 1994 to 165 in 2001 and, of that latter number of engines, just ninety-seven were in service (the system still had four steam engines). The number of freight wagons in service over that same period had fallen from 12,521 to 10,206, while passenger carriage numbers were down from 658 to 580 (although only 250 were in operational condition). Workshops were lacking spare parts and since 1992 there had been almost no investment in rolling stock or infrastructure. 'Even maintenance of infrastructure is problematic and often carried out by using materials from existing double track sections to restore single track sections elsewhere,' the report noted. The average speed of passenger trains in 2000 was 32 km/h.

Russia

Total route length (2014): 87,157 km including 806 km narrow gauge 1,067 mm (3ft 6in) located on Sakhalin Island
Electrified: 40,300 km
Locomotive depots (2010): 135
Tunnels: 150

Rossiiskie Zheleznye Dorogi AoA (RZD, or Russian Railways) is the state-owned operator of the nation's railways. The company has thirteen regional sections, including the West Siberian Railway, Moscow Railway, Far Eastern Railway, North Caucasus Railway and Sverdlosk Railway.

A 2014 report by the European Bank for Reconstruction and Development (ERBD) described Russia's railways as 'world class by any measure. It is an immense network, stretching across eight time zones from Central Europe to Central Asia, from Kaliningrad on the Baltic Sea in the west to Sakhalin on the Sea of Japan in the east, and from Murmansk on the Barents Sea in the north to the Black Sea in the south'.

Almost half the network is electrified. It is the world's third largest network and, after China and India, the third largest rail employer (934,000 people in 2012, down from 2.2 million in the early 1990s). RZD is by far the largest player in the Russian rail system with private companies providing freight services, manufacture and repair of loco-motives and rolling stock.

Rolling Stock (2012)

Locomotives: 20,300
Electric multiple units/Commuter carriages: 15,600
Long distance passenger carriages: 24,100
Freight wagons: 1.2 million (of which around 530,000 were gondolas.

At the beginning of 2016, Russian Railways had a fleet of 20,871 locomotives, of which 6,515 were non-operational. The operator is planning to reduce the overall fleet to about 18,000. Between 2007 and 2013 the various freight operators bought more than half a million new wagons.

ERBD noted that Russia needed more powerful, energy-efficient locomotives and more efficient wagons suited for specific commodities and logistics operations.

In 2012 rail cargo accounted for eighty-five per cent of freight shipments in Russia, forty-four per cent if one included all the oil and gas going by pipeline.

Tajikistan

Total route length: 799 km (main lines, with 1,380 km when other track included).
Passengers (2014): 460,000
Freight (2014): 6.81 million tonnes
Staff (2014): 5,770

There are two distinct sections of railways in Tajikistan operated by Tajik Railways (Rohee Ohani Tojikistan). The most important one, in the southwest corner, is connected to the Uzbekistan system and serves the capital, Dushanbe. The northern section is a line running through the narrow waist of Tajik territory between Uzbekistan and Kyrgyzstan and runs via the city of Khujand.

According to studies, very little rail activity in Tajikistan is gener-ated by domestic traffic. Almost all passenger traffic is carried on trains from Dushanbe and Khujand connecting with services coming from or going to Moscow. Similarly, freight movements are dominated by transporting exports (almost all being aluminium) and imports—the latter dominated by wheat from Kazakhstan and fuel from Russia.

In late 2016 there was opened the final 41 km of the new 119 km line between the capital Dunshanbe and the southern city of Qurghonteppa, thus allowing trains from the capital to travel to the south of the country without a circuitous route through Uzbekistan.

Turkmenistan

Total route length: 4,980 km

The rail system of Turkmenistan was not conceived as a network to primarily serve the needs of transport within that republic; rather, it was built as part of the vertical structure of the Union of Soviet Socialist Republics and the primary aim, as in so many other regions of the then Soviet Union, was to connect Moscow with each of its regions. As analysed by a Japanese aid team that inspected the Turkmenistan system in 2006, 'for this reason, the construction of transportation routes to the surrounding countries lagged behind, creating a bottleneck in Turkmenistan's economic growth'.

When the Soviet Union fell apart in 1991, and the former Soviet republics became independent after sixty-seven years of being ruled from Moscow under the communist government, the rolling stock was divided among the railways of each of the post-Soviet era republics. Turkmenistan received 331 locomotives, but more than half of those had been built before 1970 and were, as the Japanese put it, 'markedly aged'. The new country had a repair workshop in the capital, Ashgabat, and there were five other depots that could conduct checks on locomotives, carriages and wagons, but there were no facilities for any major overhauls; any stock needing such work had to be sent to Uzbekistan. Moreover, there was no senior management: the railway lines in what is now Turkmenistan had, during the late Soviet era, been administered from Tashkent, Uzbekistan.

In December 2014 the Kazakhstan-Turkmenistan-Iran transnational railway corridor was completed. In February 2016 the first freight train from China passed through Turkmenistan and Kazakhstan on a 10,000 km journey to Europe from Zhejiang province.

Turkmenistan has built a new railway from the town of Atamyrat into Afghanistan; of that 85 km of track, just 3.5 km has been laid inside the Afghan border (to the town of Aqina). It is proposed that the line be continued across northern Afghanistan to connect with the Tajikistan rail network—but no one knows when, or even if, that will be completed.

Ukraine

Total route length: 20,950 km
Stations: 1,500 (128 are considered major stations)
(All figures include territory occupied by Russia)

Ukrainian Railways had, as of 2014, made fewer reforms that had either the Russian Federation or Belarus. And, due to its financial difficulties, it is unable to make the size of investment needed to fully modernise the network and rolling stock. As the Asian Development Bank described it in 2014, Ukraine's wagon fleet is 'old, inefficient and unsuitable for some purposes'.

One project offering hope for the future is the completion of a new tunnel through the Carpathian Mountains to connect Ukraine with Slovakia and Hungary. The boring of the 1.8 km tunnel had been completed at time of writing and lining and track-laying was due to be finished by early 2018. This route is expected to handle about sixty per cent of freight traffic moving between the country and Central Europe.

This new tunnel will replace the Beskyd tunnel, 131 years old and built when this part of Ukraine was within the Austro-Hungarian Empire. Not only it is a bottleneck because there is just a single track, but the Beskyd tunnel leaks; in winter the water freezes into massive icicles as a consequence of which trains sometimes cannot move through the tunnel.

Just under half the Ukraine network is electrified. The railway employs about 350,000 people.

Rolling Stock
Locomotives: 4,000 (about half electric)
Passenger carriages: 5,300, of which 3,160 are operational
Freight wagons: 75,000

Uzbekistan

Total route length: 4,593 km
Stations: 267
Passengers (2014): 17.3 millions
Freight (2014): 65 million tonnes
Staff (2014): 58,200

Joint-stock company O'zbekiston temir yo'llari was formed on November 7, 1994 on the basis of the former Central Asian railroad located in the territory of the Republic of Uzbekistan.

In June 2016 there was the official opening of the Pan-Angren line. This provided Uzbekistan direct access to its part of the highly fertile Ferghana Valley (which is divided between Uzbekistan, Tajikistan and Kyrgyzstan). Previously, Uzbek trains had to traverse part of Tajikistan to reach Uzbek territory in the valley, another legacy of the Moscow-centric railway planning of the Soviet years. It is expected that in the first year operation of the 124 km line will carry about 600,000 passengers and ten million tonnes of freight. It was built by China, with the World Bank financing the electrification, and constitutes a significant engineering achievement: it involved the boring of 19.2 km (11.9 miles) Qamchiq tunnel, twenty-five bridges and six viaducts.

It was announced from Tashkent that, over the following five years, it was intended to build and rehabilitate 960 km of railway and electrify more than 900 km of route length. As the news reports explained, the break up of the Soviet Union left Uzbekistan in the early 1990s with the situation that some of the lines that link the northwest and southwest sections passed through Turkmenistan—that being no problem when the Soviet Union existed but subsequently it became one when the various Central Asian parts of the U.S.S.R. had become independent nations.

The new lines would be aimed at providing connections within the Uzbek borders.

HISTORICAL SNAPSHOTS

The first railway line in what is present-day Uzbekistan was opened in 1880. In 1904 a line was completed from Orenburg in southern Russia, across what is now Kazakhstan, to Tashkent. It was opened for traffic in 1905. It meant that anyone in Tashkent could now reach St Petersburg within a week.

By 1913, in the waning years of Tsarist Russia, the railway system in this province was using 531 locomotives, 495 passenger carriages and 7,593 freight wagons. It must be added that the locomotive fleet consisted largely of small, low-powered engines and the passenger cars were four-wheelers. But there was a workshop operating in Tashkent to service the rolling stock.

Several new lines were completed in the first two decades of Soviet rule and the Uzbek Soviet Socialist Republic (within the Union of Soviet Socialist Republics) was connected to its Turkmen, Tajik and Kyrgyz equivalents.

The last steam engines were retired in 1974.

* * *

Luxury plans. In August 1993 *The New York Times* carried, in its travel section, news of the launching of a luxury tourist train in Russia. Of the four itineraries proposed by the promoters, one involved a fifteen-day journey from St Petersburg to Tashkent, Uzbekistan (the others being to Archangel on the White Sea, a tour of the Baltic states and a tour of medieval Russian towns by train).

Today the same company operates a rail tour based on Tashkent and travelling over nine days only within Uzbekistan. The Orient Silk Road Express, which has accommodation in three classes—Ali Baba cabins with washrooms at each end of the cars; the Aladdin class cars are similar but have air conditioning, while those able to afford the Kalif class have an en suite bathroom. There are restaurant cars sufficient to cater for all passengers at a single sitting, and these cars operate as bar cars in the evening.

Country Profile: Pakistan

Total route length: 7,791 km (11,881 km with sidings, yards, double-track)

Gauges: 7,479 km—broad gauge 1,676 mm (5ft 6in)

312 km—narrow gauge 1,000 mm (3ft 3⅜in)

Double track: 1,409 km

PAKISTAN RAILWAYS IS PRIMARILY a passenger operation. (Pakistan Railways has a five per cent market share of national freight haulage.) In fiscal 2015 the system carried 52.9 million passengers, of whom 50.5 million travelled in standard cars; only 78,655 passenger journeys were in air-conditioned sleepers, 108,757 in air-conditioned sitting cars.

Rail traffic has long been dominated by a few main lines. From 1978 rail traffic volumes fell over the following two decades, with lines closed, services cancelled and corruption continuing. The system was hobbled by political considerations with governments fearing to increase fares lest there be civil unrest and civil service rules that were antithetical to operating a commercial transport business.

In August 2016 the government confirmed that 172 of its diesel locomotives were unserviceable and defective.

The Pakistan system has 13,841 bridges, almost all of which date from colonial times.

In 2014, Muhammad Asim and Qanita Imtiaz Nafees, members of the business school at Nazeer Hussain University, Karachi, summed up the then present situation thus: 'Over the past many years, Pakistan Railways has been facing problems and is now on the verge of bankruptcy. With (a) budget deficit of billions of dollars, eroding market share and corruption scandals, the future of Pakistan Railways—once the lifeline of the country—is grim. At the time of independence both India and Pakistan inherited the railway network laid down by the British. While Indian Railways has emerged as a highly profitable organisation, contrary is the situation for Pakistan Railways that is struggling for its survival'.

In August 2015, the newspaper *Dawn* ran a scathing report on Pakistan's railways, noting that 'the latest statistics from Pakistan Railways paint a disappointing picture. Down from a 100 million passengers, Pakistan Railways carried a mere 47 million passengers in the 2013-14 fiscal year. From 11 million tonnes of freight in 1986, the volume was down to 1.6 million tonnes. Despite the drastic decline in services, Railways still carried a workforce of 80,000 employees'.

* * *

'Ah, what wouldn't I give to be able to get on, say, Khyber Mail from Lahore at 8.00 a.m., watch the countryside slide past, eat a leisurely meal in the dining car and sleep in the comfort of the air conditioned coupe. The next morning, get into the toilet, shave and shower and be ready for business in Karachi! I remember a time, only twenty years ago, when I at the fag end of a journey would be somewhere in the middle of the country like Sadiqabad or Rohri. I would go to the railway station and there would be seven or eight (possibly more) trains headed for Lahore before the day was out.'

—*Salman Rashid, author and fellow of the Royal Geographical Society*

Rashid claims Pakistan railways has been destroyed on purpose, that successive political leaders have sought support from the road transport players. Ayub Khan (President 1958-1969) subsidised diesel, an act that handed road hauliers a huge cost advantage over the railways.

Pakistan Railways retained three steam locomotives to haul the tourist train Steam Safari that runs on the Khyber Pass rail line. The locomotives are British-built between 1916 and 1923 and are 2-8-0 HG/S class. Here are two views of 2473 at Lahore station ready to depart with its train. *Salman Rashid.*

As Rashid notes, railway operators do not make money from passenger traffic, but from freight—and by taking away the freight business, condemned the railway to failure. Writing in 2013, he argued that Pakistan Railways was never likely to make a comeback, due partly to antiquated tracks that existed on many sections. He recalls a trip along the line from Quetta to the Iran border in 2009 where the track was still equipped with the same rails laid when the line was opened in 1914: there was no ballast in place and trains took days to traverse the distance at speeds under 20 km/h.

Rolling Stock (2015)

Locomotives

Broad gauge: 446 Diesel, five steam

Narrow gauge: Seven steam

In 2012 it was reported that only seventy of Pakistan's Railways 500 locomotives were operational, not only from mechanical problems but lack of fuel and damage caused during civil unrest.

Coaching stock

Passenger cars: 1,740 (including 281 used for luggage, parcels, mail, horses, and 282 brake vans).

Freight wagons

Total 15,452, including 4,357 covered, 4,485 open, 503 special uses (livestock, timber, explosives), 628 department wagons, 1,755 container, 3,336 tank, 388 brake vans.

Four- wheel wagons: 10,118

Eight-wheel wagons: 5,334

Developments in 2016

February: The government announced it planned to acquire 500 new locomotives.

June: It was announced that $8.2 billion (most of that financed by loans from China) would be spent to upgrade the Karachi-Peshawer main line by 2021. New track, bridges and culverts would enable axle-loads to be increased on thar 1,872 km route.

July: It was announced that 800 new hopper wagons would be supplied by China, the first batch constructed in China but then manufacture being transferred to works in Lahore. The wagons will be used to carry coal destined for power stations.

August: It was announced an order had been placed to buy fifty-five locomotives from the U.S.

October: The introduction of e-ticketing in Pakistan. The first two months of operation saw Rs 100 million ($954,000) in tickets being purchased online.

* * *

In January 2017 Pakistan Railways took delivery of the first seven of fifty-five GE Transportation locomotive built in Erie. GE Transportation has its most advanced plant in Forth Worth, Texas, but most of its export locomotives come from its Erie, Pennsylvania, works. The five new locomotives are to be used on coal trains with a maximum 12,000-tonne load.

Historical Snapshots

The Pakistan Railways' website contains the following brief description: 'It was on 13th May 1861 that first railway line was opened for public traffic between Karachi City and Kotri, the distance of 105 miles (169 km). The line between Karachi City and Kiamari was opened on 16.6.1889. By 1897 the line from Kiamari to Kotri was doubled.

'The railway line from Peshawar to Karachi closely follows Alexander's line of march through the Hindu Kush to the sea. Different sections on existing main line from Peshawar to Lahore and Multan and branch lines were constructed in the last quarter of nineteenth century and early years of twentieth century.

'The four sections i.e. Scinde Railways, Indian Flotilla Company, Punjab Railway and Delhi Railways working in a single company were later on amalgamated into Scinde, Punjab & Delhi Railways Company and (this) was purchased by the Secretary of State for India in 1885 and in January, 1886, it was named North Western State Railways which was later on renamed as North Western Railways.

'At the time of partition (in 1947), North Western Railways (of) 1,847 route miles (2,972 km) was transferred to India leaving route miles 5,048 (8,124 km) to Pakistan.'

* * *

Railways Divided. The August 1947 partition of India and Pakistan (which then comprised the present day Pakistan in the west and, to the east of India, East Bengal—the present day Bangladesh) broke up what was one of the world's largest state enterprises, Indian Railways. Staff members were given the choice of which railway they wished to work for: 83,000 opted for Pakistan Railways and 73,000 opted for Indian Railways. The latter was badly affected because the preponderance of drivers and firemen were Muslims, who naturally preferred to join the Pakistan system. In addition, the communal violence that was sparked by the partition led to huge movements of people both ways across the new borders, with Pakistan's railway network transporting three million refugees in the first ten weeks of independence.

The 8,124 km of railway system left to Pakistan consisted of 6,880 km of broad gauge routes, 507 km metre gauge and 737 km of 762 mm gauge track. In 1961 the government adopted the present day name of Pakistan Railways.

Railway Miscellany

Slovakia has the greatest station concentration in the European Union calculated on the number of stations per 1,000 km of line. The rating of concentrations is as follows:

Slovakia	260 stations (per 1,000km of route length)
Austria	254
Slovenia	221
Croatia	197
Germany	169
U.K.	160
Belgium	151
Greece	144
Poland	142
EU average	*141*

Source: Austrian Federal Railways

229

FAST FACT: SWISS RAIL USE

The Swiss are, per head of population, by far the heaviest users of railways in the European Union. These are distances—in kilometres—travelled by train per head of population in 2014.

Switzerland	2,429 (km per head of population)
Austria	1,426
France	1,361
Sweden	1,244
Denmark	1,261
Germany	1,115
United Kingdom	1,002
Italy	792
Hungary	783
Finland	708
EU average	*961*

Source: Austrian Federal Railways

Footnote: The Swiss railway 'miracle' is not a totally valid perception. The inability of the roads and terrain to facilitate road transport meant plenty of freight work for rail without the need to compete to get the business, but with the caveat that freight had to be packed in such a way as to be within the railway loading gauge.

And, notwithstanding the high use of the network, Swiss Railways almost went broke in the 1920s and had another troubled financial period after 1945, both situations resolved by the state writing off debts. Cantons and even municipalities had long subsidised, where necessary, private railway operators to keep them afloat (as late as the 1960s there were more than 150 private rail operators, mostly running branch lines and cable railways).

FAST FACT: COSTLY BRITAIN

According to 2014 data, the United Kingdom led the European Union in train travel costs. The cost per kilometre (in U.S. cents) was:

Great Britain	16.7
Finland	10.3
Germany	9.3
Spain	8.2
Austria	7.8
Latvia	5.2
Croatia	4.1

FAST FACT: WHY U.S. LINES WERE PROFITABLE

'Only the American railroads can claim to make a handsome, smacking profit,' *The Economist* reported in July 1966 after looking at the financial state of the world's railway system. Outside of the United States, the magazine could find only two rail systems that were in the black: the Swiss Federal Railways and the Canadian Pacific Railway.

If it were not for subsidies, it was calculated that the French rail system in 1966 was, before the subsidies were added in, making losses equivalent to £200 million. The Dutch and Japanese railways, which had a few years previously been making profits, were by 1966 running in the red. The only national system close to breaking even, and thus joining the Swiss and Canadian ones, was the Swedish one.

And *The Economist* knew why: the only thing railways could do profitably was to carry bulky items over long distances. American railroads had an average freight haul of 748 km, three times the European average; the poorly performing companies were those with the 'heavy burden' of commuter services. The exception to the distance rule was Switzerland, but that country was unique because the difficulties of the terrain gave rail an advantage over road transport.

The Americans had another factor running in their favour: they did not have to run uneconomic services decreed by politicians, as was the case in Britain, France, Japan and Germany. That political influence in Europe and Japan had also led to over-manning, with still large workforces employed in Europe and Japan.

Britain: Railway Builder in Latin America

IN 1914 AT A meeting held at River Plate House, 10 Finsbury Circus, London, Frank Henderson, as chairman, presented a report to shareholders on behalf of the Central Railway Company of Montevideo Limited, a company founded in London and which began operations in South America in 1878.

Traffic volumes had been falling consistently since August 1913 and Henderson added that, generally speaking, the outlook for Central could not be considered very promising. Uruguay's trade had been hit by the outbreak of war in Europe. The chairman then read a telegram bearing the latest information: 'Traffic still slack owing to general trade depression, bad roads and inclement weather. Building operations paralysed. Shearing later and clip lighter. Cattle in excellent condition and brisk traffic expected … Wheat sown later and increased area prepared for maize. Prospects depend considerably on demand for wool and hides … strictest economy being exercised'.

Uruguay did not have the gauge mix that bedeviled some other Latin American countries, most of the network being laid to the standard gauge. In 1935, *Railway Wonders of the World*—a pioneering part-work publication of a genre that would become popular in the 1960s—reported that the total for standard gauge lines was 2,809 km (with 2,390 km of that controlled by British interests) with a narrow gauge 2ft 6in (762 mm) line running a distance of 45 km.

The Central Uruguay line system extended over 1,576 km of route length. The company's lines formed the main artery running north from the capital, Montevideo, to a point on the border with Brazil and providing a connection with the latter's rail network. The company was established in 1876 and thereupon began building lines in Uruguay, as well as acquiring other existing routes.

At the time the article was written, the company owned 129 locomotives, most British built and all oil burners. There were 199 passenger carriages (twelve of them being sleeping cars and thirteen being restaurant coaches), eighty-four brake vans and 2,222 wagons. The motive power included 2-6-0 engines made by Beyer, Peacock and 4-4-4 and 2-4-0 locomotives from the Vulcan Foundry. Uruguay nationalised its railways in 1951.

This photograph was published in the weekly publication *Railway Wonders of the World* in October 1935. The caption read: 'Track renewals in the yard of the Central Uruguay Railway Station at Montevideo. The track seen above is spiked in accordance with the general American practice. The lines converging on the city of Montevideo carry a heavy suburban traffic.' *Courtesy John Clarke who has created a website containing every issue of the publication.*

* * *

Britain, after all, had in the nineteenth century taken on much of the task of financing railways, tramways and public utilities in the former Spanish and Portuguese colonies of South America. It was Barings and Rothschild banks that, between 1823 and 1825, provided the first wave of loans that were used to buy arms (to prevent Spanish re-conquest) and also to finance mines in Bolivia and Colombia. Between 1815 and 1830 it was estimated that something in the order of £20 million was subscribed in the London market for investment in Latin America. Another wave of investment had begun in 1846 with the plan to construct the Central Argentine Railway; by 1876, more than £27 million had been invested by the British in Argentina, accounting for ninety per cent of all foreign money inflows into that country. By 1940, South America accounted for about one-fifth of all British foreign investment.

Of the roughly $2.2 billion worth of foreign investment in Brazil at the beginning of the 1935-1945 war, about forty-eight per cent was British money, while about a quarter of the total came from the United States. As American historian Frank D. McCann of the University of New Hampshire has written in an account published online through Tel Aviv University, 'foreigners controlled street car lines, electric power, coal and oil importation, much of the flour milling, all of cement production, many of the tugs and barges in Rio's harbour, and telegraphic communications with the rest of the world. A British company had owned the sewers of the older parts of Rio since 1857. Many of the movie theatres in big cities were owned by Paramount, RKO, Twentieth-Century Fox, who actively discouraged development of the national cinema industry'.

* * *

But there were gains for British investors from the process of Latin American governments wanting to take control of infrastructure and utilities owned by foreigners. In liquidating their investments in various railway operations, they got rid of some of the least profitable of their assets. The only railway owned by British interests that, in 1949, paid a dividend as much as six per cent was Dorada Railway, which operated a short line in Colombia. At the end of the Second World War, British money was still tied up in minority holdings of a number of less than satisfactory rail investments, including Mexican National Railways, the International Railways of Central America and the Guayaquil and Quito Railway.

The financial pages of London newspapers covered all the public companies that owned railway operations abroad, and there were many. In 1914-15, for example, there was highly detailed reporting of the annual meetings (in London) of such a variety of companies as the Great Western Railway of Brazil Railway Company, the Manila Railway Company (1906) Limited, the Interocean Railway of Mexico Limited, the Argentine Great Western Railway Limited, the White Pass & Yukon Railway Company, the Salvador Railway Company, the Bombay, Baroda & Central India Railway Company, and the Antofagasta (Chili) and Bolivia Railway Company.

In addition, private investors poured money into these companies. One London businessman, Charles Morrison (who was to leave an estate of £10 million in 1909), owned bonds, debentures and shares in Anglo Argentine Tramways, Argentine Great Western Railway, Buenos Ayres Central Railway (the second word of the company name is not a misprint here or in other examples following), the Buenos Ayres Great Southern Railway, Cordoba Central, Buenos Ayres Extension Railway, Cordoba & Central, Dorada Extension Railway, Entre Rios Railway and United Tramways of Montevideo.

Things, quite often, did not go smoothly. At the 1914 annual meeting of shareholders of the Buenos Ayres Western Railway Limited, convened at River Plate House, 10 Finsbury Circus, London, the chairman, Sir Henry Bell, Bt, regretted that the directors had to put before the proprietors (as shareholders were, rightly, called) the most unsatisfactory report they had issued for many years. In previous years the company had suffered from droughts and locusts, but he thought this was the first time in the history of the company that the traffic had so 'utterly collapsed' from too much rain.

In 1948 the administration of President Juan Peron nationalised seven British and three French railway companies operating in Argentina. This was the beginning of the end for European control of the country's railways, the foreign involvement having begun eighty-six years earlier) The first British company into the country had been Buenos Ayres Great Southern, founded in 1862 and which opened its first line in 1865, the 114 km route between the capital and Chascomus; the Central Argentine Railway was founded in 1863, and then in 1873 came the Buenos Ayres and Pacific Railway. In 1890 there was formed the Buenos Ayes Western Railway; there were several other smaller operations controlled from London. The three French railway companies were small and primarily freight carriers. Alongside this, there was the continuing expansion of Argentine State Railways, set up in 1886.

At their maximum extent, the British companies controlled more than sixty per cent of the track length in this South American country. But the shine went off them as investments in the late 1920s when, firstly, they began to face competition from road carriers and then, second, came the financial slump in 1929, at which point these companies ceased paying dividends. As if that was not enough, the advent of world war in 1939 made it impossible for the companies to update their equipment and infrastructure through lack of raw materials.

FAST FACT: ARGENTINA—THE FORGOTTEN RAIL GIANT

Route length: 36,917.4 km
Gauges: 26,391 km—broad gauge 1,676 mm (5ft 6in)
               2,745.1 km—standard gauge 1,435 mm (4ft 8½in)
               7,523.3 km—narrow gauge 1,000 mm (3ft 3⅜in)
               258 km—narrow gauge 750 mm (2ft 5½in)
Electrified: 149 km—broad gauge
               41.1km—standard gauge
(All figures 2014)

"It is not generally realised that Argentina has the fifth longest railway mileage of the countries of the world,' The Times of London began a report on 10 March 1943. By this time, the country's total route length had reached almost 30,000 miles (48,280 km), of that, more than 16,000 miles of track were owned by British companies. Most of the British-owned railways had been built to the 5ft 6in gauge, while other lines were mostly of the narrow gauge. The largest of these companies was the Buenos Ayres Southern

Railway Company, which controlled 4,736 miles (7,042 km) of lines, and its trains served the capital, with its main line running south through Bahia Blanca to Carmen de Patagones. The second largest operator was the Central Argentine Railway with more than 3,000 miles (4,828 km) of track, much of that serving the most important wheat growing areas; it carried about fifty million passengers a year along with 11.5 million tons of freight. It was the first company to electrify a section of line in Argentina.

Not Just Trains Involved

BRITISH RAILWAY COMPANIES WERE sometimes much more than just railway companies. In the 1930s, the Great Western Railway in Britain had £400,000 invested in the Birmingham & Midland Omnibus Company, and substantial interests in several other bus companies and road haulage contractors. GWR owned eleven steam vessels that operated between Wales and Ireland and between England and the Channel Islands. It owned six hotels and 'innumerable' docks in South Wales. The London and North Eastern, apart from working 10,240 km of track, operated 396 km of canals, owned thirty-seven steam boats operating from England to Belgium, Holland and Germany; in addition the LNER owned twenty-six tugs and 159 other vessels. On top of that, there were twenty-eight hotels in England and Scotland and docks at several ports also in its portfolio.

It was not just shipping and road services that railway operators used to increase their revenues. New Zealand Railways in the 1930s went into the publishing business—to both produce revenue and encourage more travel. This was a typical advertisement placed in newspapers across the country.

The London, Midland and Scottish Railway had a fleet of forty-three steam vessels, some of which were employed on the Irish mail service that operated between Holyhead and Dún Laoghaire. This of all the Big Four, was the largest hotelier, operating thirty-one establishments including Liverpool's famous Adelphi. Southern Railway also had a large fleet of ferries and in 1936 introduced a Channel train ferry, these vessels being able to accommodate either forty goods wagons or twelve sleeping coaches; if the latter were being transported, the passengers could remain in their beds until the coaches reached Paris.

Spanish Muddle

IN 1926 SPAIN HAD almost 17,000 km of rail lines (16,976 km to be exact) but these operations were divided up between about one hundred companies. Of the total route length, 11,662 km of broad gauge (otherwise known as Iberian gauge) was operated with steam-hauled trains, and 40 km of route powered by electric trains. There were 4,009 km of steam-hauled narrow gauge operations, with 180 km electrified. Add to that 15 km of rack and funicular railways and about 100 km on the island of Majorca. Railways by then had mostly been built close to the coasts as the mountainous terrain in the centre had made railway construction costly. An enormous burden for all the railway operators was the price of coal: the cost of hauling it over rail in difficult topography was greater than the cost of mining it. In fact, such was the cost of rail construction that the government subsidised the companies building the lines.

Much of the construction had been financed through foreign investment: the two main companies, Caminos de Hierro de Norte (3,692 km in route length) and the La Compañía de los Ferrocarriles de Madrid a Zaragoza y Alicante were run from Paris. Other railway operations were owned by British and Portuguese companies.

There were three locomotive manufacturers in Spain: the Euskalduna de Construcción y Reparación de Buques de Bilbao company, a Spanish subsidiary of Babcock and Wilcox, and Maquinista Terrestre y Maritima.

Alaska Railroad: One of a Type

Total track length: 775.5 km

THE ALASKA RAIL SYSTEM was unusual in the United States in being run by the Federal Government, being operated by the Federal Railroad Commission until handed over the State of Alaska under the Reagan administration (although the sale had first been proposed by President Richard M. Nixon). The line consists of the 756 km main route from the ice-free port of Seward, via Anchorage, to Fairbanks. In 1923 President Warren G. Harding travelled to Alaska to drive the last spike. In 1943, due to wartime transport requirements, a 19.5 km spur was laid to another port, Whittier, which involved drilling of two tunnels through the Chugach Mountains, one of which in 1999 became the only tunnel in the U.S. to be shared by rail and road traffic.

In 1985 Alaska became the only state to own a railroad, paying $22.3 million for the then sixty-one year old system, including fifty-seven locomotives, fifty-two passenger cars, 1,669 freight cars and 149 miscellaneous rail vehicles.

* * *

In August 1970 *The Wall Street Journal* printed a story filed by reporter James E. Bylin about the Alaska Railroad (then still operated by 'Uncle Sam' as the paper put it), also known as 'The Moose Gooser'. Bylin began:

> Is this anyway to run a railroad? Operate your train at a snail's pace average of 30 miles an hour. Drop off or pick up passengers anywhere they want, even between stations. Don't accept reservations. If too many people show up, merely hitch up another car. That's the way Uncle Sam runs his only railroad, and it's just fine with Alaskans.

The 'stop anywhere' policy was to meet the needs of most of the (few) people who lived along the rail line—hunters, fisherman, natives, homesteaders and others. The train was their only means of being able to connect with the outside world, and there was clearly no need building an actual railway station structure to serve a handful of occasional travellers.

The train obtained its nickname for all the moose that also live along its length—and which frequently get in the way of trains. When trains killed a moose, the beast's meat was dressed and donated to orphanages and other charitable institutions (in 1970 this meat had amounted to about twenty-seven tonnes, which gives some idea of the level of moose fatalities).

At that time, too, it cost $21.35 for a seat in one of the air-conditioned carriages against the Anchorage-Fairbanks airline ticket at $36.75. Of course, many of the passengers were not going as far as Fairbanks, and then there were always plenty of tourists who took the train for the scenery.

The *Journal* noted that, unlike trains in the Lower 48 (the forty-eight mainland states), this railroad had maintained a traditional dining car with a wide range on its menu. This includes bacon, eggs, potatoes, toast and coffee for $2.25; homemade chilli for $1.25; or you could go the whole hog and, for $4.75, be served oyster soup followed by sirloin, salad, potatoes, vegetable and roll. Cocktails were poured at $1.25 a time and beer cost 75c a bottle. A jukebox had a choice of records, although mostly country-and-western. 'Uncle Sam even provides free reading material for passengers, including *Playboy*, *Crime Detective* magazine, *True Frontier* and assorted comic books,' Byline added.

Korail: Happy Passengers Wanted

KOREAN RAILROAD CORPORATION WAS founded on 18 September 1899; it became Korail on 1 January 2005. In 2005 its average daily passenger total was 3.5 million and its freight load 102,000 tonnes. In 2004 Korail launched its high-speed train service, named Korea Train eXpress (KTX).

Korail may be the only rail system that has happiness as two of its three main goals: one of those goals is a happy staff, another happy passengers. Regarding the latter, Korail notes that through various concessions 'we have eased the people's burden and encouraged various customers to use the railroad'. Those concessions are:

KTX comfortable to Mom: Purpose—Encouraging birth. Target—Pregnant women. Benefit—Providing executive seats at the price of standard.

Multi-child happiness: Purpose—Encouraging birth. Target:—Families of at least five persons. Benefit—Discounting KTX fares by thirty per cent.

Way to go, Youth: Purpose—Supporting young people to find jobs. Target—Job seekers, 25-33 years of age. Benefit—Discounting KTX fares by thirty per cent.

Youth Dream: Purpose—Supporting youth's movement. Target—13-14 year olds. Benefit—Discounting KTX fares.

Test-takers of the scholastic ability test: Purpose—Supporting test-takers entrance examinations. Target—Test-takers and their companions. Benefit—Discounting KTX fares.

Rail-ro Young Pass: Target—Encouraging domestic travel. Target—University students 25-28 years old. Benefit—Discounting Rail-ro fares by fifty per cent. (Rail-ro is an open ticket that allows multiple rides on Korean railways.)

Japan: From Bullet Trains to Honorary Stationmasters

IN ADDITION TO THE 'big seven' railway companies (the six regional passenger companies, one national freight operator) that resulted from the break-up of Japan National Railways in 1987, the country has sixteen other major private railway operators, six private companies in mid-size range, and more than seventy regional small railways. Probably the most famous of the last group is the Wakayama Electric Railway in the Kansai region, its 14.3 km line located south of Osaka (and with twelve intermediate stations along that route). The company, confronted with falling passenger numbers, had the idea in 2007 that they could boost the number of tourists using the line by appointing a calico cat, Tama, as honorary stationmaster at Kishi station, the line's terminus. Tama, who went on duty at the station complete with a tiny stationmaster's cap, died in 2015 (and is now 'honorary divine station-master'). She was replaced by a similarly coloured cat, Nitama. In 2017, to cater for Wednesday and Thursday traffic each week—Nitama's days off duty—a third cat was appointed, called Yontama, to greet trains on those days of the week.

FACT FILE: JR HOKKAIDO

Total route length:	2,569 km
Gauges:	2,420 km—narrow gauge 1,067 mm (3ft 6in)
	149 km—standard gauge 1,435 mm (4ft 8½in);
	Hokkaido Shinkansen line
Electrified:	511 km
Stations:	435
Tunnels:	169

This company, which services the northern island of Japan, has faced serious financial problems. On 26 March 2016 it launched the Hokkaido Shinkansen but passenger levels were disappointing in the first days. In the following November the company stated that it was making unsustainable losses on about half its network—1,237 km of tracks, to be precise, comprising thirteen sections on ten routes. These sections each saw fewer than 2,000 passengers a day (with three sections averaging just ten passengers a day). In fiscal 2015 all of JR Hokkaido's fourteen routes operated at a loss. The company wants to see the fifty-six local governments affected to switch to bus operations on the worst routes and taking over track maintenance on the others.

Rolling Stock

Locomotives:	35
Railcars:	466
Passenger carriages:	21
Freight wagons:	28 (for rail maintenance only)

On 21 July 1983 this mail and passenger train paused briefly at Naebo station in Hokkaido. From the angle of the umbrella in the doorway of the lead carriage, a passenger is about to alight and walk across the tracks to the platform. Naebo is served by both the Hakodate main line and the Chtose line *John Beckhaus*.

No tractive effort being wasted here: a DUM hauls a tanker wagon, KuKi 3482, through the yards at Naebo in 1983. *John Beckhaus*.

The more modern face of Hokkaido as a local service negotiates the points to reach a platform at Sapporo, the main city on Hokkaido and headquarters of the Hokkaido Railway Company, on 31 May 2008. *John Beckhaus.*

A bucolic scene of a local train wandering through the countryside of Hokkaido, bypassing a disused railway tunnel. *Hokkaido Railway Company.*

New Zealand: Profile of a Colonial System

BY 1905, NEW ZEALAND had a population just moving above the 900,000 mark and yet it had constructed 2,374 miles (3,820 km) of main lines in both islands and a considerable number of branch lines; it was also in process of double-tracking lines that served its four major cities (Auckland, Wellington, Christchurch and Dunedin).

True, the main trunk lines on the two islands were incomplete. The North Island Main Trunk (Auckland-Wellington) would be finished in 1908 but it would be 1942 before the trunk line along the eastern coastline of the South Island system would be completed, at which time it became possible to run trains from Picton on Cook Strait and the northern end of the island to Invercargill in the far south. However, and even before the colony's population was still short of the one million mark, considerable investment was being pumped into New Zealand Railways (NZR), not only expand the network and the fleet, but to lift the standard of operations.

In 1905 the Minister of Railways, Sir Joseph Ward, delivered the annual NZR report to the Parliament in Wellington, giving members a highly detailed account of where the rail system stood.

At the beginning of the 1904-05 year, NZR had 377 locomotives, 809 passenger carriages, 301 brake vans, 12,375 four-wheel wagons and 760 bogie goods wagons. During the year the various workshops around the country had produced fourteen new locomotives, fifty-five new carriages, eleven brake vans and 445 new wagons. By 1906, the minister told the House of Representatives, another sixty carriages would be completed along with 299 wagons and five more brake vans.

By 1905 132 stations were equipment with tablet machines; the sections being controlled by tablets being increased. Twenty-eight stations by then had interlocking signals and points.

Pintech's gas lighting system had been installed in all bogie carriages and many brakevans. Creosote plants had been built in both islands to coat wooden sleepers before they were laid. In the year under review, ninety miles of main line track had been re-laid with 70lb rails, five miles of branch line had been re-laid with second-hand rails taken off the main lines.

Westinghouse braking had by this time been installed on 343 loco-motives, 752 carriages, 217 brake vans, 9,708 wagons and six travelling cranes. Cushioning had been placed on what had been bare wooden seats in 498 second-class carriages and 304 existing carriages had gone through the workshops to have lavatories added. (It should be noted that not all the second-class cars received cushions; in the 1960s Wellington's suburban system had insufficient electric multiple units for morning and afternoon peak hours. NZR had several consists of old carriages hauled by electric locomotives to supplement passenger capacity to stations on the Hutt Valley line, some of which still sported bare wooden seating—as this writer remembers only too well.)

The average late running on long distance trains was 1min 07sec over the year. Some 392 excursion trains had been run during the year for school, factory or friendly society outings. NZR was continuing to reduce fares and freight charges to encourage more people to use trains; in the case of goods traffic the dominance of agriculture in New Zealand's economy at that time was a vital consideration for the railways. Lime for manure was carried free of charge, and freight rates for butter, cheese, honey, New Zealand-grown fruit and sheep-dip were among those items by now carried at lower rates than previously.

There were also fare concessions for a range of users: newspaper reporters, teachers, delegates to religious bodies, pupils of technical schools, and judges at agricultural shows. And NZR was in the process of attaching numbers to seats in carriages used on long distance services so that passengers could reserve their places.

The New Zealand system in 1904 carried:

8,514,112 passengers
825,468 parcels
15,651 horses
38,592 dogs
110,924 cattle
3,412,984 sheep
77,768 pigs
109,174 tons of firewood

FAST FACT: TWO STATIONS THAT NEVER SAW A TRAIN

On the shores of Lake Wakatipu in the South Island, New Zealand Railways had three designated railway stations. Two of them, though, never saw a train. Kingston was the terminus of the only railway to reach the lake; but Queenstown and Glenorchy served only NZR's lake steamer service.

NZR built a railway line to the southern tip of the lake, with trains running to the railhead at Kingston, 40 km from the resort settlement at Queenstown. Even then Queenstown was a tourist attraction but the mountainous terrain made it economically impossible to construct a line to serve it. Instead, NZR operated lake steamers from Kingston, the vessels meeting trains and transporting holidaymakers across the lake. The Queenstown wharf had a NZR station, complete with stationmaster, for passenger traffic, and for handling of freight to and from several farming properties dotted around the large lake. One of the ferry stops was the small lakeside town of Glenorchy, which also had a designated railway station. The rails from the end of the wharf to the goods shed were laid to allow a wagon to be pulled ashore carrying cargo unloaded from the steamers.

The wagon pictured here was M295, built around 1880. It appears the wagon was damaged in rail service so was sent to Glenorchy to run up and down the shortest rail section in the NZR (less than 100 metres). The wharf was no longer required once a road was built in 1962 to link Glenorchy with Queenstown but when the wharf and goods shed were restored, so to was the section of track. When this photo was taken in 2016 the wagon was still awaiting new decking and sideboards. *Photo: Claire Henderson.*

Early railway publications

BARELY TWO MONTHS INTO the Second World War and, with tourism rail travel in Europe no longer possible, the centenary occurred of the first edition of *Bradshaw's Railway Time Tables and Assistant to Railway Travel*.

As *The Economist* magazine commented, Bradshaw reflected the natural eccentricity of the English character:

> In what other country would fanatics be found who glory in the reputation of having memorised its long columns, although modestly admitting to be a little shaky on their Irish locals? Where else would back numbers of a railway timetable be sought after by collectors and command a premium?

In fact, Bradshaw was not alone in seeing the publishing potential of railway information. In 1830 *A Guide to the Liverpool & Manchester Railway* had been published. H. Belcher brought out *Illustrations of the Scenery on the Line of the Whitby & Pickering Railway*. James Drake authored *Drake's Road Book of the Grand Junction Railway from Birmingham to Liverpool and Manchester*. While these were not really what you would now call 'railway' books, but were largely travel guides, there were occasional rail tips. In *Osborne's Guide to the Grand Junction, or Birmingham, Liverpool & Manchester Railway* published in 1838, E. C. Osborne advised sightseers to travel outside on trains, protecting their eyes with gauze spectacles. 'I shall suppose you mounted on the box seat,' he wrote. 'You look round, and see several engines with red-hot fires in their bodies and volumes of steam issuing from their tall chimneys. One of them moves slowly toward you. The huge creature bellows, at first, like an elephant. Deep, slow and terrific are the hoarse heavings that it makes.'

It was Bradshaw who first conceived the idea of timetables rather than simply scenic guides (although the early books had a great deal of useful information about such things as accommodation at various places and the postal delivery times). So it was in October 1839 that the seminal book appeared. The problem for Bradshaw was that railway operators were prone to make arbitrary timetable changes;

eventually the companies agreed to make changes only at specified intervals. Bradshaw invented the method of printing train details, including intermediate stations, in vertical columns. By 1889 the *Bradshaw's Railway Companion* ran to 948 pages, expanding further by 1914 to 1,200 pages. The complexity of the guide shrank considerably in 1923 when many of the British railway companies were grouped into four large operations. The last edition of *Bradshaw's* appeared in 1961 but in 2012, thanks to Michael Portillo's television series, *Great British Railway Journeys* (his travels following journeys recommended by the book), a facsimile edition of one edition of *Bradshaw's* was published and became a big seller on Amazon. Portillo, a former British politician who served in several cabinet posts, including Secretary of State for Transport, used the Bradshaw guide as he travelled for the television series (and repeated this in a series on European railways).

French Grouping

FROM THE FIRST OF January 1938 all French railways were brought under a national umbrella, the now well-known Société Nationale des chemins de fer Français or SNCF. It had been judged by the government that the one region that had up until that point been managed by a state railway body had proved a success, and that the entire system should be converted to state control. It was also considered imperative that some action be taken to stem railway losses, the cumulative deficit as of 1937 being the equivalent of £200 million. Up until that time, there had been five regions:

Ouest (Western): Its trains departed from and arrived at Gare St Lazare for services to Normandy (including Rouen and Le Havre) and to suburbs on the right bank of the Seine. Gare Montparnasse handled this company's trains serving Brittany, the west of France and western suburbs of Paris, and Gare des Invalides (now an RER and Metro station) was for trains to Versailles. This region had also begun running one-car diesel railcars, known as Autorail, the journey between Paris and Lyon being reduced to 1hr 15min.

Sud-Ouest (Southwest): The P.O.-Midi railway (Paris, Orleans and the South). Its expresses used Gare du Quai d'Orsay while Gare d'Austerlitz was for this company's trains to the Loire Valley, Bordeaux, the Massif Central, the Pyrenees and the Spanish border, while Gare du Luxembourg was for suburban trains.

(Gare du Quai d'Orsay was built in 1900 with sixteen rail tracks, complete with a hotel above. It was closed in 1939 because its short platforms could not accommodate the longer electric trains. The building now houses the Musée d'Orsay. This station-turned-museum bears a plaque commemorating the station's use in 1945 for the trains bringing back from Germany French prisoners-of-war and forced labourers.)

The plaque reads: 'Between April and August 1945 a large number of camp survivors from prison camps, concentration camps, forced labour camps, all victims of Nazism, were on their return welcomed at Gare d'Orsay, the largest French repatriation centre. *Claire Henderson.*

Sud-Est (Southeast): Until 1938, this region was operated by the Paris, Lyon and Mediterranean Railway (PLM) company. This operator's train used Gare de Lyon for lines to the Rhone Valley, Marseilles, the Alps, the Riviera and connections to Swiss and Italian railways.

Nord (North): Previously called Chemins de Fer du Nord, this company operated from Gare du Nord to northern France, Lille, Channel ports including Dunkirk, and connections to Belgium and Germany.

Est (Eastern Region): Operated by the Eastern Railway Company and the Alsace and Lorraine Railway Company. Trains ran from Gare de l'Est serving the eastern region, the Ardennes, and connections with southern Germany and Switzerland.

Use Radio in Train Operations? Leave it With Us

RAILWAYS, EVEN WHEN THEY were seen as a modern technological development in themselves, have often been loath to embrace other technologies. It was not until 1889, when an excursion special in Northern Ireland became decoupled on a steep grade with ten carriages rolling back down the hill and into a following train (with eighty-eight people killed) that the British government enacted laws to force the railway companies to adopt basic safety measures that had been available for years and, indeed, were widely in use in the United States. These were interlocking of points (switches) and signals so that, for example, when the points were against an oncoming train, so were the signals; block working so that trains on any one section of line could run in the knowledge that no other train was on that section; and continuous brakes where, with the brakes applied in the locomotive cab, the brakes applied to each and every wheel on the train. The companies spent decades resisting these innovations until the growing list of fatalities forced the government's hand. (Experts at the time said the Northern Ireland disaster could have been avoided had the train been equipped with continuous brakes.)

When it came to radios, the Americans also led the way. By 1924, vessels plying the Great Lakes of North America were in voice contact with other ships. Yet by 1944 it was still commonplace for freight trains to have to stop, then a crew-member walk the entire length of the train to communicate some information to either the engineer or the brake man in the caboose.

Radio progress had been slow in the United States. In the 1920s there had been experiments with wireless connections between moving trains and railroad signal towers. At the beginning of 1928 a fifty-watt transmitter had been installed in a New York Central locomotive, the set being powered by the headlight generator, and railroad officials were able to communicate with the driver. The trainmen (guards) in the caboose at the rear also had such a transmitter, this one powered from a generator attached to the axle. Everyone expected this to be the end of an era in which the driver and trainmen communicated by lantern, flags or use of the locomotive whistle.

Not so: it was a full sixteen years before, in 1944, the Denver & Rio Grande Western Railroad experimented with FM radios to provide communications between each end of the train. It cost $1,500 per train to install the equipment. That year the editor of the magazine *Electronic Industries* was complaining that U.S. railroads had made too little use of the same type of electronics then available on almost every ship and aircraft. Instead, trains were still being stopped so that trainmen could walk to the locomotive to deliver a message.

By 1937 telephones within trains had been adopted by some railway companies. In the United States by the 1930s some companies had telephone communications between locomotive and caboose but in 1936 the Chicago, Burlington & Quincy Railroad took the technology one step further by installing telephones in each Pullman car so that passengers could call and reserve a table in the dining car rather than walking through several cars only to find all the tables taken. In 1937 the Southern Pacific announced that its new City of San Francisco train would have telephones in every compartment as well as in the dining and observation cars. (In 1935 Japan's Ministry of Railways had announced it was to install telephones on trains. The trial use would take place on the Tokyo-Hamamatsu stretch of the Tokaido line. All carriages would be equipped with antennae to receive and transmit telephone calls from passengers on board.)

* * *

This is not say that railways were unimaginative. What about the water trough? The Pacific-type locomotives used on long distance trains in Britain had tender capacity for 5,000 gallons (just under 19,000 litres) and replenishing that supply would have involved additional, time-consuming stops just as railways were fighting to reduce travel times to keep passenger business. Hence the introduction of water troughs: a scoop under the tender could be lowered when the engine approached one of these troughs and, within fifteen seconds, could pick up at least 1,500 gallons. Another innovation to eliminate unnecessary stops was a tender with a narrow corridor through it allowing engine crews to change while at top speed.

Then there were slip carriages. An express could be equipped with a special type of coupling by which a guard could release one or more carriages from the train without the express having to be stopped, the now separated coaches being brought to a gentle halt at a platform by use of hand brakes. Thus the Cornish Riviera could detach a coach at Westbury, another at Taunton, and not have to make its first stop until Exeter. This practice was adopted by several companies but eventually discontinued due to the cost of employing extra guards needed to remain with the detached carriages.

Mails on Rails

'The track … was very rough and the cars, being short, got off the tracks quite often. Mr. H. W. Farley, the master mechanic, put two iron rods along the top of the car for the postal clerks to hang on to while the car was off the track and it provided to be an excellent safety appliance'
—a description in *Montana: The Magazine of Western History* of the first eastbound mail van being hauled by the Hannibal & St Joseph Railroad (later part of the Burlington system) on 28 July 1862.

THIS FIRST DAY OF operation of a dedicated mail van in the United States saw the Hannibal & St Joseph RR load mail at Palmyra, the junction with the Chicago, Burlington and Quincy Railroad, and proceed west behind the company's locomotive No. 1. As the magazine of the Montana Historical Society recalled on the centenary of the first run, the track of the Hannibal & St Joseph RR 'left much to be desired so far as standards of construction and maintenance were concerned'. The mail car derailed on that run.

At one end of the first postal car were small boxes, each marked with the name of a station between Hannibal and St Joseph. A table in the centre was used for mail sorting. As the journal noted in 1962, 'the basic design of postal cars has not had to be changed substantially to this day'.

Mail was first carried on American trains in 1832, but in the form that the bags were loaded and stacked on the floor of a standard van and they remained untouched until being unloaded at their destinations. It was not until that run in 1862 that postal items were sorted inside a moving train. It was a practice that would continue for 115 years.

In 1838 Congress designated all United States railroads as postal routes.

The website of the U.S. Postal Service tells us that a parcel post service was added in 1913 but the volume soon outgrew the available space in the railway vans, so parcel sorting had to be done at especially established terminals before the items were loaded on trains. By 1930 more than 10,000 trains were moving mail across America. However, the Transportation Act of 1958 allowed the discontinuance of loss-making passenger services, which meant a severe cut to the number of passenger trains available to carry mail; by 1965, only 190 trains were carrying mail. The last railway post office, running between Washington D.C. and New York (run by Penn Central and Conrail) made its final run on 30 June 1977.

But, shortly after, there was a partial reprieve: the increase of the volume and weight of catalogues and advertising mail during the 1980s saw those items return to the rails, with Amtrak carrying them on many of its routes.

* * *

In Britain what became known as the Travelling Post Offices went back to 1838 when the Post Office attached a converted horsebox to a train running from Birmingham to Warrington on the Grand Junction Railway. Apart from its interior sorting equipment, the van (16 feet or 4.9 metres long) was fitted with an exterior device that interacted with line-side apparatus, allowing mail bags to be caught while the train was in motion; the apparatus was improved in 1848 but the design remained unchanged well into the twentieth century, it consisting of hinged arms that held the bags to be dropped; at the same time a large folding net on the side of the rail vehicle was opened out and caught the mailbags hanging from the line-side apparatus. These vans were designated as a Travelling Post Office (TPO).

By the mid-1930s there were seventy-three TPOs operating on the British railway network using 156 sorting vans, with 132 stations equipped with the apparatus to allow mailbag exchanges at speed. At this time the Royal Mail was handling six million letters and 150 million parcels a year—and eighty per cent of this mail travelled by train.

As featured also around this time in the magazine *Railway Wonders of the World*, the first company to run a special mail-only train was the Great Western Railway in 1855 (although, later, first class passenger coaches were added). In 1859 the London & North Western and Caledonian Railways co-operated to run a nightly train in each direction between London and Aberdeen, initially hauling three sorting vans and three 'mail tender vans' as well as some first-class carriages. By the mid-1930s this service, known as the West Coast Postal, had thirteen sorting coaches, six with mail-exchange apparatus and the remainder for storage of parcels.

Safety was important. Sorters had to be physically fit and be able to maintain balance on a moving train, but all corners inside the vans had rounded corners.

The train was staffed with about forty postal workers. They left Euston in London at 8.30 p.m. and arrived at Aberdeen at 7.52 a.m. the next morning, stopping at Rugby, Tamworth, Crewe, Preston, Carlisle, Carstairs Junction, Stirling and Perth (all of which stations received and dispatched such volumes that these could not be handled by automatic equipment), with mail being exchanged by apparatus at thirty-three other stations.

The operators had to be skilled in the use of the strong receiving nets with leather pouches of mail weighing up to 60lb (27kg) being transferred; even in fog, the failures of exchange were extremely rare.

Crewe was one of the key points at which the train stopped, as that station was served over any single night by ten such travelling post office services (the others starting from or terminating at places as far afield as Cardiff, Birmingham, York and Holyhead). York was served by seven arriving and six departing TPOs while Bristol had four departures and four arrivals.

The last TPO in Britain ran in January 2004. By this time only 20 million of the 80 million letters being posted throughout the United Kingdom were being transported by trains, with 55 million being sent by road and the remainder by air. Rail was an expense the Royal Mail no longer wanted to bear. At the end, only a handful of TPOs were still in service (serving London, Carlisle, Newcastle, Swansea, Plymouth, Dover, Norwich, Bristol, Penanze, Cardiff and Glasgow).

The sorters could handle 1,200 letters an hour and were able to fill bags for individual postmen's rounds to be dropped at stations along the way. But they cost money: they received a supplement above the normal sorter's wage, and they had to be accommodated in guest-houses when away from home. Moreover, the postal vans could not be attached to the fastest passenger trains then being introduced, nor even to some freight trains, as the vans could not travel faster than 90 mph if the sorters were to be able to carry our their task.

(Footnote: the TPO frank on envelopes was very much prized by stamp collectors.)

* * *

TPOs spread to other countries. In 1873, for instance, Switzerland required all railway companies to haul these postal vans without charge, although cantons throughout the country did receive a royalty on sale of stamps (55.9 million items being posted that year).

India—naturally—followed British practice. In 1908 the *Times of India* reported that new carriages were being completed for the Bombay-Punjab Special Postal Express. The three cars (all 62 feet or 18.9 metres long) consisted of a van for sorting newspapers, one for sorting letters and the third to store mail bags after sorting. The vans, the paper added, were 'brilliantly lit by electricity and have fans throughout'.

In 1936 a reporter from *The Irish Times* travelled on an overnight TPO between Dublin and Cork.

It was some time before I could stand steady without seizing hold of something every time the train swayed. This swaying did not trouble the sorters, however, and as the speed gradually increased to sixty

miles an hour the letters continued to flow through their hands to the
pigeon holes at more than thirty a minute—letters telling of love and
laughter, death and sadness—they were just 'pieces of mail' to these
quick-fingered men.

He listened to cries about drops to be made at approaching stations
(one of the first being 'four bags for Sallins') and asked how, in the dark,
the sorters knew where they were. 'By sound', came the reply; they
listened to all the noises, such as passing over culverts, through cuttings,
the whoosh past a wayside station, and so on, becoming familiar with
the noises of their nightly run.

In 1878 New Zealand introduced the first Railway Travelling Post
Office between Christchurch and Dunedin (the South Island cities);

Mail sorters pictured hard at work in 1939. The names on the sorting boxes
suggest that this postal van was attached to a passenger service between the capital,
Wellington, and the city of New Plymouth—not only is New Plymouth listed on
a box, but also towns on the line such as Stratford and Eltham. *National Library of
New Zealand.*

the direct rail connection between the North Island's major cities, Auckland and Wellington, was not completed until 1908 due to the difficult terrain in the centre of the island. By 1881 New Zealand Railways was providing fifty mail services, and the development of these helped to make it possible for a parcel-post service to be introduced in 1887.

* * *

The Australian colony of Victoria introduced postal vans in 1865 and mail was carried in New South Wales from 1870, many of the overnight trains from Sydney to regional centres bearing appropriate names such as the Forbes Mail and Coonamble Mail; the post office in the central NSW city of Dubbo had separate posting boxes, one for letters to be delivered along railways to the west, the other for those to be delivered to Sydney and intermediate stations on that line to the state capital. The last NSW TPO ran in 1984.

In February 2016 the *Central West Daily* newspaper based in Orange, New South Wales, published an article about the deteriorating postal service in Australia. It began:

> Can anyone remember when trains had a travelling post office van known as a TPO with mail workers sorting letters along the way? You could mail a letter to Sydney at Orange railway station up to midnight and it would be delivered next morning, an overnight service. Sorted mail was also dropped off at stations where the train stopped. Australia Post, as the Postmaster-General's Department had become by then, scrapped the TPOs in 1984 and bought its own fleet of road trucks because of so many damaging railway strikes in the early 1980s.

'Crookedest' Lines

WHAT WAS THE 'CROOKEDEST' railroad line in the United States? It seems there was some competition for the title.

In January 1920 the *Los Angeles Times* reported that the country's crookedest line was about to be scrapped. Application had been made to the State Corporate Commission for discontinuance of the United

Verde & Pacific Railroad, a twenty-six mile narrow gauge (914 mm or 3ft 0in) line connecting the United Verde copper mine with the Santa Fe, Prescott & Phoenix Railroad system (which in 1911 had become a subsidiary of the Atchison, Topeka & Santa Fe) at Jerome, Arizona. 'This line is the one renowned in a western story on which the engineer could borrow a chew of tobacco from the conductor in the caboose at a dozen curves on the way through the Black Hills,' the paper reported. 'There were many forty-five degree curves but these later were straightened a bit.' In all, the line ran through 186 curves

Crookedest? Maybe not. In 1949 the *Christian Science Monitor* reported thus from Quinwood, West Virginia: 'Once upon a time there was a railroad. It was the world's crookedest railroad, so they said, with enough twists to start a pretzel factory and enough ups and downs to qualify for a well-kept roller coaster". It took an hour to travel two miles. 'And, brother, that is slow for a railroad' the paper noted. The Nicholas, Fayette and Greenbrier Railroad was built by

By the time this photograph was taken, the Nicholas, Fayette and Greenbrier's line had been (at least partly) straightened. On Labor Day weekend in 1954 No. 1419, 2-8-2 engine, hauls a loaded coal train. *Donald A. Kaiser, courtesy Alexander Campbell.*

pick and shovel in 1909. At one point, the trains of thirty-five freight wagons carrying coal had to be cut into four to negotiate the grade and the curves. There was a series of switchbacks, built one under the other. In 1927 the line was bought through a joint venture between the New York Central and Chesapeake & Ohio. By 1943 the line could not cope with the amount of coal needing to be transported due to the laborious system of train running so major earthworks were undertaken to straighten the line. 'Now forty cars make it across the mountain in a few minutes,' wrote the *Monitor*.

In 1935 the British magazine *Railway Wonders of the World* designated as the crookedest railway in the world the Mount Tamalpais Scenic Railway in California. It ran 8.19 miles (13.2 km) and, in that distance, contained 260 curves. The area was a favoured outdoor outing for San Franciscans. The line had a ruling grade of 1 in 14.3. Trains were hauled up the mountain by Shay geared locomotives at eight miles an hour (12.9 km/h); the engines were oil burning to avoid sparks that could have caused forest fires. The big thrill for many passengers was the means of descent: open gravity cars ran down the line controlled by double hand brakes. The line opened in 1896 and closed in 1929, a fire in the latter year burning many ties (sleepers); given that, by that time, many locals preferred to drive their cars up the mountain rather that take the train so there was little economic justification to rebuild the line.

The 'Lunatic Line' and other rail enthusiasms of 1902–03

THE BUILDING OF THE line across Kenya to Uganda was begun from Mombasa in 1896 and reached Kisumu on an arm of Lake Victoria in 1901, where a port was developed at the rail terminal. The first trains reached there in 1903. In 1931 the line was extended to Kampala, Uganda (in 1929 the operations had been transferred to the organisation, Kenya Uganda Railways & Harbours).

The project was referred to by its opponents in the British Parliament as the 'lunatic line' due to the huge expense of laying a railway through forbidding country, with malarial swamps and hostile tribesmen. In all, about 4,000 men (mainly Indian labourers) lost their lives during the construction, including about 100 killed by lions. (The last run of what was dubbed the Lunatic Express travelled from Nairobi to Mombasa on 28 April 2017.)

But: back to 1902.

Further south from Kenya, there were plans to continue the 'Cape-to-Cairo' rail dream by building a new section northward from Victoria Falls. 'The supreme grandeur of Victoria Falls is destined to make it a rival of Niagara in attracting tourists, a fact of which the interested railway authorities have by no means been unmindful,' wrote B.H. Meyer of the University of Wisconsin (see bibliography). Before the close of 1903 the South African Chartered Company would, he said, have spent £2 million, one half of that being for a steel bridge over the Zambezi and the construction in that area of three branch lines. The other half of the money was 'to be devoted to a continuation of the Cape to Cairo railway from Victoria Falls northward to the great bend in the Kafu River' in Uganda.

Meanwhile, in the British colony of Gold Coast (now Ghana) about 15,000 local men were employed building a railway into the Ashanti region. The narrow gauge (1,067 mm) line was being laid at the rate of up seven miles (11.2 km) a month.

Other colonial powers were similarly working to build railway networks. In the first quarter of 1903 the Reichstag in Berlin appropriated funds to extend the 1,000 mm Usambara railway in German East Africa (now Tanzania) to stop the British taking trade from the German territory with their Uganda railway, the terminus of that system being just 160 km from the German line. 'Traffic on this road has been ridiculously light,' noted Meyer. In 1903 the line had earned 156,700 marks, against running costs of 346,682 marks. The number of coloured passengers was ten times the number of whites using the trains, he reported.

A British syndicate had in 1902 secured a contract to build a line from the Atlantic coast of Portuguese West Africa (now Angola) and extending nearly 1,400 km eastwards.

International rail rivalry was alive and well in China, too. In June 1902 the American-China Development Company was granted an eighty-year concession to build a line of 699 miles (1,125 km) in length between Canton (now Guangzhou) and Hankow (now Hankou).

This railway was to replicate the ancient trading route between northern and southern China. Meyer reported that it was hoped that the company, run entirely by Americans, would complete the project in three years.

Meanwhile, the German-Chinese Railway Company had been incorporated in Berlin, backed by Deutsche Bank, Dresdner Bank and ten other financial institutions. Another player, the Russo-Chinese Bank, had raised a loan of forty million francs in Paris for the construction of the Ching-Tai railway, a western branch of the line between Hankow and Peking (now Beijing) that had been constructed largely with French and Belgian money. In June 1903 the British government asked for 'favourable running powers' over certain lines and to be given preference to provide capital for another planned railway.

In November 1902 a transcontinental railway act was passed by the Australian parliament (then sitting in Melbourne until a new national capital was developed at Canberra). This was not what is now known as the Trans-Australian line running east-west across the continent, but a narrow gauge track crossing the continent from south to north, linking the railhead of the South Australian Railways line at Oodnadatta (close to the edge of the Simpson Desert) to Pine Creek, the railhead of the isolated 233 km North Australia Railway line from the northern town of Darwin. The gap between the two railheads was 1,930 km. The new line was to be narrow gauge of 1,067 mm, the gauge of the existing lines at either end. As at 1902 Australia had more than 12,800 km of line to this gauge, against 4,830 km of standard 1,435 mm track and 6,440 km of broad gauge (1,600 mm). This new narrow gauge track was never completed, although extensions were laid from both ends, from the south as far as the new railhead at Alice Springs and from the north to a tiny settlement of Birdum. (A new standard gauge line to link Darwin to the rest of Australia was not completed until 2003.)

Work was still proceeding in 1903 on the trans-alpine railway to link Argentina and Chile. Meanwhile, in Buenos Aires the Argentine government announced that the eight broad gauge companies operating lines in Argentina were to be combined, while Buenos Aires had signed an agreement with Bolivia to build a railway to link the two countries. Bolivia had just completed its first state-owned line, a 92 km track between La Paz and Lake Titicaca. Peru was studying a rail route that would run from its section of the Amazon to the Pacific coast.

Meyer reported that English railway management had been receiving criticism due to their adherence to antiquated types of cars and locomotives and the lack of adequate statistics about their operations. 'A competent European critic has recently characterised English railway statistics as the poorest of any in the civilized countries of the world', he wrote.

Prussia's government was continuing to acquire railway companies, and in 1903 there were just 2,110 km of primary and secondary railways still left in private hands.

But, Closer to Home, Prevarication

IN 1906 *THE SPECTATOR* magazine said of yet another attempt to promote passage of a bill through the House of Commons to authorise a channel tunnel: 'It is possible to admire pertinacity of purpose and devotion to an idea, however foolish; but it is difficult to believe that the promoters of the Bill to be presented to the House of Commons during the coming Session have any hope of succeeding where others have consistently failed'

By then it was an old issue. A French engineer, Albert Mathieu, had as early as 1802 proposed a tunnel, lit by candlelight and wide enough for horse-drawn carriages to ply between England and France. The first design for a tunnel accommodating steam-hauled trains came from another French engineer, André Thamé de Gamond, in 1856; he proposed a twenty-one mile (33.7 km) tunnel, ventilated by tall chimneys whose tops would rise above sea level. A British engineer, William Low, came up with his own plan in 1860: it allowed for double tracks, and the suggestion that trains entering the tunnel would bring fresh air in behind them. In 1881 serious tunneling got under from each end; before it was abandoned in 1883 after 3.5 km had been dug; by that time British concern about the tunnel being used by French invaders had become sufficiently aroused (the two countries were in dispute over a number of foreign matters including the Suez Canal and colonial claims).

The House of Commons was, by 1906, consistent in rejecting any bill to authorise a tunnel, such legislation having been rejected in 1882, 1884, 1881, 1887, 1888 and 1890, while in 1893 another bill was withdrawn before it reached a vote.

The Spectator, however, did see some merit in the idea, noting that it would be extremely satisfactory for passengers to find themselves getting from Dover to Calais in half an hour 'instead of spending nearly an hour and a half on a steamer, and possibly suffering lamentably from sea-sickness'. However, the writer also suspected that many people would still prefer the brightness and fresh air of the sea voyage.

But the writer was no old fogey: the article then proposed building rail ferries, whereby carriages would be run on the decks of the ships and then offloaded at the other end to continue their journey behind a locomotive of the other country. The writer concluded that that, if there were to be a tunnel, it could more usefully be constructed between Scotland and Ireland.

Medicine Train

RAILWAYS HAVE OVER THE years had hospital trains and rail ambulances, but there has been nothing quite so bizarre—and still largely forgotten—as the trains used by California to rid itself of mental patients who had come from other parts of the United States. In May 1958 *Time* magazine published a reported headlined "Medicine: Train Ride". It described a train that had departed Sacramento headed initially to Arizona with 220 mental patients aboard, those patients having been committed within the first year of their arrival in the state, and so had not achieved the twelve-month residency qualification for care in California's own hospitals. Two trains a year left on such a mission.

Time would never have made it up. But, strangely, I could find no references to such a practice through an extensive online search, and an extensive one at that (apart from the searches throwing up the same *Time* report that had provoked the search). But then I came upon a brief item in the *Los Angeles Times* dated 9 June 1939. It had a report from Oklahoma City with complaints that California was 'dumping' mental patients and that a hospital at Norman, Oklahoma, had taken in patients sent from Stockton, California. California's State

Commissioner of Lunacy, Dr Aaron J. Rosanoff, was quoted, saying that his state's law required the deportation of the non-resident insane and 'two trains a year go east carrying about 150 patients each'. So *Time* had got it right.

Then Rosanoff makes another appearance in the *Los Angeles Times* in May 1942, again defending deporting these 'unfortunates' (as the paper so characterised them). He said reciprocal arrangements for such transfers had been made with forty-six states. The complainant was again Oklahoma, this time after the latest deportation train had reached Oklahoma City. The local police chief had refused to allow eight patients to disembark until ordered to do so by a county judge.

It seems that the only detailed account we have of these trains is from the weekly newsmagazine. The train that departed Sacramento in May 1958 was described in *Time* as consisting of fourteen old carriages (mostly Pullmans). For each passenger there was a supply of tranquilisers, and there was the equipment for electric shock treatment. Each car had its doors locked and there were handcuffs for instances where patients tried to escape at stops.

At Phoenix the car carrying Arizona patients was uncoupled. The other cars were taken off along the way; by the time the train reached St Louis, Missouri, it was down to four carriages. The run ended at Boston, with one lone carriage remaining of the original fourteen.

Royal Railwayman

BULGARIA HAD A RAILWAY enthusiast as a monarch. Not only did he like trains, King Boris III (reigned 1918-1943) was a qualified engine driver and, in 1933, became a member of the Bulgarian Railroad Engineers' Union. As the *Christian Science Monitor's* correspondent in the Bulgarian capital reported about the union issue, 'three hard-handed engine drivers from Sofia called upon him in the palace to present him with his card and give him a pin'. After that formality, they all sat down and talked about Bulgarian locomotives.

In October 1930 the King was travelling from Sofia to Varna (an important Bulgarian port on the Black Sea) on an express train when the locomotive caught on fire (the details of which were not explained in the newspaper reports at the time). The King dressed the driver's wounds and then drove the locomotive to the nearest river 'where water was obtained and the fire extinguished', according to the Reuters report. Once the locomotive was fit to operate, Boris drove the train the remaining 96.5 km to Varna.

In 1937, on a visit to Britain, King Boris drove the *Coronation Scot* on a special run from Euston to Bletchley at the invitation of the London Midland and Scottish Railway Company (with the company's driver, a man called Bishop, supervising on the footplate). Boris drove the engine at speeds up to 88 mph (141.5 km/h) with nine coaches attached.

The King was also keen to take part in any new rail line opening. In 1930 drove the first train on the 40 km Tvartditza-Sliven line, a railway that would later be extended to provide a direct connection between Sliven and Sofia.

In 1939 he celebrated the twenty-first anniversary of his ascension to the throne by taking charge of the locomotive on a line into what was known as the Valley of the Roses, an area famous for its flowers. (Boris also marked the anniversary by granting political amnesty to 176 political prisoners, including communists, Macedonian revolutionaries and the men behind an attempted army *coup d'etat* in 1934.)

New Zealand's Railway Crockery Crime Wave

'WHERE IS THE MISCHIEF to end?' asked the weekly magazine *New Zealand Free Lance* on 15 February 1908. It seemed that railway travellers were light-fingered with the property of New Zealand Railways' refreshment rooms, the average licensee having to pay about £50 a year (a good slice of their profit) to replace 'borrowed cups (never returned), appropriated saucers, missing knives, forks, spoons, etc.'. The magazine instanced the case of Mr. Thomas F. Thompson who ran the refreshment room at Kaitoke, just north of Wellington on the then line (which included the famed Rimutaka Incline) to the Wairarapa region.

He had spent £160 2s 6d (that's 160 pounds, two shillings and sixpence, or what would today be $320.25) between May 1905 and December 1907 for replacements. Of the 8,496 cups with which he had begun his lease, only 400 remained at the end of the above period.

The Free Lance agonised that, if that sort of thing was going on at refreshments rooms throughout New Zealand, 'our name for honesty must be "mud".' If a man or a woman can take a cup from a railway refreshment room without any pang of conscience, he or she would just as well take the saucer also. It was all very well to complain about the cost of a sandwich or cup of tea, but what other action could the poor licensee take to stay afloat?

The magazine called for detectives to patrol stations and trains and for prosecutions to be brought against those pilfering.

Country Snapshot: Madagascar

Total route length: 848 km
Gauge: Narrow gauge 1,000 mm (3ft 3⅜in)

THE ISLAND OF MADAGASCAR has two separate railway systems. The northern system which connects the capital, Antananarivo, with the coast is under concession to a private company, Madarail SA. There are three lines on this system: Antananarivo-Côte Est (372 km), Moramanga-Lac Alaotra (160 km) and Antananarivo-Antsirabe (153 km).

Madarail or Madagascar Railways is a freight carrier in the North-East Network of Madagascar. It is an important actor in the transport of products such as chromites, hydrocarbons, building materials such as iron and cement, and foodstuffs such as rice, cereals and fruit. Not only does it transport goods, it also ensures the maintenance of the track, its renewal and the development of railway infrastructure.

The southern system is managed by a parastatal company. It has a single line running from Manakara on the coast to Fianarantsoa (163 km).

In 2016, the British travel documentary maker Simon Reeve, in an interview with *The Guardian* newspaper, described the train from Fianarantsoa to Manakara as the maddest journey he had ever been on. 'The track was built in colonial times and thousands of workers died during its construction; it was a wicked project. But now it helps Malagasy farmers in the hinterland shift out their crops of coffee and fruit … The route has dozens of tunnels, viaducts, valleys, bridges and steep inclines. It's totally chaotic—health and safety doesn't exist: we stood on the cowcatcher on the front of the train. There are no proper lights, the toilets leak and it takes twelve hours, but it was magical.'

In a 2015 study, the African Development Bank stated that the railway infrastructure was in generally poor condition due to lack

Two scenes at Andasibe taken in 2010. A freight working approaches a road crossing just outside the town; an earlier photograph shows all three lines occupied at the town's station. *Tim Davis.*

of maintenance (and in spite of a national $49 million investment program that spanned 2003 to 2010 led by the World Bank and its International Development Agency arm—a scheme that did not allocate funds to the railways).

The study said the rail tracks used three different weights of rail, there were damaged wooden sleepers and many bridges and cuttings were in need of urgent stabilisation. As a result, train speeds barely exceeded 20 km/h.

On the northern system the government obligated the operator to offer passenger services and losses were covered by subsidies.

* * *

In 1958 William A. Hance, associate professor of economic geography at Columbia University, noted that in 1955 the railway system, though only 848 km long, carried 44.1 per cent of all imported goods. 'Notwithstanding their small extent, the rail lines serve four of the eight leading cities of the island,' he wrote two years before France gave the country its independence. 'They are well-equipped, well run, and in recent years have operated at a slight profit. They provide a welcome contrast with the inadequate roads and ports'.

Of the section now known as the Antananarivo-Côte Est line, he described parts of the lines as tortuous, with most of the sharper curves having a radius of between eighty and 120 metres.

Of the southern line, he recorded that it had forty-nine tunnels (totaling 5.3 km), forty-five bridges and two viaducts (172 and 200 metres high respectively).

At the time of Hance's visit, power units had been modernised: the wood-fired steam locomotives had been replaced with twenty-one diesel units, eighteen autorails (railcars) and eighteen switching (shunting) engines.

The main exports moved by rail were rice, manioc, coffee, graphite, peanuts and preserved meats. On the journeys inland, the trains carried cement, fuel, beverages, iron and steel, and flour. There were 2.33 million passenger journeys in 1955.

Rolling Stock (2014)
Locomotives: 17
Freight wagons: 260

Postscript: Railways in 2042?

I F YOU WERE ASKED to predict how railways would look twenty-five years hence, you would probably be thinking in terms of some improvement of how they look today—high speed rail (only faster), a completed Asia-Europe trunk railway that speeds trains from Singapore to Paris.

But, if the experience of F. H. Hardin is anything to go by, you might be well off the mark. Hardin, the chief engineer of motive power and rolling stock on the New York Central system, was asked by the *New York Times* in 1923 to visualise what railways would be like in 1948.

He said that, at some stage, complete electrification would come but, in the foreseeable future, it was too costly. Oil would become a railroad fuel—but no mention by Hardin of diesel locomotives, just the conversion of steam engines from coal burning, but then only in parts of America where oil was produced. Hardin presumed that steam would still be the primary motive power in 1948 (it was, but giving ground fast as diesel train sets and locomotives were becoming more common) and contented himself with envisaging improvements to steam. Design would change: the headlight above the boiler would be replaced by a powerful searchlight placed much near track level; the smokestack would disappear and be replaced by a small opening 'probably in an entirely different position'.

Grade (level) crossing would be a thing of the past by 1948, and lines would be built without tunnels (just blast upwards to remove what ever was above). Locomotives would be unmanned, the trains controlled from signal boxes; a third rail would be laid through which electric currents could be transmitted to apply brakes.

Long-distance trains would have a theatre car for putting on plays, showing movies and staging concerts for passengers.

But Hardin did get it right in some respects. He predicted radio contact between the caboose and locomotive, radio communication between locomotives, signal boxes and train dispatchers (and, remember, this was only three years after the first commercial radio station had gone to air in the United States).

Still, anyone now making predictions about rail in 2042 would no doubt end up being well off the mark.

Acknowledgements

I am most grateful to those who responded to my requests for photographs and other information, given they received emails out of the blue from someone of whom they had never heard: Alexander Campbell who had purchased West Virginia photographs from Donald A. Kaiser;, Henry Posner II of the Railway Development Corporation; Nao Nakata of Hokkaido Railway Company; Bill Linley who helped with Newfoundland pictures; David Longman who has a collection of photographs taken in Cuba; Salman Rashid of Pakistan; Michael Homola at Austria's postal service; Professor Jenny Edwards of Sydney's University of Technology who provided photos take by her husband in Madagascar (he was on a wildlife tour but managed to capture the local rail scene); Mike Morant sent photos of Japanese steam locomotives; David Kellor copied a caboose photo I sought; John Clarke helped (see his great site with all copies of *Railway Wonders of the World*), while Thomasz Galka and Antoni Bochen of Quixi Media provided scenes from Poland; Charles Dix supplied the photo of old 4113; and Patrick Rudin of Germany supplied the Paraguay shots.

Especial thanks go to John Beckhaus in Sydney for his photos used in this book. John has been most generous over the years, supplying pictures for various railway book projects of mine dating back to the 1980s. Another Australian railway authority, John Hoyle, pulled me up on several mistakes in the text (I take full responsibility for all the others); he also has been a great help over the years.

Claire Henderson, as well as enduring the time I spend beavering away on such projects, is a handy person to have when a photograph needs to be properly framed and I am the only alternative photographer.

* * *

I want, finally, to dedicate this book to my old friend Bob Stott. Back in 1971, when I was chief reporter of *The Dominion* (the morning newspaper in Wellington, New Zealand) and he was my deputy (as well as the paper's highly esteemed transport reporter), Bob suggested that what the country needed was a commercial rail magazine to complement the various enthusiast publications. So, with little thought of the risk involved but wisely keeping our day jobs, we launched *Rails*, a monthly magazine which, fortunately for us, captured enough subscriptions to survive (although it was a close run thing a couple of times). Bob and his wife Jan took over completely after I moved to Australia and kept the magazine going for more than thirty years, an astonishing achievement. Both have been great friends over the years—and this is a belated thank you.

Bibliography

Alderoft, Derek H., "Innovation on the Railways: The Lag in Diesel and (Electric Traction", *Journal of Transport Economics and Policy*, Vol. 3, No. 1 January 1969)

Alexander, Edwin P, *American Locomotives: A Pictorial Record of Steam Power 1900-1950*, Norton, New York 1950

Aldrich, Mark, "Running Out of Steam: Federal Inspection and Locomotive Safety", *Journal of Economic History*, Vol. 67, No. 4

Allen, Cecil J, "The Future of Railways", *Journal of the Royal Society of Arts*, Vol. 113, No. 5105 (April 1965)

Blasenheim, Peter L, "Railroads in Nineteenth Century Minas Gerais", *Journal of Latin American Studies*, Vol. 26, No. 2 (1994)

Aoki, Eiichi, *Technological Innovation and the Development of Transportation in Japan*, United Nations University Press (1993)

Barns, Kathleen, "Soviet Union Improving Railway Network", *Far Eastern Survey*, Vol. 8, No. 25 (20 December 1939)

Bogart, Dan, and Chaudhary, Latika, "Regulation, Ownership, and Costs: A Historical Perspective from Indian Railways", *American Economic Journal: Economic Policy*, Vol. 5, No. 1 (February 2012)

Bromby, Robin, *Australian Railways: Their Life and Times*, Highgate 2014

——*Rails That Built a Nation*, Grantham House 2003

——*The Railway Age in Australia*, Lothian 2004

——*Ghost Railways of Australia*, Lothian 2006

——*New Zealand Railways: Their Life and Times,* Highgate 2014

Dominguez, Luis V, and Ceballos, Manuel Diaz, "Main Lines and the Making of a Nation", *Railroad History,* No. 190, 2004

Fournier, Leslie T., "The Canadian National Railway versus the Canadian Pacific: A Comparative Study", *Journal of Political Economy,* Vol. 39, No. 3.

Gardiner, Juliet, *The Thirties, An Intimate History,* HarperPress 2010

Geographical Journal, The, "Railway Surveys in the Yemen", Vol. 43, No. 1 (January 1914)

Ginio, Ruth, *French Colonialism Unmasked: The Vichy Years in West Africa,* University of Nebraska Press, 2006

Hall, Derek R, "Albania's Growing Rail Network", *Geography,* Vol. 69, No. 3 (June 1984)

Hance, William A, "Transportation in Madagascar", *Geographic Journal,* Vol. 48, No. 1, 1958

Harvie, Christopher, "The Politics of German Railway Design", *Journal of Design History,* Vol. 1, No 3/4.

Hayward, R.M., "The Question of the Standard Gauge for Russian Railways 1836-1860", *Slavic Review,* Vol. 2, No. 1 (1969)

Kato, Shinichi, "Upgrading Narrow Gauge Standards", *Japan Railway & Transport Review,* December 1995.

Keuchel, Edward F, "Coal-burning Locomotives: A Technological Development of the 1850s", *The Pennsylvania Magazine of History and Biography,* Vol. 94, No. 4 (1970)

Maggi, Stefano, and Gras, Rutger, "Sahara's Lost Railroads", *Railroad History,* No. 183, Autumn 2000

Marx, Thomas G, "Technological Change and the Theory of the Firm: The American Locomotive Industry, 1920-1955", *The Business History Review,* Vol. 50, No. 1 (1976)

Mellor, R E H, "A Basic Railway Passenger Network in the United States", *Geography,* Vol. 58, No. 2 (April 1973)

——"Through railway links between USSR and its neighbours" *Geography,* Vol. 49. No. 4 (November 1964)

Meyer, B.H., "Foreign Railway Events in 1902-03", *The Annals of the American Academy of Political and Social Sciences,* Vol. 23 (January 1904)

Middleton, William D; Morgan, Rick; and Diehl, Roberta L, *The Encyclopedia of North American Railroads,* Indiana University Press (2007)

Mierzejewski, Alfred C., "Hitler's Locomotives", *Railroad History,* No. 186 (2002)

Mirski, Michael S, "The Soviet Railway System: Policy and Operation", *Russian Review*, Vol. 13, No. 1 (January 1954)

Nishiyama, Takashi, "War, Peace and Non-weapons Technology: The Japanese National Railways and the Products of Defeat, 1880s-1950s", *Technology and Culture*, Vol. 48, No. 2 (April 2007)

Norton, Hugh S, "The Locomotive Industry in the United States 1920-1960: A Study in Output and Structural Changes", *The Railway and Locomotive Historical Society Bulletin*, No. 113 (1965)

Pearson, R.E., "Closure of the Newfoundland Railway", *Geography*, Vol. 74, No. 3 (June 1989)

Puffert, Douglas J, "The Standardization of Track Gauge on North American Railways 1830-1890", *Journal of Economic History*, Vol. 60, No. 4 December 2000.

Reutter, Mark, "The Lost Promise of the American Railroad", *The Wilson Quarterly*, Vol. 18, No. 1 (Winter 1994)

Roth, Ralf and Dinhobl, Gunter, *Across the Borders: Financing the World's Railways in the Nineteenth and Twentieth Centuries*, Ashgate Publishing (2008)

Schreiber, Gerhard; Stegeman, Bernd; Vogel, Detlef, *The Mediterranean, Southeast Europe and North Africa 1939-1941; From Italy's Declaration of Non-belligerence to the entry of the United States into the War*, Oxford University Press (1995)

Solomon, Brian, *North American Railroads - The Illustrated Encyclopedia*, Voyageur Press (2014)

Stargardt, Nicholas, *The German War—A Nation Under Arms*, The Bodley Head, London (2015)

Stevenson, David, "War by Timetable?—The Railway Race Before 1914", *Past & Present,* No. 162 (February 1999)

Stopler, Gustav, "German Military Transport", *Proceedings of the Academy of Political Science*, Vol. 20, No. 2

Thomas, Benjamin E, "The Railways of French North Africa", *Economic Geography*, Vol. 29, No. 2 (April 1953)

Travis, Anthony S., "Engineering and Politics: The Channel Tunnel in the 1880s", *Technology and Culture*, Vol. 32, No. 3 (1991)

Westward, J N, "The Vladikavkaz Railway: A Case of Enterprising Private Enterprise", *Slavic Review*, Vol. 25, No. 4 (December 1966)

Westwood, J.N., "The Railway Flying Squads of 1914", *The Slavonik and Eastern European Review*, Vol. 55, No. 2 (April 1977)

Westwood, J, *Soviet Railways to Russian Railways*, Springer 2001

Index

OTHER BOOKS BY ROBIN BROMBY
(and available at Amazon in both e-book and paperback format)

New Zealand Railways: Their Life & Times

New Zealand railway builders surmounted many obstacles: the terrain, a sparse and scattered population, two islands separated by an often stormy stretch of water, demands from every small settlement for their own railway line. But build a railway system—and a comprehensive one at that—New Zealand did. This is the story of that railway, from its heyday to the day of reckoning as losses had to be confronted.

By 1953 the pattern was clear. The era of railways as the mainstay of land transport throughout New Zealand was ending. One by one, most of the rural branches would disappear over the next forty years; passenger train travel—other than commuter services in Auckland and Wellington—would almost disappear to a stage where there are just a handful of tourist services on the most scenic lines; all but the largest towns would lose their railway station.

But, until then, the railways of New Zealand were part of almost everyone's life: you caught the train to visit friends and relatives in other parts of New Zealand, you depended on the trains to carry the bulk of the freight that moved to and from the ports. This is their story. Profusely illustrated with photographs and maps. (*E-book and paperback*)

Australian Railways: Their Life and Times

'Picture a small wayside country station. It is unmanned but there is a siding with a few empty four-wheeled wagons; these may have brought bagged fertilizer for local farmers, or they may be left there for a farmer to load bales of wool or bags of wheat. On the platform sit cream cans—full, as it happens—so there must be a train due to collect them and cart them off to the nearest butter factory. Until that train arrives, there will be hardly a sound apart from the wind in the trees behind the station. Then, eventually, we hear the train approaching; it glides to a halt, the cream cans are rolled into the van, the van doors are slammed shut, the locomotive whistle is heard, and the train is on its way again. Within a few minutes, the place is once more silent.'

The nightmare of three different gauges, the daunting challenge of building railways across vast open spaces often with no water supplies, the follies of railway lines that were rarely used—all this is the saga of Australian railways, the sheer hard work and suffering of those who gave their life in service to the railways. Brimming with anecdotes and colorful stories, *Australian Railways: Their Life and Times* documents the old, the odd and the now forgotten. Complete with rare historic photographs. (*E-book and paperback*)

Fighting on Empty: How Hitler and Hirohito Lost the Economic War

Nazi Germany, Imperial Japan and Fascist Italy all embarked on their Second World War plans of conquest without one vital factor: sound economies that could absorb and withstand the stresses of total war. In this groundbreaking study, Robin Bromby shows how all three Axis powers went into battle with seriously flawed economies, inadequate industrial capacity and deficient food security. When they invaded much of Europe and East Asia, the Nazis and their partners only compounded the problem: they had made few plans to manage their conquests and failed to harness captured factories and farms.

It was a fatal flaw: their war plans were doomed. Despite the legend of a beleaguered Britain, that country was the largest economy in Europe and was soon building more aircraft than Germany—and had its empire on which to call. Japan's lack of economic planning was breathtaking and the strains soon began to show. And then came the Americans with all their economic power. The Axis was finished.

Fighting on Empty reveals a largely ignored, but crucial, aspect of the Second World War. (*E-book and paperback*)

German Raiders of the South Seas: The extraordinary true story of naval deception, daring and disguise 1914–1917.

Far from the mud and slaughter of the Western Front, there was another face of the Great War—an oddly stirring and thrilling one, characterized by chivalry and remarkably few casualties. This is the story of how three German naval surface raiders disrupted British shipping across large swathes of the Indian and Pacific oceans between 1914 and 1917. Attempts to supply critical cargoes and much needed reinforcements for the trenches in France and Belgium were hamstrung by German daring on the high seas.

Were it not all real and true, it would make wonderful fiction: the buccaneering crew of the *Emden* casting a shadow of fear over an ocean; the survivors of the battle with the Sydney sailing a leaking copra schooner from the Cocos Islands to the East Indies; the *Wolf* steaming undetected around the coasts of Australia and New Zealand laying mines that later would claim merchant shipping, then capturing a passenger vessel and sailing it to the East Indies; victims the captain of the *Seeadler*, von Luckner, sailing a small boat halfway across the Pacific to Fiji, and then later making a dramatic escape from a New Zealand prisoner of war camp.

In the first days of World War I a German light cruiser detached itself from the East Asiatic Squadron with the mission to raid and harass Allied shipping. The ship, SMS Emden, not only became world famous in its two months of raiding, during which it sank sixteen ships and captured others, but demonstrated the vulnerability of Australian, New Zealand and Empire shipping links. (*e-book and paperback*)

The Farming of Australia: A saga of backbreaking toil and tenacity

This is the story of triumph over a dry, hot and often infertile land. Australia's farmers have overcome difficult terrain and the tyranny of distance to make the country an important food bowl. This is the story of 200-plus years of ups and downs from savage droughts and daunting challenges to the triumphs of irrigation and imagination and inventiveness. (*E-book and paperback*)

Go to **www.highgatepublishing.com.au** for further details and free extracts.

Printed in Great Britain
by Amazon